W0016926

Women's Studies Quarterly

An Educational Project at The Feminist Press at The City University of New York in Cooperation with Rochester Institute of Technology

Guest Editors for Current Issue
Lee Quinby, Hobart and William Smith Colleges

Editor
Diane Hope, Rochester Institute of Technology

Editors Emerita
Nancy Porter, Portland State University
Janet Zandy, Rochester Institute of Technology

Publisher
Jean Casella, The Feminist Press and The Graduate School and University Center, CUNY

Editorial Board
Lynne Derbyshire, University of Rhode Island
Jean Douthwright, Rochester Institute of Technology
Lisa Freeman, Kansas State University
Dorothy O. Helly, emerita, Hunter College and The Graduate School, CUNY
Barbara Horn, Nassau Community College, SUNY
Alice Kessler-Harris, Columbia University
Wendy Kolmar, Drew University
Linda Layne, Rensselaer Polytechnic Institute
Tobe Levin, University of Maryland, European Division, and J.W. Goethe University,
    Frankfurt am Main, Germany
Kit Mayberry, Rochester Institute of Technology
Carol J. Pierman, University of Alabama
Lee Quinby, Hobart and William Smith Colleges
Carol Richardson, Rochester Institute of Technology
Deborah Rosenfelt, University of Maryland, College Park
Sue V. Rosser, Georgia Institute of Technology
Carole Anne Taylor, Bates College
Mari Boor Tonn, University of Maryland
Bonnie Zimmerman, San Diego State University

Managing Editors
Molly Vaux and Livia Tenzer

Copy Editor
Romaine Perin

Editorial Assistant
Lamar Clarkson

Contents

POETRY

FEMINIST TRANSFORMATIONS OF THE TECHNO-PROFICIENT CURRICULUM AND CLASSROOM

Editorial

A look back on the second half of the twentieth century makes it clear that innovations in information and biological technologies have dramatically altered the landscape of women's everyday lives. Questions about the concrete effects of these transformations on women and their responses to these changes have prompted this special issue. Feminists have contributed greatly to our understanding of gender and technology, both how technology is gendered and how it transforms traditional notions of gender, but we need greater understanding of how women of varying backgrounds and current circumstances are dealing with demands that they learn to use the new technologies. And even though a fair amount of attention has been spent on the ways in which biotechnologies are reshaping our bodies and processes of reproduction, we need a better grasp of women's agency in this regard.

At this point in time, advanced industrial nations account for 81.6 percent of information technology use. The remaining 18.4 percent includes all developing countries combined, a discrepancy that reinforces the already rampant inequities between advanced capitalist nations and developing ones (Seven Billions of Netizens Project, online). The focus of this special issue is women's acceptance of and resistance to changes in the workplace and in their private lives where this technology is currently most entrenched. Contributors to this issue include teachers, scholars, Web designers, librarians, and poets, who focus primarily on such concerns as confidentiality of data, uses of prosthetic devices, the impact of surrogacy, and the pedagogical value of the Internet. The emphasis here is on providing a grounded discussion through case studies and interviews with women—as users of biological technologies and as both leaders and workers in the field of information technology—in order to give firm foundation to the abstract formulations of cyberculture studies that have emerged over the past decade and a half. In other words, this volume's emphasis on the uses and impact of technology is intended as an examination of hands-on technological work that valuably joins with available theoretical work. The intent is thus to encourage dialogue and debate between users and theorists in areas ranging from biomedical science to computer training. In that vein, many of the authors of the essays confront current notions of cybertheory as well as the new technologies,

demonstrating the necessity of ongoing interplay between embodied
activity and abstract formulation. As Donna Haraway has long argued,
beginning notably with her groundbreaking essay from 1986, "The
Cyborg Manifesto," feminists must become adept in thinking about
the changes that digital and biological technologies make in and
throughout the world. The contributors here take up that task by
focusing on issues of medical technology, computer and information
access, and education and training.

It is clear from these diverse approaches that confrontation with the
new technologies entails grasping the complexity of women's relationship to the *old* technologies. The relationship between women and
technology is hardly minimal, but it has been largely ignored. Feminist
historians of technology have shown that, in Autumn Stanley's words,
"women invent. Women have always invented. . . . Women still invent.
They invent significant things. They create breakthroughs and fundamental inventions. . . . And they do all this in the full range of human
endeavor and technology" (quoted in Noble 1999). Nevertheless,
women have not been acknowledged for their contributions, in part
as David Noble has indicated, because of the "religion of technology"
that emerged out of the Latin Church and gave shape to an intensely
misogynistic Western science. The masculinization of science and technology, Noble argues, "historically had no reference in reality (at least
up until the relatively recent monopolization of the useful arts by professional engineering), only in mythology" (212).

As technology gradually became understood as a male domain—
despite the fact that women continued to participate in technological
labor, and, as Sadie Plant has indicated, despite innovations of women
such as Ada Lovelace, the first programmer—the ideology associated
with technology absorbed values of transcendence over bodies, soil,
and work. This aspiration to transcendence has been accentuated in
the new technologies. In much of today's cybertheory, it is common
to find assertions about disembodiment in cyberspace even though
there is ample evidence to the contrary, in carpal tunnel syndrome,
severe eyestrain, and other bodily symptoms. When we begin by asking technology workers about these issues, disembodiment does not
emerge as a primary issue.

Issues surrounding women's embodiment do, however, constitute
a key area of controversy and concern within technoculture. Part one
of this volume begins with the issue of surrogacy, which has long been
at the center of feminist discussions about technological reproduction
and is in many respects emblematic of the complexity derived from
biomedical interventions. Elly Teman takes up this topic from the

unique perspective provided by the Israeli state-funded and -regulated practice of surrogacy. Although she acknowledges the work done by feminists who have criticized extensions of patriarchal control and commodification of women's bodies through reproductive technologies, she discovers several avenues of agency and empowerment in the ways that Israeli surrogate mothers think and speak about their experiences.

Within feminism and cyberculture studies, linkages between technology and human beings have come to be known as cyborgian from the influential work of Donna Haraway. Much of Haraway's theorization has been critical of the transcendent aspirations of science and technology of the modern era. But Sharon Betcher's reading of Haraway shows that the cyborg is more complicit in the discourse of transcendence than formerly thought. From the perspective of one who is herself a prosthetically-enabled disabled person, Betcher finds in Haraway's theorizations a gravitational pull toward holism that participates problematically in the "salvation history" of technoscience. Susan Hawthorne further examines the dangers of transcendent technoscience, which, in its universalizing of human experience and knowledge, fuels forces of globalization that exacerbate conditions of bodily exploitation for women in general and for women in developing countries in particular. Against these rising forces that colonize and commodify women's bodies, she advocates an alternative vision of "wild bodies."

The writers in part two turn to two other primary issues that emerge as key for women: access and training. Stephen Newton's essay addresses both these issues from the perspective of several women who are acknowledged leaders in information technology. In his interviews with such female "geeks" as Ellen Ullman and Aliza Sherman, Newton asks how they were able to break through the gender barriers that keep many women from gaining technological expertise. Most of them attribute their own success to their persistence in the face of recognized obstacles to technological proficiency.

Such obstacles are the focus of the essays by Mary Virnoche and Dolores Fidishun, both of whom recount difficulties women face in confronting information technologies in the workplace. Virnoche's study of human-service workers demonstrates that numerous other factors intervene to make the transition to computer technology problematic, including inefficiently slow equipment and concerns over the confidentiality of clients. Fidishun's interviews with middle-age and older librarians show that self-perception is also a crucial factor in gaining expertise. It made a difference for the women she interviewed whether they regarded themselves as "people servers" or "information providers."

Another form of access is documented in the essay by Anna Sampaio and Janni Aragon. Their research into software filtering systems indicates that topics of concern for women, sexual education and breast cancer, for example, are often blocked out by filtering systems. To avoid a construction of women's "Body" in cyberspace that results from the filtering out of valuable information in efforts to block ever-increasing cyberpornography, they argue for "increased access to and advocacy for and by women on the Internet at the grassroots level, in academic centers, and in boardrooms" (141). The final essay of this section, by Joan Korenman, gives an overview of one of the most, if not the most, valuable Web sites for women on the Internet, that of the Center for Women and Information and Technology. While the center's primary mission is to serve women who work in information technology, its resources extend far beyond that scope, including such materials as hundreds of women's studies syllabi, a job information list, and news articles about women in technology.

The tension between desire for technological assistance and exasperation about technological intrusion are the focus of all the poems in part three. Encapsulating various forms of ambivalence, the poems by Dorothy Howe Brooks, Carole Cole, Maria Proitsaki, and Judith Rose grapple with the promise and perils that the new technologies have already wrought.

As reliance on the new technologies expands exponentially, new pressures on education also come to the forefront. The focal point of Part IV is how feminist insight can help forge links between technological research, pedagogy, and the creation of an inclusive curriculum. Engineering is one of the prime areas in which these links must be strengthened. Recognizing the need to diversify engineering as a field in terms of both race and gender, the Accreditation Board for Engineering and Technology has developed Engineering Criteria 2000 (EC2000). In 1990, Sue Rosser devised twenty pedagogical criteria for "female-friendly science." In her essay in this volume, she compares her criteria to criterion 3 of the EC2000 to analyze and assess its value. Her essay provides essential ways for science and technology programs to review their own efforts at recruiting and retaining women.

Within women's studies classrooms, issues of technology can take several directions. As Ivy Schweitzer indicates, studying cyberfeminism entails not only examining issues of techno-identity, but also expanding the classroom itself to engage in online discussion and marshal electronic resources. Her essay provides a valuable introduction for teachers who may be beginning the process of online teaching and for those wondering whether it is useful to do so when the topic is not technology per se. From a less sanguine perspective, Lori Amy and Laura Milner argue against what they see as a premature and unreflective push toward technology in education. By scrutinizing the "technology literacy mandates" that promise technological breakthroughs in learning, they redirect the rhetoric of being simply for or against technology to ascertain ways in which social divisions are actually aggravated by technology and to look for ways in which technology can be used to further ethical education.

The final contribution provides an abundance of resources for further thought and access to issues involving the new technologies. Sidney Eve Matrix's annotated bibliography is wide-ranging in its focus on five major categories of cyborg theory and cyberspace. Her syllabus Cyberfeminism and Technoculture is included as an example of how she has used these sources.

As the contributions in this special issue make clear, it is paramount not only that women confront the myriad ways in which these new technologies are so rapidly making an impact on our lives, but also that we add our feminist visions and voices to this process.

REFERENCES

Haraway, Donna. 1985. "A Cyborg Manifesto: Science, Technology, and Socialist-Feminism in the Late Twentieth Century." *Socialist Review* 80: 65–108.

Noble, David F. 1999. *The Religion of Technology: The Divinity of Man and the Spirit of Invention.* New York: Penguin Books.

Plant, Sadie. 1997. *Zeroes and Ones: Digital Women and the New Technoculture.* London: Fourth Estate.

Seven Billions of Netizens Project. "Seven Billions of Netizens." Online. Available: <http://geocities.com/ResearchTriangle/4485/>. June 25, 2001.

Lee Quinby holds the Donald R. Harter Chair in the Humanities at Hobart and William Smith Colleges in Geneva, New York. During the time she edited this issue she also held the Visiting Caroline Werner Gannett Chair on the Millennium at the Rochester Institute of Technology. She is the author and editor of several books, including Anti-Apocalypse, Millennial Seduction, *and the coedited* Feminism and Foucault.

Technological Fragmentation and Women's Empowerment

Surrogate Motherhood in Israel

Elly Teman

Introduction

In 1991 the Ministers of Health and Justice in Israel nominated a public committee to prepare a proposal for legislation on in-vitro fertilization and surrogate motherhood (Benshushan and Schenker 1997, 1832).[1] Following the cancellation of strictures banning surrogacy in Israel after twenty-five childless couples petitioned the high court of justice in Jerusalem in 1995, the Israeli Law of Agreements for the Carrying of Fetuses was born. March 7, 1996, marked the day that Israel became the only country in the world besides the United Kingdom to allow state-controlled surrogacy (Benshushan and Schenker 1997, 1832), and the first and only country in the world where all surrogacy contracts are legislated by a government-appointed committee (Kahn 1997, 171).

The Israeli surrogacy law has also made Israel one of the few countries in the world to legalize surrogacy at all. Surrogate motherhood—a practice whereby a woman agrees to carry a child to term for a couple who will then keep the child as their own[2]—has been prohibited by law throughout much of the world. Countries where surrogacy is illegal include Australia, France, Germany, the Netherlands, and Scandinavia; it is also outlawed in parts of the United States (Schenker 1991).

The banning of surrogacy stems from its controversial nature and the negative attention it has drawn on moral, ethical, legal, and social grounds. In the vast body of literature on the subject, it has been asked whether there is something intrinsically immoral about surrogacy (Brennan and Noggle1997) and what these ethical questions are (Baslington 1996). Surrogacy has been compared to prostitution and regarded as dehumanizing women's reproductive labor (van Niekerk and van Zyl 1995). Surrogacy has also been viewed as changing the cultural meanings of motherhood (Snowdon 1994) and kinship (Macklin 1991), and as threatening women's and children's basic human rights (Brennan and Noggle 1997).

In the context of women and technology, surrogacy has been used as a severe example of the tightening of male control over female reproductive processes (Corea 1987). Viewed as a vehicle for the economic exploitation of women, surrogacy has been seen as exposing women to the capitalist commodification of their bodies and subjecting them to patriarchal subordination (Faquhar 1996). Surrogacy has also been scrutinized as an extreme case study of the technological colonization of women's bodies (Baird 1997).[3] Regarded as a practice that reinforces male values and enables the social controlling and monitoring of women's lives (Arditti 1987), surrogacy has been drawn upon to argue the case of women's inalienable rights (Langer and Pedrosa 1995).

The numerous arguments for and against surrogacy in the vast literature on the subject are only vaguely based on the actual experiences of surrogate mothers and commissioning couples. Primarily drawing from statistical samples and media accounts, such as the famous Baby M case,[4] these arguments rarely focus on the agency of participants in surrogacy arrangements themselves. While surrogacy has been explored from an anthropological perspective in the United States (Ragone 1994; Roberts 1998; Cussins 1998), the present study entails the first comprehensive ethnography of surrogate motherhood in Israel. Based on interviews with seventeen surrogate mothers and commissioning mothers, along with multiple hours of participant observation, the following discussion is an attempt to outline the surrogacy experience from the perspective of the female actors themselves.

Specifically, I argue that the narratives of Israeli surrogate mothers could be viewed as a prime example of the medicalization, commodification, and technological colonization of women's lives. Their narratives read as a testimonial to their willingness to accept capitalist, nationalist, male medical control of their reproductive bodies. However, within these "accepted" avenues of subordination, I suggest that Israeli surrogate mothers redirect, transform, and shape their own experiences. In the following discussion I will outline three cyborg[5] practices through which surrogate mothers call upon and maneuver within the realms of medical technology, capitalist commodification, and technological colonization of the human body in order to distance themselves from "nature." As a result, these practices become tools of resistance, enabling them to assert control over their bodies within the given patriarchal framework of the Israeli surrogacy law. In this way, I argue that surrogates override common definitions of nature and motherhood, and direct these definitions away from their pregnant bodies and onto their commissioning mothers.

The first of the three practices that aid Israeli surrogate mothers in using, resisting, and shaping technology from within is the acceptance and encouragement of the medicalization of their bodies. Surrogates narrate pregnant bodies controlled by doctors and synthetic hormones. However, drawing upon their stable, medically controlled bodies, these surrogates define their own "artificial" relationship with the incubated child. Technical medical jargon thus assists them in their own attempt to "control" nature. The second practice, commodifying, refers to a practice whereby surrogates associate commodity terms with their reproductive parts. Adopting the commodity jargon of capitalist society, these surrogates once again override nature by emphasizing their distance, as objects, from nature. Last, the practice of "creating the third body" reads as the cyborgification of the surrogate's body. From within the context of technological colonization of the body, the surrogate imagines her own body as cyborg, constructing an imaginary "third space" outside of her body and locating the pregnancy within it. With this third space the surrogate uses technology to "naturalize" the commissioning mother's relationship with the fetus by detaching it and transferring it to her.

A short overview of the Israeli context will help to establish the patriarchal setting within which these practices take place and enable the further development of this argument.

Surrogacy in Israel: An Overview

Israel is a particularly interesting place to study surrogacy, not only because of its novelty, but also because of the unique cultural meanings attached to motherhood and reproduction in Israel (Kahn 2000). Israeli society is driven by a pronatalist ideology of compulsory motherhood, an ideology that Israeli women participate in fully, to the effect that they will do anything in order to have a child (Kahn 2000). This strong reproductive impulse is rooted in a variety of factors, including the biblical directive of Jewish tradition to "be fruitful and multiply," and the emotional needs of a people in a permanent war society (Yuval Davis 1989). Out of this backdrop, motherhood has emerged as a role and a symbol that bears major national significance, especially within the context of the Israeli-Palestinian conflict, where motherhood has been celebrated as a "national mission" (Berkovitch 1997). Israel has more fertility clinics per capita than any other country in the world. Furthermore, the Israeli nation-state actively encourages Israel's "cult of fertility." While surrogacy is largely privatized in the rest of the world, with costs often exceeding seventy thousand dollars, the medical expenses of surrogacy—like those of other new reproductive technologies—are heavily subsidized by Israel's national health insurance (Kahn 1998).

The Israeli surrogacy law is strongly patriarchal (Shalev 1998). The surrogacy approval committee, nominated by the government health minister, includes seven members: two gynecologists, one internal specialist, a clinical psychologist, a social worker, a lawyer, and a clergyman, according to the religion of the parties involved (Benshushan and Schenker 1997, 1832). Through the law, patriarchal state control over women's reproductive bodies is reinforced with the aid of the national, religious, legal, and medical arms of the state (Shalev 1998).

On the national level, the law dictates which types of families can be created through surrogacy: only married, heterosexual couples in which both partners are Israeli citizens are eligible for consideration. Moreover, couples must undergo psychological and genetic testing to prevent the birth of "unhealthy" fetuses to "unsuitable" couples from "inappropriate" wombs. The selection of couples is based upon an interview before the committee plus the assorted documents with which the commissioning couples must provide the committee. These include medical and psychological reports attesting that they are "suitable for the process," notice of any criminal records, proof of their Judaism, and complete details of the state-required monetary payment to be exchanged between couple and surrogate (Benshushan and Schenker 1997, 1833).

The law aims to ensure that surrogacy remain extremely limited in practice: couples eligible for surrogacy must prove that the female partner is unable to become pregnant or carry a pregnancy to term, or that she is at a severe health risk during pregnancy. At the same time, the law also necessitates that the commissioning father be the sperm donor. This insistence on patrilineal continuity through surrogacy further establishes the patriarchal nature of the law.

On the religious level, Israel's surrogacy law was significantly influenced by the Halakhic considerations of the Orthodox rabbinic establishment that controls all matters of family law in Israel.[6] Religious considerations led to the requirement that surrogates be single, widowed, or divorced, in order to prevent the illegitimacy of the child according to Jewish law. Because Jewish law sees the religion of the child as determined by the religion of the birth mother, the surrogate mother must be of the same religious denomination as both members of the commissioning couple. The committee may consider an inter-religious agreement only if all the parties are not Jewish. The law prescribes that the surrogate be an Israeli citizen between ages twenty-five and forty and have given birth prior to the surrogacy arrangement. Coupled with the insistence on the surrogate's unmarried status, these religious considerations increase the exploitative possibilities of the practice (Shalev 1998).

On the legal level, the surrogacy law regulates the practice in terms of contract and criminal sanctions, thus degrading the surrogate to the status of property (Franklin 1995, 327). The law necessitates that a contract be signed between the parties in the presence of the state-appointed committee. By insisting on contractual agreements and on the surrogate's monetary reimbursement for her services, the law establishes surrogacy as a commodifying practice. Moreover, couples are required to present proof that they have insured their surrogate-property with a special "pregnancy insurance" offered by an Israeli insurance company for the protection of the surrogate's reproductive organs during pregnancy. Criminal sanctions accompany the law prohibiting the public exposure of the names of any persons involved in surrogacy contracts in Israel.

Medically, the law prohibits any genetic connection between the surrogate and either member of the commissioning couple, though adopted relatives are permitted. Halakhic considerations concerning incest stand behind this clause. The clause eliminates the possibility of "traditional" surrogacy—by which the surrogate mother herself supplies the female gamete—for no genetic connection whatsoever is permitted between surrogate and future child. This leaves the surrogacy option open only to couples where the woman has an intact ovary or frozen eggs, and the husband is able to supply his own sperm (Roberts 1998).

Moreover, this necessitates the intervention of medical technology in each and every surrogacy arrangement in Israel. While traditional surrogacy is done by artificial insemination and does not require any complicated medical procedures, gestational surrogacy is enabled through the technologies of egg extraction, in-vitro fertilization, and fresh or frozen embryo transfer. These complicated medical procedures ensure the medical establishment's complete medical control over the surrogate pregnancy. Thus, it is incorrect to assume that the state is not present throughout the pregnancy, even though it officially steps out of the picture after the contract has been approved and until a state-appointed social worker becomes involved in the fifth month of pregnancy.[7] Indeed, the state is ever present in the medical process, which cannot be undertaken without the help of the controlling hand of the medical arm of the State.

As of this writing in May 2000 there have been nineteen children born of surrogacy arrangements to sixteen surrogate mothers; three of the aforementioned births resulted in twins. More than seventy-five couples have contracted with surrogates and provided documents for the surrogacy committee's approval. Of these, more than fifty contracts have already been approved.

Methodology

The following research is based on seventeen in-depth, open-format interviews and many hours of participant observation with six Israeli surrogate mothers and eleven Israeli commissioning mothers. Typically, the interviews took a narrative form, whereby the woman interviewed would respond to the request to "tell your surrogacy story from wherever it begins." Most interviews were conducted in the woman's home and lasted an average of two hours. The interviews were recorded and transcribed verbatim, then translated from Hebrew to English. The women were diverse in terms of age, geographical location, education, occupation, and ethnic affiliation. Surrogates and commissioning mothers were both between the ages of thirty-four and forty-two. Geographically, they spanned the entire length of the country, from south of Beer Sheva to north of Haifa. While three commissioning mothers held bachelor's degrees and eight held steady jobs, only one surrogate had a bachelor's degree and all worked in temporary jobs. All the women interviewed were Jewish and all but one had been born in Israel. Still, they associated themselves with a wide variety of ethnic heritages, among them Russian, Georgian, Yemenite, Moroccan, Egyptian, and Kurdish. Finally, while surrogacy in the United States is an option limited to the very wealthy, in Israel it is potentially open to all levels of society, since it is subsidized by the state. This study does not intend to be a broad overview of surrogacy in Israel. Indeed, the practice is at too early a stage in its development in the country for any such assumptions to be formed.

My contacts were initially formed with informants through the help of mutual acquaintances. This later developed through the "snowball effect," as my informants themselves would often introduce me to other women in their situation. Because my intention was to explore the surrogacy experience from the female perspective, I did not pursue interviews with their male partners. Still, the times that commissioning fathers were present while I conducted participant observation enriched my understanding of the gendered nature of the women's narratives.

Medicalizing

Emily Martin (1992, 21) in "The Woman in the Body" claims that
women are profoundly alienated from science, because they are less
involved in the production of science than are men. Still, ethnographic
studies have revealed that when pregnancies are medically managed,
most women learn to redescribe their bodily changes through the language of medical technology, rather than dating their pregnancies
experientially (Martin 1992). Surrogacy narratives, which arise from a
practice that requires that both surrogates and commissioning mothers undergo a complex medical regime of corporeal preparation, regulation, and bodily change (Konrad 1998), are saturated with medical
metaphors. These narratives, however, do not echo with a sense of
alienation from science by their protagonists. Rather, surrogates incorporate medical terms and images of technoscience into their narratives with a strong sense of familiarity. The confidence with which they
use medical metaphors is not far from that of the medical professionals from which they are adapted.

The employment of medical rhetoric in surrogacy narratives thus is
not solely an artifact of male medical control of female reproduction.
Rather, it is an avenue of expression for surrogates to rewrite their own
bodily experiences in their own terms, by interpreting the dominating
medical discourse in accordance with their own personal thoughts and
experiences.

Consequently, I use the term *medicalization* to describe the way in
which surrogates use their own understandings of the medical regi-
men that they undergo to direct the surrogate pregnancy away from
their own body and toward the commissioning mother, all the while
distancing "nature" from themselves and inscribing "nature" on the
commissioning mother's experience.

One aspect of medicalization involves imagining that the body carrying the surrogate pregnancy is artificial. The transfer of fresh
embryos between commissioning mother and surrogate requires that
the "naturally" occurring balance of hormones within the surrogate's
body be converted, attended to, and contained by medical represen-
tatives (Konrad 1998). Consequently, surrogates often refer to their
body during surrogacy as artificial, creating a distinction between this
"medically managed" body and the individual, "natural body" that they
inhabit regularly. Sima separates between her own body and the "artificial" body that carried the surrogate pregnancy by explaining that
her own system was "suppressed" through medical management:
"Before [the embryo implantation procedure] you get ten days of

injections, every day, in order to suppress your system . . . your biological system. To suppress it and prepare your womb for absorption
of something else, (something) strange, in an artificial way."

Like Sima, other surrogates also felt that the medical management
of their pregnancies helped them to "switch off" (Konrad 1998) their
individual bodies and replace what they had formerly deemed to be
their "natural" reproductive system with the "artificial" control of the
medicalized surrogate pregnancy. Accordingly, surrogates claimed that
the artificial pregnancy that they carried did not give rise to the natural emotional attachment that they normally associated with pregnancy. Orna, for instance, explains how the hormone injections that
she receives transform her body into a "clean slate" (Konrad 1998) and
dismiss all connotations of motherhood from her body:

> It is not mine. It is all artificial. . . . The hormones do it all instead of
> me. My brain doesn't even know that I am pregnant. My brain is sup-
> pressed with the shots that they give me. It turns my brain back to
> zero. Then all that is needed is given through pills. Through hor-
> mones . . . the brain is the injections. Instead of the brain ordering
> one, two, three, the hormones need to go up, need to go down, and
> then the injections do everything.

The metaphor of genetic kinship is repeatedly engaged by surrogates to emphasize their nonconnection to the fetus and to coun-
teremphasize the "natural," genetic connection between the
commissioning couple and child. Rinat, a surrogate, explains that she
holds no biological or emotional investment in the future child. She
validates her disconnection from the fetus with scientific explanations
drawing from her interpretation of the medical technology of in-vitro
fertilization:

> Some [neighbors] said, "Oy vey, she is giving away her children."
> They just couldn't digest that it wasn't mine. Nothing of mine is
> there. Nothing, nothing is mine here. It is only theirs [the couple's]
> . . . nothing of him, not my blood. No. It is all theirs . . . what was
> put into me is a whole baby. It is ready. A baby that is formed from
> the sperm and egg together and was created as a baby and only
> then inserted into my stomach. And then what is attached to me is
> just in the placenta and the umbilical cord. But nothing else is
> mine. Nothing, nothing is mine. . . . And that is why I am telling
> you, that you don't have feelings [for the fetus] like you would
> expect.

Another surrogate also uses her own interpretation of genetics and of in-vitro fertilization to prove that there is no biological precedent for the formation of a "natural" bond between herself and the child she gestates. Her confidence in the medical technology refutes any claims of women's perceived alienation from science. She embraces scientific discourse to explain her "biological" distance from the fetus in an assured, didactic manner:

> The egg and the sperm aren't mine, right? There are cells, I just develop those cells. I mean, the cells divide with his genes. For instance: when you get a blood transfusion, you don't change all of your blood. . . . The blood that they give you, it helps you make more of your own blood. It has to be the same type of blood, because you can't mix two different types of blood, but it just helps your own body recover by itself. It is the same thing here. You have a cell, an embryo, and it just needs a little help from outside in order to develop into a fetus. The genes of the child aren't mine . . . I feed him, develop his genes. But not mine. My genes are something else. His looks, his personality, he takes nothing from me. It is all there in four little cells, eight cells, the first cells, everything is already there. Even the shape of his nose is in those two cells. . . . I have nothing to do with this embryo. I have no genetic connection to him . . . I have no connection to him.

By imagining the child as a whole unit simply transferred into her body for the length of the pregnancy, she imagines a separation between the two bodies: the fetal body and her own. Rinat, further distancing herself from the fetus, imagines a third, intermediary body existing within her own, yet in a space specifically allocated for the pregnancy, attached but separate from her own body. It is the hormones, she claims, that both cause and enable this separation of bodies:

> It isn't regular. You have to take their hormones, because the hormones aren't yours. And you start to get bloated. . . . In the beginning I got a bit round . . . and I am usually very small in my pregnancies! See, now, [pointing to her stomach, currently pregnant with her own child], from the beginning of this pregnancy, mine, till now, I've gained one kilo or so. With them [pointing to her two youngest children playing on the floor], I lost weight during the pregnancy. . . . But here [pointing to a photo of herself pregnant, with her arm around the commissioning mother] I weighed seventy something kilos from the injections and the hormones that they gave me . . . suddenly I got a bottom, I got a tummy, I got thighs . . . from

the hormones. The hormones change your body. And my hair fell out. I would go like this [scrunches her hair] and it fell . . . because of the hormones. They aren't yours. The hormones that enter your body are strangers. They give them to you in injections. It is hormones for the baby to develop well.

Rinat describes a body invaded and taken over willingly by a foreign power's control, yet she marvels with wonder at the miracle of it. She excitedly demonstrates how a second and third body emerge from her own. She appropriates this description to emphasize how her own body and her own experiences of pregnancy and motherhood differ from the artificial, physically dissimilar body she carried in surrogacy.

Rinat's words strongly ring of the internalization of the technological, patriarchal medical management of women's bodies and give rise to long expressed concerns over the "artificial invasion" and appropriation of control over the female body by the new reproductive technologies (Klein 1987, 65). Surprisingly, these concerns do not mirror Rinat's and other surrogates' own views of the situation. Instead, they grasp at the possibility of medicine enabling the extraction of "nature" from their bodies during surrogacy and its replacement with "artificial," controllable substance. Indeed, these women affirmatively accept the medical control over their bodies and all of its most criticized effects willingly. These include the separation of pregnancy from nature and the notion that a woman's connection to her pregnancy is neither vital nor necessary (Raymond 1993, 48). They accept these consequences, however, only in order to subvert them, and to reshape the surrogacy experience in their own way. It is precisely the distance from nature and the distancing of motherhood from pregnancy that help surrogates strengthen and preserve their own view of themselves as mothers and enable them to naturalize motherhood for another woman—the commissioning mother.

Through the medicalization practice, these women are not simply internalizing the "far removed" and "mystified" technological jargon that medical practitioners implement in controlling women's reproductive processes (Klein 1985, 67). Moreover, they are not alienated from their bodies as helpless victims of medicalization. Instead, these women appropriate and subversively shape medical rhetoric in order to direct and control their own surrogacy experience. Medicalization, in summary, becomes a vehicle of empowerment for the surrogate by transforming the unpredictable and uncontrollable natural process of pregnancy and birth into relatively controllable technological phenomena (Davis-Floyd 1992, 2). The artificially controlled body thus enables these women to direct their bodies in the way they feel is most beneficial to themselves. Specifically, it enables them to make the choice to disconnect from the fetal body, and often the "pregnant body," that they gestate. This pattern—of distancing nature from the pregnant body and maintaining control from within a subordinating context—is strengthened through the use of commodity rhetoric, as explored in the following section.

Commodifying

The boundaries of the surrogate-fetus relationship are assessed and determined by surrogates through the rhetorical definition of their own role in the pregnancy in commercial terms. This process, which I term *commodifying*, makes use of the capitalist framework by which things, as well as relationships between persons and things, are often described in Western society. Surrogates use the capitalist framework of commodities to concretize and affirm their distance from the fetus and from nature. H. K., for instance, commodifies her role in surrogacy as that of babysitter: "The egg and the sperm aren't mine. I just serve as a womb for rent, and it is just like I give my son to a babysitter to watch over him and she feeds him, dresses him, and takes care of him. So what, will she think for a minute that he belongs to her?"[8]

H. K., as quoted above, takes the commercial situation of the paid caregiver to show how she can care for and look after the fetus that she gestates without becoming emotionally attached. Osnat, another surrogate, also incorporates the babysitter metaphor to create a clear definition of her relationship with the fetus she gestates, establishing at once the monetary, temporary, and caregiving components of the relationship: "Physically it was like a regular pregnancy, but mentally I knew that I was just a babysitter, not more."

Redefining their role as babysitter, surrogates can continue to locate the pregnancy and their role in it outside of nature and biology. While emphasizing the surrogate's own caring, nurturing characteristics within the temporal relationship with the fetus, the babysitter role allows her to show an active interest in the child's welfare. However, at the same time it allows the surrogate to maintain that her interest in the child is not rooted in a natural "bond" but in her desire to dutifully fulfill the tasks of her labor (Roberts 1998, 106).

Rosa, a would-be surrogate who appeared in a March 1996 broadcast of the *Yael Dan Show* on Israel Television's Channel Two, described why she wanted to become a surrogate. In her explanation, she presents her role as babysitter, also describing her womb as a "boardinghouse."

She claims that she would "love and caress a child that she carried in her womb, like someone who received something very valuable to guard, knowing that she would give it up at the end, that it wouldn't be hers. . . . 'I understand that it is something that will be with me for a few months and then it will be gone, shalom. Like a boarder in my house, like a boarder in my body'" (Kahn 1997, 187).

Like Rosa, surrogates often engage in a vocabulary of "containers" and "hotels" for the purpose of describing their nonconnection with the part of their body that they have partitioned off. Specifically, surrogates draw upon this vocabulary to imply that just as a container is not expected to have feelings for the substance it contains, so they do not hold any emotions for the surrogate child that they carry. In this respect, Orna relates how she was able to distance herself from the child she gestated throughout the surrogate pregnancy:

> You have to remind yourself all of the time that you are providing nothing more than a hothouse for him [the fetus] . . . like a hotel in which one stays and leaves without feeling. . . . I put it in my head that it won't have any physical or mental effects on me. That it would have no influence on me, and the fact is that it worked. . . . I had no feelings . . . no side effects. . . . I didn't feel like I was pregnant. . . . It's just like it's called, a *pundak* [inn]. It's a boardinghouse for nine months.

In this statement, Orna plays upon the Hebrew word for surrogate mother, which literally means "innkeeper." She alternately calls her womb a hothouse, a hotel, an inn, and a boardinghouse. With the help of this objectifying terminology, Orna explains the lack of physical effects that the pregnancy had on her, comparing her lack of maternal feelings for the fetus to the lack of emotional attachment that an inanimate object has on its tenant or owner.[9]

Additional commodity-linked vocabulary was prevalent in surrogates' narratives. While one surrogate claimed that she was "only a receptacle tank, an instrument," another surrogate said that she saw herself as "a growth cell for a woman who has no womb. That is all." Still others described their wombs as "vessel" or "incubator." H. K. compared her womb to a car for rent: "It is like someone rents you a car and takes money from you, I am renting my womb and I want money in exchange. . . . It is actually the same rental process, that ends with the termination of the connection [with the car/fetus]."

Surrogates implement similar commodifyng techniques regarding the fetus. Thus, surrogates often talk of the fetus as "the fetus," "their baby," or "it," but not as "him" or "her," even when the future child's sex is known to them. As with the medicalization technique, surrogates use commodity metaphors to distance the surrogate pregnancy from nature. By defining the child as "it," surrogates create a reality that does not call for emotional connection. Specifically, while they perceive a mother to "naturally" fall in love with her child, they would not have the same expectations in an interaction with an object or "thing."

Similar findings in a study of surrogacy in the United States showed surrogates calling themselves "incubators" and "baby machines" (Roberts 1998, 204), yet again in an affirmative, confident fashion, and in a context uninformed of the oppressive connotations with which such metaphors resonate. The practice of commodifying thus helps the surrogate to present herself as an "incubator" who cannot connect emotionally with the child, while the commissioning mother—as both "genetic" and human (not object)—is "naturally" expected to connect with the child[10] (Roberts 1998).

Claiming that surrogacy is a practice that commodifies children and objectifies and exploits women's reproductive capabilities, antisurrogacy activists employ the metaphors of "mother machine" and "human incubator" (Corea 1987) in a negative connotation to further their arguments against surrogacy. Concurrently, surrogates use these commodity metaphors in a positive light to show how they cope with the pregnancy and to enable themselves to part with the child. Thus, the same objectifying rhetoric is at once seen as oppressive and as enabling by the actors themselves.

Inasmuch as the academic arguments use commodity metaphors to characterize surrogates as helpless victims, surrogates use these metaphors to show their power, strength, and altruistic greatness, as well as their control of their bodies, emotions, and actions. Moreover, while the academic arguments use these metaphors to draw a picture of surrogacy as a cold, technological practice in which a commissioning couple exploits a surrogate, the use of commodity metaphors by surrogate mothers themselves is done in order to enable a "natural," human bond of parenthood for a couple in whom the surrogate has invested her friendship and caring.

Seen together, the use of medicalization and commodification by surrogates to replace nature with the unnatural, artificial arm of technology leads us to the image of the cyborg: half human, half machine. It is precisely this surrogate-cyborg that helps surrogates to transform the commissioning mother-child relationship into a more natural one (Roberts 1998, 204). This will be explored in the following section.

Creating the Third Body

The third body is the concept that I draw upon in order to describe how surrogates speak of the surrogate pregnancy as an event occurring both inside their bodies and in a separate body altogether. Drawing upon the other practices that have aided her in distancing her pregnant body from nature, the surrogate thus imagines her body as a hybrid fusion between human and technospace. Visualizing her body as a cyborg entity, the surrogate imagines the pregnancy as "other," attached to, yet detached from her own body. This "third space" can then be removed and attached to another body, creating yet another hybrid entity.

Surrogates narrated an instinctive feeling from the very start of the surrogate pregnancy, identifying it as different from pregnancies they had experienced before. Positioning the pregnancy at a liminal distance, one surrogate claimed that she did not feel the baby inside her at all. This maneuver, she said, allowed her to detach herself from all sensations associated with the pregnancy and eliminate the development of emotional attachment toward the child, which she had in her "own" pregnancies:

> My babies moved inside me all the time. I even felt them when they weren't moving. . . . When you are pregnant, with your own, your own child, you get attached to the child, even before he is born. I mean, you feel him move, every kick, every movement makes you bond with him. So in my subconscious I just didn't bond. I detached, completely. It isn't mine, it isn't my child, I won't feel him. I won't become attached at all. And it was great. I didn't bond. I didn't bond with [the fetus] at all.

The surrogate, as cyborg entity, makes herself dichotomously into both human and machine, whole and hybrid fusion. As cyborgs, surrogates create the attached space carrying the fetus either in their body or adjoined, and either as a whole separate entity, or as one specific imagined part. One surrogate even claimed that "it isn't the same womb" carrying this pregnancy as the one that carried her own child.

As the fetal body becomes mutually exclusive from her own, the surrogate can distance herself from any embodied occurrences surrounding the fetus. Orna created a third space by dividing her body into three separate parts: she allocated her womb to a location she imagined as completely detached from the rest of her person. *Her* body, she claimed, she could *feel*. But although she could physically acknowledge the existence of what she sees as her *nonbody,* whatever occurred in this disowned section she did not feel with her *heart*:

> So I was like this. Me [points to her chest and upward], not me [indicates area from chest to midthigh]. Completely disconnected. I totally disconnected myself from my stomach. I mean, whatever I felt in my stomach, I didn't feel. I mean, I was always saying that I am divided in three. From here to here is me, from here to here isn't me, from here to here is me. And everything to do with my stomach, I ignored. Very simple. I got fat, so I got fat. I didn't pay any attention to my stomach at all. No touching. It was fun to see the ultrasound, to feel him move, because he was moving, because he was alive. But not to feel him move with my heart.

The construction of a "second body" as the third space housing the pregnancy is enabled by the comparison of physical descriptions of bodily responses to prior pregnancies with descriptions of the surrogate pregnancy. In this manner, the cyborg surrogate is able to "prove" that the pregnancy is not, or did not occur in, her "real" body. Rather, the narrative attests to the pregnancy occurring in the "detached" body she conjured up for the purpose of surrogacy. Rinat differentiated between her own pregnancies and the surrogate pregnancy by the fact that during this birth she had cramps:

Rinat: Suddenly I go to bed, lay in bed, and I have cramps. In my own births I don't have cramps . . . not in the births of any of my children . . . suddenly I felt these pains.
Elly: You had contractions here but not with your own kids?
Rinat: If I ever have birth pains, I get them in my back. And these didn't come in my back. Here I really felt pains in my stomach.

Whether the third body is felt or suppressed, it is constantly referred to as behaving differently from how the surrogate's "own" body "naturally" reacts. One surrogate pointed out that the surrogate delivery lasted only three hours, while her "own" deliveries usually lasted the entire day. Almost all the surrogates interviewed claimed that their bodies did not produce milk after they gave birth to the surrogate child. While Orna claimed that "the next day the doctor gave me two pills to dry up the milk, but there was almost no milk to dry up," another surrogate asserted that she had "no milk! The doctor said, you have no milk! I said, no. He said, that is impossible, it doesn't make sense. And he checked. Nothing. Nothing!" Rinat also claimed that her body did not produce milk after this birth. She uses this as a validation for "proving" the distance of both the fetus and pregnancy from her body:

Rinat: I would talk to him and I would, whatever I did for my own babies I did for him.
Elly: But you didn't fall in love with him?
Rinat: No, even when he was born, I had no milk.
Elly: You had no milk?
Rinat: I'm telling you, it was something from another world. Even the milk you get after you give birth, when your breast fills up and everything, nothing.
Elly: And now, with this child, your child [she is about to give birth again], you will I am sure.
Rinat: Of course I will.
Elly: And now you are in love with your child?
Rinat: What kind of question is that! From the minute that I found out that I was pregnant!
Elly: That is strange. You didn't feel like a mom, you had cramps, and no milk.
Rinat: And that is completely different from my own pregnancies, and every woman has those things when she is pregnant!
Elly: I guess your body knew that it wasn't your kid.
Rinat: Yes it did. [Rinat points to a photo of herself on the hospital lawn just hours after giving birth.] Look.
Elly: You look as though you haven't given birth at all.
Rinat: Yes. And that was not long after. Yes, I got out of bed right away. After an hour I was back on my feet.
Elly: And your stomach went down so fast?
Rinat: Yes. Right away.

The child, as is evident in Rinat's account, was erased from her body immediately after delivery. The third space, now finally completely detached, does not remain etched in the embodied memory of the surrogate.

The cyborgian restructuring of the body enables Orna to present the detached third space—and the fetus and pregnancy associated with it—to her commissioning couple. Accordingly, Orna dismisses her commissioning father's embarrassment at seeing her partially unclothed during an ultrasound by assuring him that he is not seeing her—Orna. What he is seeing, she claims, is "only" a stomach dividing between himself and "his" child: "I said to him [the commissioning father], don't be shy, just remember, this is yours [pointing to her stomach]. Don't even think about this stomach, it is nothing, just a stomach, only think about what is inside it."

One surrogate divulged that when she was pregnant with her own children, her stomach was huge, and she gained at least thirteen kilos. During this pregnancy, on the other hand, her stomach remained small, while her commissioning mother "gained the weight instead of me!" Another surrogate claimed that while she usually maintained her small frame or even lost weight while pregnant, she gained more than twenty kilos while pregnant with the surrogate child. Her commissioning mother, however, developed a skin rash common to pregnant women and suffered from postpartum depression after the birth. By simultaneously placing the pregnancy in a space disconnected from their own bodies while still emphasizing their commissioning mother's sympathy pains, surrogates quietly aid in attaching their third space to the commissioning mother.

Likewise, Dafna, a commissioning mother who lived far away from her surrogate and could not follow the pregnancy closely, recalled how her surrogate never ceased to remind their fetus that she and her husband were the intended parents, even though they were not physically nearby: "She asked us to record a tape of our voices talking to our child, so that she could play the tape to the baby in her stomach. And she really would play the tape on a walkman and press the earphones to her stomach. And she said that when she [the fetus] heard our voices, she would turn her head toward us."

As in the example above, technology is used in order to enable "nature" and the "natural" bonding process between mother and child—only in this case, this natural bonding occurs through another woman's body. Often surrogates encourage their commissioning mothers to speak to their stomach and to caress it. Surrogates can then at once acknowledge their emotional and embodied responses to the pregnancy, but at the same time pass them on to the "natural" mother to whom they believe that these feelings belong. One surrogate claimed that she shared all the cramps, vomiting, and initial responses to pregnancy with her couple, not hesitating to phone them the minute she felt the fetus move. "Everything I did was for them," she claimed, "because it was their child."

By transforming her body into a transparent intermediary, the gestational surrogate takes on another form of cyborg identity, making "herself into a model on which pregnancy and birth are purely instrumental phases of [the commissioning couple's] reproduction whom she is helping" (Cussins 1998, 58).

One way of surrogates' transferring the third space to their commissioning mother is by insisting that she accompany them to each and every doctor's appointment. "I want her to go through everything," Masha relayed. "I told her that it is important to me that she be there at all of the ultrasounds. It is not my pregnancy. So I want her to experience it as much as she can." Likewise, surrogates often gave commissioning mothers complete responsibility for making doctor's appointments, obtaining medicines, and speaking with the doctor during checkups.

By creating the third body, surrogates direct the "natural" mother-child bond to where they feel it naturally belongs. Thus, during narratives both of ultrasound and of the delivery itself, the surrogates whom I interviewed barely mentioned themselves at all. Instead, they concentrated in their narratives on their commissioning couple's reactions to the child, stressing the "natural" bonding that occurred between commissioning mother and child, whether in the flesh or on screen. Sealing off the transfer of the third space to the commissioning mother, surrogates maintained that the latter kept the ultrasound photos of the incubated fetus. This, in turn, implies the use of technology to re-create nature.

Emily Martin (1992, 21) argues that science is a "male-biased model of human nature and social reality." Women, she claims, suffer the alienation of parts of the self more acutely than do men; women's bodies are fragmented into body parts by the cold, hard, impersonal, male practices of scientific medicine. Accordingly, studies of women in childbirth in the United States have represented the feelings of fragmentation and objectification as the negative, forced consequences of medically managed pregnancy and childbirth (Martin 1992, 84).

The preceding examples read as extreme instances of the technological fragmentation of the body, as surrogates imagine their wombs as detached from their bodies and even a second body emerging from their own. However, it seems that these women's descriptions of their complete disconnection from the pregnancy occurring inside their bodies is not experienced in the negative manner that Martin suggests. Instead, one can view the cyborg third space as these women's deliberate manipulation of the technological framework encompassing them to maintain their own control over their bodies. Whereas anti-surrogacy literature claims that "technodocs" dissect and market women's bodies by dismembering them into separate reproductive parts that can be reassembled (Klein 1987, 66), here we see an account of the opposite. By creating the third space, surrogates are essentially dividing their bodies in order to maintain the wholeness of motherhood.

Specifically, creating the third body subverts the notion that the separation of pregnancy and motherhood deconstruct the mother-child bond. By making their bodies into fragmented, cyborg entities, women are actually encouraging the bonding process, only with another woman. It is indeed the colonization of nature by technology that enables these women to override, copy, and redirect nature to the person/place that they deem most natural.

Conclusion

The three practices explored above have shown how surrogate mothers in Israel maneuver within the oppressive frameworks of medicalization, commodification, and technological colonization of women's bodies to ultimately exercise their own control over their bodies and the outcomes of their actions. All interrelated, the first two practices explore how the child and pregnancy are detached from the surrogate's body and from "nature" through the surrogate's use of technical jargon. The third practice, in turn, shows how the detached pregnancy and child are transferred to the "natural" commissioning mother.

The transferring of the child returns and draws upon the medicalization technique, inasmuch as the surrogate is able to begin the transfer of the child by transferring all genetic and biological connection to the pregnancy to the commissioning couple. By repeatedly claiming that the genes, blood, and cells making up the fetus are not hers but the couple's, the surrogate symbolically attaches the child that she has detached to them.

Next, by way of the commodifying technique, surrogates facilitate the bond between commissioning mother and child by classifying themselves as containers whose sole purpose is to "incubate" the child until the "natural" mother can claim him. By describing their roles in the pregnancy as "objects," surrogates detach themselves from "nature" and transfer the "natural," human role of mothering to the commissioning mother.

As these two practices conjoin in detaching the child from the surrogate's body, the third practice, of creating the third space, steps in to allocate an imagined body/space to the pregnancy and fetal body. This third space is then passed on to the commissioning mother, as the surrogate actively encourages her to attach both the pregnancy and the fetus to herself.

As a result of these three practices, surrogates emphasize that motherhood is primarily a relationship. They de-biologize motherhood by situating it outside of the pregnant/birthing body. This is not the negative effect, however, of technology or contractual issues, but the empowering attempt of these women to redefine nature. In the end, this results in the subversive removal of motherhood from the body through the medium of a patriarchal practice that is meant to firmly situate genetic heredity in the body (Raymond 1993, 38).

The employment of technological metaphors, then, also becomes a method of their own empowerment, for they use the technocommodity system in their own favor. Incorporating societal belief in the superiority of technology over nature, they use the idea of technological colonization of their reproductive processes in their own favor, showing their own superiority over nature and their own control of their bodies (Davis-Floyd 1992). With these metaphors, they call upon technologies that markedly aim to increase male control of women's bodies, and assist in them to denaturalize the surrogate pregnancy by using the imagery of machines, instruments, and commodities to describe their bodies during pregnancy. They take the images of women as laboratories and of "test tube women" that are often seen as reinforcing the degradation and oppression of women and turn them on their heads.

Inasmuch as I wish to locate the surrogate as agent in a place of pure empowerment, I argue that surrogacy cannot be touted as purely a "choice" for women. Instead, I maintain that these women's agency can be considered as acts of empowerment within the given patriarchal framework (Holmes and Hoskins 1987). The surrogacy narratives show us an example of women who seem to willingly "collude with the technodocs" (Klein 1987, 69), yet by navigating within that framework, they shape their own reality. The question of who is really in control—whether it be the doctor, women, or law—is replaced by a much more ambiguous picture of degrees of control and degrees of freedom. Finally, surrogate mothers in Israel ultimately gain control over their own bodies through the same channels through which patriarchy attempts to mold women into its image (Klein 1985, 65).

NOTES

The research for this project was made possible by grants from the Minerva Center for Human Rights, Hebrew University of Jerusalem; The Association of Israeli Academic Women; The Laifer Center, Hebrew University of Jerusalem; and the Shaine Center for Sociological Research, Hebrew University of Jerusalem.

Furthermore, this project could not have been completed without the generous support and guidance of my advisor Meira Weiss; the comments and encouragement of Don Seeman; the supportive advice of Tamar Rappaport, Edna Lomsky-Feder, and the graduate student peer group that they host; the editing assistance of Rhisa Teman; and the prioritizing help of Avi Solomon. I also thank the women who opened their homes to me, told me their stories, and let me share in their lives.

1. For a detailed discussion of the social, moral, legal, and ethical implications of the Aloni Commission Report, see Shalev 1998; Corinaldi 1995.

2. Surrogate motherhood can take any of three forms. In "traditional" surrogacy, the surrogate is artificially inseminated with the sperm of the commissioning father, thus giving birth to a child conceived of her own egg. In gestational surrogacy, eggs are extracted from the commissioning mother's womb, fertilized through the technology of in-vitro fertilization in a petri dish with her husband's sperm, and then implanted in the surrogate's womb. In this case, the surrogate gives birth to a child with no genetic relation to her. Gestational surrogacy necessarily requires that the commissioning mother be fertile. However, a third type of surrogacy can be undertaken when the commissioning mother is infertile but wishes that there be no genetic connection between the surrogate and the fetus. In such cases the surrogate is implanted with an embryo created from the commissioning father's sperm and the egg of an anonymous donor.

3. For detailed discussions of the feminist arguments for and against surrogacy, see Andrews 1988; Baker 1996. In addition, for detailed discussions of the ethical debate on surrogacy see Cahill 1988; Baslington 1996; McNaughton 1997; Macklin 1991.

4. The Baby M case was the result of the surrogacy contract between Mary Beth Whitehead and William and Elizabeth Stern. Whitehead, who was also the genetic provider of the ovum, carried the child to term and then decided not to give up the child. A much publicized legal battle ensued. In 1987 William Stern, the biological father, sued Mary Beth Whitehead to force her to return the child as the surrogacy contract stated. The lower New Jersey court awarded custody to the Sterns. Later, the New Jersey Supreme Court overturned the decision and awarded custody to William Stern, prohibiting his wife from adopting the child, and granting Whitehead visitation rights (Ragone 1994).

5. Cyborgs are symbiotic fusions of organic life and technological systems (Davis-Floyd and Dumit 1998).

6. For a discussion of the Halakhic issues surrounding surrogacy, see Shifman 1993. For a discussion of the Israeli surrogacy law and the Jewish and Israeli legal aspects involved in its creation, see Corinaldi 1995; Shalev 1998.

7. After the surrogacy contract is approved, the committee is no longer involved unless unique circumstances occur. For instance, a couple who has received the committee's approval for their contract with a certain surrogate mother needs to apply again from the start if the couple wish to change surrogates or even to pursue a second round of surrogacy with the same surrogate. A successful round of surrogacy does not assure that the committee will approve repeat surrogacy of the same couple and surrogate. In fact, in one such case the request for approval of a second contract between a surrogate and couple who had already pursued surrogacy together was rejected by the committee because the surrogate had passed the age limit of forty years old. The committee has intervened in a case

involving the death of the commissioning mother and the subsequent termination of the contract, as well as in a case involving the plea of a commissioning couple for the committee's permission to terminate the pregnancy after fetal testing indicated that the seven-month-old-fetus was developing abnormally.

8. "Like one rents a car and takes money, I rent my womb," (*Tsomet Hasharon* [*Sharon Intersection* (local weekly newspaper)], 19 January 1996.

9. Interestingly, most of the words that Orna chooses to describe her objectified state are in the Hebrew female form, hinting at her view of her surrogacy role as that not just of a container but of a gendered container.

10. It is not surprising, then, that a social worker involved in numerous surrogacy arrangements claimed that the most difficult surrogacy experiences she had witnessed were those involving ova donation, when the commissioning mother did not provide the genetic material herself. This is supported by the fact that surrogates repeatedly emphasize the strong connection between the commissioning mother and the fetus and the commissioning mother's strong internalization of the pregnancy, in opposition to their own nonconnection to the fetus and pregnancy.

REFERENCES

Andrews, Lori B. 1988. "Surrogate Motherhood: The Challenge for Feminists." *Law, Medicine and Health Care* 16 (1–2): 72–80.

Arditti, Rita. 1987. "The Surrogacy Business." *Social-Policy* 18 (2): 42–46.

Baird, Patricia. 1997. "Individual Interests, Societal Interests, and Reproductive Technologies." *Perspectives in Biology and Medicine* 40 (3): 440–51.

Baker, Brenda. 1996. "A Case for Permitting Altruistic Surrogacy." *Hypatia* 11 (2): 34–48.

Baslington, Hazel. 1996. "Anxiety Overflow: Implications of the IVF Surrogacy Case and the Ethical and Moral Limits of Reproductive Technology in Britain." *Women's Studies International Forum* 19 (6): 675–86.

Benshushan, A., and Joseph G. Schenker. 1997. "Legitimizing Surrogacy in Israel." *Human Reproduction* 12 (8): 1832–34.

Berkovitch, Nitza. "Motherhood as a National Mission: The Construction of Womanhood in the Legal Discourse in Israel." *Women's Studies International Forum* 20 (5/6): 605–609.

Brennan, Samantha, and Robert Noggle. 1997. "The Moral Status of Children: Children's Rights, Parents' Rights, and Family Justice." *Social Theory and Practice* 23 (1): 1–26.

Cahill, Lisa Sowle, "The Ethics of Surrogate Motherhood: Biology, Freedom, and Moral Obligation." *Law, Medicine and Health Care* 1988, 16 (2): 65–71.

Corea, Gena. 1987. "The Reproductive Brothel." In Gena Corea, ed., *Man-Made Women: How New Reproductive Technologies Affect Women*, 38–52. Bloomington: Indiana University Press.

Corinaldi, M. 1995. "Towards the Practice of Surrogacy in Israel" *Medicine and Law* 14 (5–6): 425–27.

Cussins, Charis. 1998. "Quit Sniveling, Cryo-Baby. We'll Work Out Which One's

Your Mama!" In Robbie Davis-Floyd and Joseph Dumit, eds., *Cyborg Babies: From Techno-Sex to Techno-Tots.* New York: Routledge.

Davis-Floyd, Robbie. 1992. *Birth as an American Right of Passage.* Berkeley: University of California Press.

Davis-Floyd, Robbie, and Joseph Dumit. 1998. Introduction to *Cyborg Babies: From Techno-Sex to Techno-Tots,* ed. Robbie Davis-Floyd and Joseph Dumit. New York and London: Routledge.

Faquhar, Dion. 1996. *The Other Machine: Discourse and Reproductive Technologies.* New York and London: Routledge.

Franklin, Sarah. 1995. "Postmodern Procreation: A Cultural Account of Assisted Reproduction." In Faye Ginsburg and Rayna Rapp, eds., *Conceiving the New World Order: The Global Politics of Reproduction.* Berkeley: University of California Press.

Holmes, Helen B., and Betty B. Hoskins. 1987. "Prenatal and Preconception Sex Choice Technologies: A Path to Femicide?" In Gena Corea, ed., *Man-Made Women: How New Reproductive Technologies Affect Women,* pp. 1–15. Bloomington: Indiana University Press.

Kahn, Susan Martha. 1997. "Reproducing Jews: The Social Uses and Cultural Meanings of the New Reproductive Technologies in Israel." Ph.D. diss., Department of Anthropology, Harvard University.

———. 2000. *Reproducing Jews: A Cultural Account of Assisted Conception in Israel.* Durham, N.C.: Duke University Press.

Klein, Renate Duelli. 1987. "What's 'New' about the New Reproductive Technologies?" In Gena Corea, ed., *Man-Made Women: How New Reproductive Technologies Affect Women,* pp. 64–74. Bloomington: Indiana University Press.

Konrad, Monica. 1998. "Ova Donation and Symbols of Substance: Some Variations on the Theme of Sex, Gender, and the Partible Body." *Journal of the Royal Anthropology Institute* 4 (4): 643–67.

Langer, Lilly, and Pedrosa Eliot. 1995. "Reproductive Technology: Life as a Commodity in the Past, Present, and Future." Paper presented at annual meeting, American Sociological Association.

Macklin, Ruth. 1991. "Artificial Means of Reproduction and Our Understanding of the Family." *Hastings Center Report* 21 (1): 5–11.

Martin, Emily. 1992. *The Woman in the Body: A Cultural Analysis of Reproduction.* 2d ed. Boston: Beacon Press.

McNaughton, M. 1997. "Ethical Issues in Surrogate Motherhood." *Human Reproduction* 12 (11): 93–94.

Ragone, Helena. 1994. *Surrogate Motherhood: Conception in the Heart.* Boulder, Colo.: Westview Press.

Raymond, Janice G. 1993. *Women as Wombs: Reproductive Technologies and the Battle over Women's Freedom.* San Francisco: HarperCollins.

Roberts, Elizabeth F. S. 1998. "'Native' Narratives of Connectedness: Surrogate Motherhood and Technology." In Robbie Davis-Floyd and Joseph Dumit, eds., *Cyborg Babies: From Techno-Sex to Techno-Tots.* New York and London: Routledge.

Schenker, J. G. 1991. "Assisted Reproduction: Formation of Laws and Regulations." In Y. Boutaleb and A. Gzouli, eds., *New Conceptions in Reproduction*, pp. 149–58. New York and London: Parthenon.

Shalev, Carmel. 1998. "Halakha and Patriarchal Motherhood—An Anatomy of the New Israeli Surrogacy Law." *Israel Law Review* 32 (1): 51–80.

Shifman, Pinhas. 1993. "A Perspective on Surrogate Motherhood in Jewish and Israeli Law." In Andrew Bainham, David Pearl, and Ros Picford, eds., *Frontiers of Family Law*, pp. 79–93. New York: John Wiley.

Snowdon, C. 1994. "What Makes a Mother? Interviews with Women Involved in Egg Donation and Surrogacy." *Birth* 21 (2): 77–84.

van Niekerk, Anton, and Liezl van Zyl. 1995. "The Ethics of Surrogacy: Women's Reproductive Labor." Journal of Medical Ethics 21 (6): 345–49.

Yuval Davis, Nira. 1989. "National Reproduction and 'the Demographic Race' in Israel." In Floya Anthias and Nira Yuval Davis, eds., *Women-Nation-State*. London: Macmillan.

Elly Teman *is a graduate student at the Hebrew University of Jerusalem, Israel. Her research interests include the anthropology of the body, medical anthropology, women's studies, and Jewish folklore. She can be reached at mslula@onebox.com.*

Putting My Foot (Prosthesis, Crutches, Phantom) Down

Considering Technology as Transcendence in the Writings of Donna Haraway

Sharon Betcher

"[I]n the era of techno-biopolitics," writes feminist historian of science Donna Haraway, "[p]rosthesis becomes a fundamental category for understanding personal and political" embodiment. For technonatural bodies, she concludes, "[e]mbodiment is . . . prosthesis" (1991b, 249 n. 7 and 195). In this essay I consider Haraway's prosthetic technology, especially as figurally established in the cyborg, from two perspectives: (1) the witness of prosthetically-enabled disabled persons; and (2) a critical examination of the Christian incarnational or embodiment practices to which Haraway herself alludes—notably, her observation that "[t]he 'hardest' science is about the realm of pure spirit" (1991b, 153). Leading us into the laboratories of prosthetic incarnationalism, she must mean (I can only assume) to take us along with the cyborg into the spiritual realms of "ether, quintessence" (153).[1]

Haraway recognizes that Western technoscience has been motivated by Christian millennialism—a "salvation history" or metanarrative of Edenic, pastoral innocence, its loss, redemption, and re-creation. Presuming its beginnings and ends to be Edenic bliss, Christianity (as Haraway analyzes it) has been driven to eradicate all unseemly characters and offensive disruptions (flux and flow, muck and mess, suffering and toil, death and disease, swampland as well as the wilds) by enacting a zealous, purificatory biologic. This mytheme, a potent narrative node that has colonized modern time and space, can be divorced (as Haraway realizes) neither from the genocidal, ecocidal horrors nor the modest remediations of suffering that have prevailed within modernity. Attempting to reprogram this "time machine" so as to commit ourselves to the midst of history (not its end/s), Haraway calls upon the figure of the "cyborg, a hybrid of machine and organism," to generate new practices of embodiment and therefore also new configurations of world-making practices that will embrace mortality

and finitude (Haraway 1991b, 149). As an hybridic and therefore transgressive implosion of animal with machine, cyborgs (Haraway hopes)
might disrupt the pretense to wholesomeness that Haraway believes
mobilizes Christian practice. This mutant "figure," she maintains, con-
fuses the naturalist categories of Christian salvation history and can
therefore mutate its incarnational technologies and salvific matrix.

Following upon the work of Merleau-Ponty, who phenomenologi-
cally located the corporeality of the soul, the term *incarnation* has been
employed in philosophical discourses to name the practice of embodiment (Grosz 1994, 219 n. 1). This usage has specifically prevailed
within feminist philosophy—in an attempt, I believe, to subvert the
biologic that has repressed women's lives by consciously evoking the
phenomenon of "spirited corporeality." While Haraway uses the term
sparingly, I choose to employ *incarnation* in this essay, because I contend that it is precisely "spirit's" relation to mortality and finitude that
Haraway fails to calculate adequately. Haraway's "cyborg figures" have,
despite her feminist and ecojustice commitments to morph the edges
of the Second Christian millennium, been metabolized by Christianity's
discourse on "Holy Spirit." Christian pneumatology, or doctrine of
Spirit, has been an idealist discourse that floats upon Christianity's
abjection of all things transient. Its transcendentalist currents—quite
easily, if surprisingly, fused with Western technological aspirations—
inflate Western technological infatuation.

'Embodiment Is . . . Prosthesis'

Postmodern philosophies, hoping to disrupt totalism, sport allusions
to the morphological fragmentation of disabled, apparently "totaled"
bodies. Among such philosophies, Haraway's "socialist, feminist, and
anti-racist environmentalism" seems most promising for one such as
myself who has unwittingly joined the Crip Nation (Haraway 1992b,
296).[2] For one who has found it difficult to walk the line of ecological
commitments with anything but my phantom foot, her insistence that,
when considering survival hopes for the next millennium, practices of
embodiment must learn to incorporate material technology seems
helpful, hopeful even (1992b; 1997). Given that and her avowed commitment to a future that includes de/monstrous, mutated, and dismembered bodies, Haraway's figural "cyborg for earthly survival"
would seem a natural affiné for the prosthetically-enabled disabled
(1992a, 86; 1991b, 212).

Haraway's "embodiment is . . . prosthesis" seems finally to invite
those of us who each day "don" our prostheses, "plant" our feet, and/or

spin our wheels into discourse. Until this time, disability has remained the province of "healing professions" and public benevolence. Despite the liberative humanitarian agenda of the past four decades, disability has not yet been "privileged . . . as a foundational category of social experience or symbolic investment [within the humanities]" (Mitchell and Snyder 1997, 1). Consequently, Haraway's poststructuralist allusion to our experience of "body" feels like an open door, the possibility for a discourse in which we might have something author/itative to offer. Such an agenda as Haraway sets might even generate affinity between the able and the disabled, could possibly open out an affinity circle in which we the disabled could contribute our constructive witness. Insomuch as incarnation presumes to be a prosthetic technology, surely disabled persons could finally garner some subjective respect. Who, after all, has spent more time in prosthetic labs than the disabled? If anyone knows how to don a prosthesis, it would seem to be one of us, who, like Melville's Ahab, has "one leg standing in three places"—a prosthesis planted in the material eternity of prosthetic titanium and carbon fiber, a phantom thick with the sinews of memory, and a set of crutches or wheels to prop up the other two (Melville 1961, 447).

Such a discourse as Haraway proposes is not then to be ignored as the disabled—the last identity group in the "PC" catechism—attempt a subject position. As the disabled, we need an allied philosophical discourse that can enable the emergence of a shared political agenda among those whose bodies are, as Haraway correctly notes, "irredeemably specific" (1992a, 87). That the identity politics and rights legislation of previous liberative movements will not work for us is attested by the fact that, during the first five years of the Americans with Disabilities Act, the unemployment rate for the disabled rose from an already scandalous 66 percent to 71 percent.[3] Further, even though technology has promised to be the "great equalizer" for the disabled, and, despite the obsolescence of the human body for the way of life within the information age, we the disabled find ourselves positioned on the edge of a sociocultural precipice.[4] Having served as high technology's "poster children" (thereby giving it figural legitimation, while disguising its hidden militarism), we now find ourselves to be socially expendable: given the socioeconomic burden we are perceived to present, genetic breakthroughs on one end of the life-spectrum, like euthanasia on the other, promise easy, if "merciful," eradication. Given this, how can we not accept the hand of friendship from a cyborg?

Although the disabled represent one of the earliest, most intimate facilitations of human and machine, the disabled have typically been

made figuratively to speak *for* a cyborgian existence without being
allowed to *speak up* or, in Haraway's terms, to "witness" (1997). This—
oddly enough—also pertains within Haraway's prosthetic practice of
incarnation. Despite her explicit rejection of discourses in which some
represent themselves as the "voice of the voiceless" (a discourse practice which, despite its social justice commitments, has itself gained its
transcendence from the marginalization and suppression of disabled
bodies), Haraway chooses as her witnesses, not the actual lives of disabled persons, but characters from the pages of sci-fi literature (see
Haraway 1992b, 311).

Haraway has consistently contested the co-constitutive technologies
of modern gender and science that originated with Robert Boyle's
demonstration of the air pump, the infamous experiment of suffocat-
ing a "bird-under-glass," which "required" the exclusion of women
from the laboratory (Haraway 1997, 24, 31). But inasmuch as gender
was "in-the-making" as that "experimental way of life built the exclusion of actual women," I must ask, what are these discursive "disciplines" of scientific theory and postmodern philosophy now making
up? What technology-in-the-making would require that we, the disabled, be wallflowers rather than witnesses (28–29)? As long as the disabled remain the bird-under-glass of scientific theory and postmodern
philosophy, and therefore of social and material technologies, one
must ask whether there still remains something that this incarnational
technology is choreographed to keep silent. When one person
becomes the object of vision (as Haraway herself notes), someone else
gets to play at transparent, transcendent objectivity (32). So, what tran-
scendentalizing move would be "disabled" by our presence in this discourse? Because I do not choose to slight the hand she extends to the
family of abjects-in-solidarity (1992a), I want to challenge Haraway's
discourse—not to refute it, but to find a "prosthetic territory" where I
can put my foot (prosthesis, crutches, wheels) down (Brahm and
Driscoll).

Inasmuch as the tenacious rhizomes of Christianity's salvation history sprout up like crabgrass in disabled bodies, enticing us to try to
master its old grave-to-glory and tragedy-to-triumph plotlines, I personally couldn't be happier than to work beside Haraway to dispense
with the "bracing discourses of salvation history" (Haraway 1997, 45).
Haraway, however, seems to assume of the term *prosthetics* as she does
of the figure of the cyborg that, by simply coupling human flesh with
machine, we have generated politically agile transgressors who "trouble kind and force a rethinking of kin" (119). Haraway consequently
presumes that the cyborg—theoretically now a "mixed breed"—has

already put its foot down on and walked away, as if a fugitive, from
Christian salvation history, that the cyborg has entered as agent into a
new prosthetic territory, which eludes the demarcation of the Next
Christian Millennium (119).

Sounding out the suspicious silence exacted of the disabled and the
reluctance of the disabled community to embrace either the cyborg
or postmodern prostheticism, I would suggest that Haraway's cyborg
may not be quite the positive perversity Haraway imagines (see
Wendell 1996, 44–45; Haraway 1991b, 149). I suspect rather that the
cyborg's prostheses represent a condensed referent of what has been
construed as "the most natural" in a certain trajectory of Christian discourse. Specifically, I am suggesting that in the cyborg we encounter
totalistic holism parading as technological hybridism. If that proves
true, then without some interpellation the cyborg may not prove
demonstrative for postmodern humanity. Postmodernism's incarnational prostheticism would then need to be reconfigured, since—as
Haraway herself has said—anything that figures itself as "natural knowledge" is readily and covertly "reincorporated into techniques of social
control instead of being transformed into sciences of liberation"
(1991b, 7–8).

Given that the studies that led to Merleau-Ponty's theoretical conjecture of the corporeality of the soul were conducted with amputees,
perhaps we the disabled can swerve incarnational technology once
again (Grosz 1994, chaps. 3–4). I will proceed, first, by reviewing the
social and material technologies currently motivating prosthetics and
then, second, by critiquing Haraway's arguments on behalf of the fugitive status of the cyborg. Finally, can we—without discarding prosthetics as a hopelessly totalistic technology—reconfigure prosthetic
incarnationalism on behalf of a "mutated experimental way of life that
does not issue in the New World Order, Inc." (Haraway 1997, 47)?

She Thought She Would Get the Chair: On the Social and Material Technologies of Prosthetic Sciences

That *prosthetics* in common language refers only to artificial limbs and
not to my wheelchair or crutches gives you some preliminary idea of
the disciplinary power operating in prosthetic sciences and, by extension, within our culture itself. To illustrate this disciplinary power, I
refer you to ad copy in the fall 1998 issue of *Enable*, a magazine with
the express mission of empowering the disabled to reach our full
potential. An ad for Universal Institute, who describe themselves as
"rehabilitation and fitness specialists," features an elderly, Caucasian

woman seated dejectedly beside a square, chrome, orthopedic wheel-chair. In successive phases, moving from parallel bars to an indepen-dent walker, she is lifted from despondency. The caption reads: "She thought she was getting the chair. Instead we gave her life."[5]

As this ad suggests, prosthetics is most often socially motivated by the "pick up your bed and walk" philosophy. Prosthetic technology seems to have one goal in mind, the uprightness of bipedism—whether or not this proves the most empowering possibility for a par-ticular body. As my body has refused to concede to this technological solution with anything much more than cosmetic "seemliness," I have become—socially speaking—a somatic heretic of our cultural belief in the power of technoscience. While learning consequently to piece together a prosthetic multiplicity of shape-shifting forms, for example, crutches for daily distance, wheels when chasing my preteen daughter through the mall, prosthetic limb when it's raining, I have been con-strued, from a social and medical perspective, as "failing to adjust."

Material technology can bedazzle us with its claims for culturally endowed transcendental transparency—its assumed beneficent whole-someness inviolate, superordinate to marks of gender, race, or eth-nicity. Perhaps it is only when you stub your (prosthetic) toe on the doorjamb to eternity that you figure out technology's "habitus"—that is, how social beliefs and values functionally energize or articulate the body in relation to its world—and eternity's perimeters (Bourdieu 1995, 52–65). It might appear, when adding cybernetics to organic bodies, that—as Haraway ascribes to cyborgs—bodies no longer "end at the skin" (Haraway 1991b, 178). And to be sure, a disabled person can in fact learn to incorporate the machine into his/her body image. Nevertheless, it is also the case that prostheses may materially consolidate skin-deep oppressions. Greeting my first terrifyingly exuberant steps in a prosthetic leg, my prosthetist emitted a troubled, if cryptically prophetic, scream: you walk like an Indian! Having been raised in the rolling farmlands of southeastern Minnesota, where only city slickers would be fool enough to dig their heels into the undulating surface of a haywagon, I toed into the earth. Because my hydraulic knee is activated by a firm heel strike, my prosthesis demands that I dig my heels into the earth. Now what story generated this habitus? Is not my prosthesis demanding somatic belief in the Christian story of the Fall from the Garden of Eden? According to normative readings of the story, from henceforth humanity would accomplish its salvation by exercising animosity toward the earth—figurally communicated by the human heel crushing the head of the earth serpent, Tiamat (Genesis 3).

Once that little lesson in orthodox soteriology began to unravel, other revelations were quick to follow. If the prosthesis demands a clean heel strike, descending hiking trails would clearly prove problematic; I was destined for the Flatlands of the Flat Earth Society— hardwood floors, cement sidewalks, parking lots, life on the level. Not only must I dig in my heel, my leg has been built with a heel-to-toe differential that demands I wear a shoe. Since my family and therefore our friendship circles have been built multiracially, this presents a bit of a problem when I am invited to the home of Korean friends. What social propriety prevails at this threshold: shall I take off not only my shoe, but also put my foot down on their doorstep?

The action of donning a prosthesis, like any "incarnation," can be shown to demand consent not only to a certain ethnic, but also to a class and gender, posture. Inasmuch as artificial limbs are specifically built to fill in for what a body "lacks," feminists should get a bit edgy.[6] "Cyborg technologies," write Gray and Mentor, "have the potential to reify in material bodies class and caste distinctions that were *only social constructions* up to now" (1995, 245 n. 7, emphasis added; see also Kaufman-Osborn 1997, 15). As habituated as we might be to certain social technologies, once they are incarnated in prosthetic machinery, they prove insidious, leaving precious little room for forgiveness, for free-flowing mimesis, for re/incarnations. Haraway seems, at times, to be cognizant of this point, for example, when she observes that "prosthetic devices . . . build in translations and specific *ways* of seeing, that is, ways of life" (1991b, 190). In fact, Haraway proceeds to argue that our technological prostheses can therefore provide ethical critique in a way more objectively revelatory than "primate vision." Obviously, I may be illustrating Haraway's point precisely: I understand the *habitus* of the Western body better than ever before. However, my question to Haraway remains: now that I know, how do I "intervene in this pattern of objectification" (195)? Where do I put my foot down? Once I don that prosthesis, it stipulates that I plant my heel on Tiamat's head; it is committed to that salvation history and demands my obedience.

Further, compulsory bipedism demands that we consent to the social amelioration of suffering by hiding it, under the veil of the prosthesis, within the individual body. Contrary to Haraway's contention that the cyborg is no longer defined by the public/private split, the staunch individualization of suffering enabled by prosthetics enforces just such a split (Haraway 1991b, 151). Prosthetics, as historian David Yuan's research correlating its use with national self-image following the Civil War has also shown, can be as much about offering an aesthetic and aseptic social response to suffering as it may be about the actual personal amelioration of such. "[O]ne of the most injurious wars in history," the Civil War, Yuan reports, "produced more amputees than any other war Americans have fought in" (1997, 71). A young nation was suddenly confronted with the problem of self-image: 130,000 of its most virile young males had been left "stumping" around. In an effort to avert "the scorn that a critical Europe might have for the struggling United States," the physician, inventor, and statesman Oliver Wendell Holmes called for the politics of "Reconstruction" to be applied to this grotesquerie of amputated virility. Holmes, in an essay in the *Atlantic Monthly* (May 1863), praises the Palmer leg, one of the first cosmetically shaped prostheses complete with an articulating knee, for "'counterfeiting [Palmer's injury] so far as possible'" (cited in Yuan 81, 75). In the process of the United States making itself appear presentable and more aesthetically refined than the Old World, American society, specifically American technology (Holmes insisted), had an obligation to "raise the coarse and vulgar to the plane of symmetry and refinement" (Yuan 82). Putting the nation back together required "a new technology," "an artificial limb that [would] convincingly *disguise* the intolerable fact of the incomplete body"—the body social, the body personal (74–75, emphasis added).

In my own experience, the day that I donned a prosthesis was the day that everyone else breathed a sigh of relief, and I lost my sense of humor. For some of us, the psychic repression that belief in the cure of the prosthetic limb can entail may be comparable to that of a gay or lesbian being forced into the closet, and the psychic relief, but social retaliation, when one refuses the cultural solution, comparable to that of "coming out." So what do the cyborg and her prosthesis keep "in the closet"?

While Haraway suggests that the cyborg figuration can, like the science-fictional wormhole, "cast travelers into unexpected regions of space," the "wormhole" in my cyborgian complex appears for public view when I take off my prosthetic foot (Haraway 1997, 12). That which forces reconsideration of the question "And Aren't I a Woman?" appears to be the etchings of futility upon my mortal form (see 1992a). That this unveiling (of the doughnut hole of my limb loss), rather than the curious, cosmetically covered endoskeletal structure standing in for my leg, should throw off the light switch of desire is a clue for me that Haraway's analysis may be slightly off course. When inclusion among the human community is being considered, the cyborg's machine/human interface seems not to be as troubling as a prosthetically unproselytized body—a disabled body refusing social comeliness or "seemliness."

To be sure, by presupposing a feminist audience and inasmuch as she specifically intends to resituate women in a technostrategic discourse, Haraway may presume that the mixing of kinds is actually not merely "cybernetics/organism," but machine/female (1991a, 6). Yet even this I do not find sufficiently disruptive, since Ivy![(tm)], though an above-knee (AK) amputee, can simply don one or the other of her dozen or so prostheses and go back to work as a New York fashion model with nothing jarred loose in the social psyche. There is a point at which the machine/female interface may be transgressive—namely, showing my "thighs of steel," revealing the black reptilian carbon-fiber endoskeletal frame as opposed to veiling the machine with a cosmetic cover. To a degree, then, I could agree with Haraway that there is an issue of "cross-dressing" here; a machine/female interface can never be as transcendentally transparent as a machine/male interface. A woman with her technological interfaces does not generate the same acceptance that a man and his machines does (see, e.g., John Hockenberry's *Moving Violations*). This does not, however, refute my point that these machine/female interfaces can still provoke transcendence, whereas removing the machine interface inevitably shuts off the light switch of desire. In fact, given "woman's" identification with "decaying flesh" in the platonic trajectory, when a woman becomes disabled, doesn't prosthetics—like some version of the chador—become even that much more socioculturally mandatory?

Thus, my suspicion: the science of prosthetics, in particular, and consequently cyborg incarnations may actually veil a discourse on compulsory holism. If so, it is not only on behalf of disabled bodies that we need to disrupt such composite holisms; without disruption postmodernism's "embodiment is prosthetic" may merely replicate idealism, all the more subtle because of its purported hybridism. Without interruption, our prostheses—for "we are all cyborgs" now—may carry this totalism, like a zebra mussel, into the next millennium.

Considering Cyborg Incarnations

Haraway begins her political project from a theoretical position not unlike that of the philosopher Luce Irigaray—namely, by theorizing from what Irigaray calls the catastrophic fold and what Haraway herself comparably calls the "split"—sites, in other words, that yield neither to radical severance nor to reductive fusion. "Splitting, not being, is the privileged image for feminist epistemologies of scientific knowledge," Haraway insists, concluding that "'[s]plitting' . . . should be about heterogeneous multiplicities that are simultaneously necessary and incapable of being squashed into isomorphic slots or cumulative lists" (1991b, 193). Whereas Irigaray "tends towards subversive figurations based on female *morphology*," for example, the two lips, Haraway—given the extensive and inescapable, even preferable, dimensions of technonature—formulates political resistance from what she, in countering organicists, assumes to be the transgressive couplings across taxonomic lines, namely, the machine-human (Braidotti 1994, 3). She writes:

> Located in the belly of the monster, I find the discourses of natural harmony, the nonalien, and purity unsalvageable for understanding our genealogy in the New World Order, Inc. Like it or not, I was born kin to PU-239 and to transgenic, transspecific, and transported creatures of all kinds; that is the family for which and to whom my people are accountable. It will not help—emotionally, intellectually, morally, or politically—to appeal to the natural and the pure. (Haraway 1997, 62)

Given that it is my "unprosthelytized" rather than my prosthetically enabled body that haunts the social psyche, I am wondering whether these "trannies" of Haraway's—in other words, these transgenic, transmutated, and transsubstantiated creatures—are as transgressive as Haraway makes them out to be. In what follows, I want to consider whether Haraway's "cyborg incarnation" has in fact escaped "salvation history," as she claims (1991b, 150), or whether the technonatural cyborg, though it disclaims all origin stories, might itself be born of the (S)pirit.

I would like to pose the theoretical possibility that, while refuting the organic essentialist, Haraway has actually backed herself into the closet of another "naturalist" discourse. Haraway claims—and I have no question—that the cyborg "has no truck with seductions to *organic* wholeness" (150, emphasis added). Haraway, however, seems to assume that by escaping organicism, she has also escaped millennial interests in "wholesomeness." Yet, as I've shown, no more than the term *organic* does the term *prosthesis* refer us to a territory uncontaminated by the mythemes of the Second Christian Millennium. Haraway's primary argument on behalf of the fugitive status of the cyborg is that, looked at from the perspective of Christianity's interest in preserving the purity of "kinds," the cyborg appears to be a taxonomically troublesome extraterrestrial (1991b, 152–55; 1997). Haraway reads Christianity as offended by this "mixing of kinds" and consequently invested in patrolling the borders between humans and animals, among the races of humans, between the sexes, and now, in terms of both the debate surrounding genetic engineering and ecological organicism, between human and machine or between earth and "technology." Read in this way, "embodiment is prosthetic" would appear to be syntactically transgressive.

However, if certain trajectories of Christianity have been invested in maintaining clearly distinct taxonomic "kind"-ship (as they indisputably have), this does not sum up the Christian project. One of the earliest baptismal formulas known to Christianity articulated a commitment to the formation of an heterogeneous community held together with pneumatic energy: "In Christ there is neither Jew nor Greek, slave nor free, male nor female" (Gal. 3:28). Baptismal commitments to an adopted spirit family—an affinity group, certainly not a nuclear family or any form of biological kinship network (Matt. 10:34 ff.)—specifically precluded soteriological exclusivism based in the delineation of kinds. In fact, the key salvific figure here—namely, Jesus as Christ—was considered a hybrid. Jesus, it was asserted, hybridically merged two natures, such that he could be both "true God, begotten of the Father from eternity" and "true [hu]man."

According to the fourth-century theologian Athanasius of Alexandria, whose writings became Christianity's creedal gene pool, the "eternal" realm, ontologically distinct from the earth, was the most natural, while the finite world was a mere artifice. As a produced artifact and therefore likely to degenerate, the material porosity and solubility of corporeality had to be prosthetically stayed by fusion with the unchangeability of what was considered the most natural material, the incorruptibility of pure spirit. "Setting his sights upon the model of a re-creation performed by [the incarnation of] Christ," scholar of late antiquities Virginia Burrus explains, "Athanasius expects the human subject to supersede his own natural mutability through the granted stability of divine incorruptibility. . . . The divinization of humanity thus comes in the (dis)guise of a put-on, a cover-up, a veil, shrouding the ebb and flow of bodily existence" (2000, 47).

If the "mixing of kinds" is—as I would therefore submit—paradigmatically Christian, what has made this heterogeneous human community possible has been the commitment to live "in the spirit"—to live, that is, "beyond the skin," by psychic divestment of the carnal body, by donning or putting on the prosthetic spirit-body. This process of becoming a virtual somatic agnostic required Christians to psychically disarticulate sexuality and to disavow territorial ties and ethnic markings, becoming thereby—it was supposed—a generic, transcendent, if also "hybrid," human (Boyarin 1993). In this vision of universal human solidarity what has been at issue is not so much the "mixing of kinds," for example, apples and oranges, Jews and Greeks, male and female; as what has to be kept out of the mix, for example, the worm in the apple, the foot in the grave, the female-engendered body, the body "close to death," as Levitical laws seem to have construed disabled bodies (see Lev. 21:16–24; Abrams 1998, 8). Psychic delibidinalization of the carnal, female realm undergirded the practice given over to achieving christological hybridity.

Haraway appreciatively reads Irigaray's mimetic critique of Plato's cave as the womb for man's "second birth" out of the body and into the mind (Haraway 1992b, 330–31 n. 9; 1997, 83). Western Christianity has had, however, its own "breeder reactor," namely the Holy Spirit, through which men have given birth to "nature 'enterprised up'" (Strathern in Haraway 1997, 102). Prior to the coming of the Spirit, writes theologian Jürgen Moltmann, "[t]ransitory time and the mortality of all the living was held to be the 'natural' condition of created things" (1992, 88). The Spirit, however (Moltmann continues), exposes finitude as a sickness amenable to remediation. Transience, in other words, is that which in terms of Christianity's doctrine of the Spirit appears most *un*natural. Just as living "in the Spirit" has required Christians to live beyond the flesh, so here: the Spirit moves Christians into a territory beyond the reach of finitude—*in the name of the most natural.*

Given Christianity's commitment to break the "bondage of transience" or "futility," so as to restore the possibility for universal, human community, (material) technology has itself been greeted as an evolution of the Spirit (see Romans 8:20–21). That the Holy Spirit has not been at all averse to the evolution of material technology, can be read in the work of the early-twentieth-century philosophical theologian Nicholas Berdyaev. In the process of "liberat[ing] man [*sic*] . . . from his immersion in elemental nature," Berdyaev observed, Christianity was "obliged to mechanize nature" so as to keep humanity from the "danger of communing" with the earth (1936, 116–17). Our christological *machin*ations have led us straight into prosthetic territories.

"Any transcendentalist move is deadly," writes Haraway (1991a, 16). When looking around for transcendentals, one cannot, I would only add, ignore their technological materialization, since—as theologian Catherine Keller has pointed out—when Columbus set sail, he bent the trajectory of Christian transcendence from the vertical thrust to "the horizontal, horizonal" (1998, 12). The "Age of Discovery" turned upon a new theological impulse that sought the transcendent not in the heavens above, but on the cusp of the next horizon—the horizon of scientific as well as of colonial discovery. Technology—begotten in the womb of Christian apocalyptic and modernist hopes for the "New Creation," the "New Heaven and New Earth," *in and through* the "discovery" and reclamation of the Garden—has been among the primary, modern modes for Western Christianity's transcendence of transience (see Rev. 21:1–4; Keller 1996, 3; also see Noble 1998, 3, 9–20). Consequently, what appears to be a transgressive technonatural hybrid from one angle may from another angle—specifically from that which inspires Haraway's own hopes for communities of abject, "dismembered," un- "kind" persons, bonded in solidarity (1992a)—well, from that angle the cyborg and her prostheses, rather than "subvert[ing] what counts for nature," may be all- "most natural" (1991b, 152). Haraway herself seems poised on the edge of such insights when she observes that "[t]he 'hardest' science is about the realm of pure spirit" and that "[s]cience made was nature undone" (1991b, 153; 1997, 33). Even going so far as to greet cyborgs as "ether, quintessence," she nevertheless fails to recognize the import of her own words: as incarnational figures, cyborgs appear to have been born of (W)holy Spirit, animated by Western Christian salvation history, and quite at home in the Garden of modernity's New Earth (1991b 153, 150–51).

As she concluded her essay "The Promise of Monsters" with a rendition of the cyborg, so throughout her 1997 text, *Modest Witness,* Haraway has enfolded the work of artist Lynn Randolph. A review of these iconographic figures (inspired by, but also reflectively woven back into, Haraway's text), suggests to this disabled person Haraway's consistent overestimation of the transcendent capacities of technoscience and her consequent unwitting commitment to a "summing and subsuming" holism (Haraway 1997, 16; 1992b, 192). In each figuration—from the Cyborg to OncoMouse, La Mestiza Cosmica, and the Millennial Children—the aesthetic loveliness of these supposedly dismembered and "disarticulated" figures stands out against their overtly contaminated landscapes. (Ironically, among the disabled, disarticulation refers to a radical amputation severed through a joint, whereas nothing comparable visibly disables the somatic innocence of Haraway's or Randolph's figures.) Remarkably, the biotech figures remain visually immune from the consequences of four decades of petrochemically and pharmaceutically "enhanced" life.

If "[s]ituated knowledges require that the object of knowledge be pictured as an actor and agent," why has the oil-polluted bayou not yet acted back—in the form of allergic rashes and asthma, at the least— upon the millennial children, who are figured instead as "whole, firm" (1991b, 198; 1997, 40)? Clearly OncoMouse, replete with a crown of thorns, serves as a christological figure, specifically a figure of substitutionary atonement. Yet why has OncoMouse—"born" of the hybridic implosion of women with biotechnology's little "warrior princess," the rodent order used to wage humanity's war against cancer—remained so, well, "well-endowed"? Frankly, I would have expected her appearance among "the clan of one-breasted women" (Williams 281). Likewise the interpolation of the Virgin of Guadalupe straddling the Texas-Mexico border: neither migrant labor nor work in a maquiladora leave a body this pristine. Many of us who have been "gestating in the amniotic effluvia of terminal industrialism" spawn tumors; we wear the infamous necklace scar of thyroid cancers (1991b, 296). Some among us enter the postgender world of the cyborg through dismemberment, for example, the loss of breasts and testicles; others by developing a compensatory musculature, for instance, bulging biceps from working crutches or wheelchair, a morphology that henceforth refuses fashionable feminine seemliness. If these icons represent "Cyborgs for Earthly Survival," if these are figures meant to gather up irredeemably suffering bodies at the end of the Second Millennium, why aren't their "freak flags" flying (Linton 1998, 3)? If the cyborg is to serve in any way as an incarnational figuration to get us out of the Second Millennium and back into the middle of history, wouldn't we see at least *three* feet sticking out from under the computer table? (I mean that question only *figuratively,* of course.)

On Prosthetic Erraticism: Reconsidering Technology as/ and Transcendence

Haraway's evocation of incarnation as *prosthetic* constitutes her attempt to calculate the "ratio" of mortality imploded with the immortal or eternal—for her, the Promethean contours of the likes of PU-239 (a radioisotope of plutonium with a half-life of 24,000 years), or, in my case, the nondisintegrative prosthetic textures of titanium, carbon fiber, bioelastic and silicon. In a footnote to her essay "Situated Knowledges," Haraway reviews the science-fiction literature of John Varley, affirming his ongoing exploration of the way in which prosthetic technologies re/mind a cyborg to finitude "despite their extraordinary transcendence of 'organic' orders" (1991b, 249). In other words, by evoking *prosthetics* Haraway intended to remand us—most appropriately, I would say—to the decisive split that Kate Soper simply writes as "Nature/'nature.'" As we "rethink . . . our conditions of flourishing" (Soper advises), we can discursively do without neither an awareness of our dependence on and the independence of various strata of the ecological terrain nor an awareness of how cultural technologies reconstrue what counts as nature (1996, 28, 23). Yet I would suggest that as Haraway has fit the cyborg with prostheses, these have actually seamed-up the split of ethical, figurative accountability all too well. Prosthetics, as *currently* socially and theologically motivated, have not been about split subjectivity, but about its cure—about wholeness or, variously, holiness.

While Haraway has pointed to this decisive dis/juncture figured in prosthetics, her own sci-fi enthrallment overwhelms a more "constructive ambivalence" toward technoscience (Keller 1996, 24). If, as Haraway rightly puts it, "severely handicapped people can have the most intense experiences of complex hybridization," disabled persons also have the most exquisite awareness of the abrupt edge and shocking disparity between the organic and the machine (1991b, 178). Unlike the able bodied, who may imagine the technologically endowed body as somehow bionic or indestructible, the disabled person becomes even more acutely aware of the need to take up what Irigaray calls "the life-death watch." Disabled persons must psychically wrestle with the exquisite loveliness of and frustration with one's own transient tissues at the same time as s/he wrestles with the physical and psychic cumbersomeness, the severe rigidity, if also acquired grace, of the technologically endowed body.

Further, what may appear to an outsider as the "natural constraint" operatively reducing disabled bodies to the bondage of natural immediacy reads far too repressively. It assumes, in my experience, a tremendous transcendentalist inflation about what makes life worth living. The exquisiteness of transient occasions and passing moments, even quite indeterminate moments—for example, Did the child in the stroller recognize me with the waving of her hand?—are why some of us put on our feet, pick up our crutches, and spin our wheels everyday.

Despite the fact that prosthetics do not generate the "reciprocational excess" or "extraordinary transcendence of organic orders" that both technoscience and an able-bodied culture want to believe in, we the disabled are also not likely to put down, in other words, lay aside or give up, our prosthetic feet, wheels, or crutches (Haraway 1991b, 249 n.7). For me, prosthetics, and consequently, incarnation, is about tipping the fierce ambivalence that is mortality toward a love of the "futility" of it all—toward a love of the flesh and of finitude, I mean.

If embodiment is prosthetic and is meant to re/mind us toward finitude, then I would like to propose the figure of the "prosthetic erratic"—the one who, self-admittedly, has her/his foot in at least three places. Barbara Hillyer, author of *Feminism and Disability*, takes the first step toward the production of this figure. For women with disabilities, Hillyer writes, "the issue is not whether to use technology but how best to integrate it with self-concept and with body awareness." She bases this observation on several studies, including "the experience of mothers of 'thalidomide babies,' who came into conflict with rehabilitation specialists about the use and interpretation of prostheses for the children's deformed or missing arms." While the professionals, assuming that a missing limb signified a somatic deficit, insisted on early initiation into and integration of prosthetic appliances, "the child's body image was already whole," Hillyer reports, "so the prosthesis was experienced as a deformation." Given the discrepancies between the professionals' and the child's own apparent, healthy body image, the mothers' response was, Hillyer concludes, "to frustrate the professionals by using the prosthesis *erratically* and at random in terms of tasks to be performed" (1993, 173, emphasis added). Interrupting the social demands for composite holism, the children and their mothers chose the path of prosthetic erraticism.

The prosthetic erratic: s/he would be a fugitive from the habitus of the upright—perhaps one like Mary Verdi-Fletcher, principal dancer of the Cleveland Ballet Dancing Wheels, who "stopped walking" and "started dancing."[7] At the least, s/he would not be socially constrained, under the threat of the "death sentence," to veil herself and would, consequently, give us a better figure of what it means to be "stitched together imperfectly" (Haraway 1991b, 193). It is from the likes of Verdi-Fletcher that I have found the courage to admit to the world my heretically unprosthelytized body, to demonstratively shift the kindship relations thereby, and to discover for myself—offstage of that performance named "seeming/seaming so together"—the physics and psyche of a triped existence. Now I with studied calculation shape-shift through my cyborgian incarnations, namely, prosthetic foot, wheels, and crutches. I suspect only the closest of friends can imagine how difficult it has been to resign from compulsory, social holism and join the "erratics."

Spinning my wheels with five sixth-grade girls on Rollerblades clinging to the back of my wheelchair handles, I crest the hill and, careening wildly, we "crack the whip." Exhausted, I kick off my leg. My daughter tickles my phantom silly; it is the only location on my body where I am ticklish. Now I'm getting my sense of humor back. Comedy, as Haraway knows, can be quite instructive regarding what carries us from here to elsewhere (Haraway 1997, 15).

NOTES

1. In Christian theology, incarnation refers to the mutual enfolding of nature and sacred (S)pirit. That (S)pirit becomes enfleshed in history has been considered the crux of the saving or healing message of Christianity. The ways in which (S)pirit has been understood to indwell or enfold the contours of the material world are, however, renegotiated according to the various cosmologies and world situations in which Christians find themselves. In classical theistic Christian doctrine, Jesus was considered to be the unique incarnation or embodiment of God. During modernity (as I develop more fully later in this essay) and with the "discovery" of North America, Western Christianity attempted to create paradise on earth, namely by assuming that the practice of incarnating Spirit would eradicate the toil, suffering, and troubles which Christianity believed to have been incumbent upon an original "Fall" from obedience to God. Here redemption from the transient earth by incarnation of divine Spirit would constitute Christianity's "salvation history." In feminist theologies and philosophies, incarnation refers much more broadly to the embodiment of spirit in the universe at large as well as among human communities practicing inclusivity and equality.

2. While Haraway is generally referred to in the category of postmodernism, she herself prefers to think in terms of the "amodern" so as to move yet another step away from salvation histories. "The amodern refers to a view of the history of science as culture that insists on the absence of beginnings, enlightenments, and endings: the world has always been in the middle of things" (1992b, 304).

3. See "1990 Law Has Not 'Accommodated' All People with Disabilities," *Sunday Star-Ledger* of Newark, New Jersey, August 23, 1998, Section 1, p. 23. This article summarizes a poll conducted by Louis Harris and Associates for the National Organization on Disability and an MIT study coauthored by Joshua Angrist.

4. See, for example, Michael Rubens, "Technology Aids Disabled: Hi-Tech Devices Are Leveling the Playing Field for the Disabled," online, available: <http://cnnfn.com/digitaljam/9809/28/disabled_pkg/>, September 28, 1998.

5. *Enable: Official Magazine of the AAPD* 2, no. 4 (1998): 89.

6. For some of us who become disabled through traumatic, midlife events, this sense of "lack" will be a self-defining trap. According to anecdotal reports within the disability rights movement, this is much less the case for those who are congenitally differently abled. Congenitally differently-abled persons tend to have a sense of themselves as "whole" without prostheses. Traumatically disabled persons arrive at this much more slowly and complexly, since many of us cannot deny the loss and its tragic ramifications, yet refuse to be defined by the dizzying doughnut hole of abjection spinning loose in the social psyche.

7. *Active Living Magazine* 7, no. 4 (1998): 11. Kitty Lunn—actor, dancer, and founder of the Infinity Dance Theater of New York City—would be another such figure. See *Enable* 2, no. 3 (1998): 27 ff.

REFERENCES
Abrams, Judith Z. 1998. *Judaism and Disability: Portrayals in Ancient Texts from the Tanach Through the Bavli*. Washington, D.C.: Gallaudet University Press.
Berdyaev, Nicolas. 1936. *The Meaning of History*. New York: Charles Scribner's Sons.
Bourdieu, Pierre. 1995. *The Logic of Practice*. Stanford: Stanford University Press.
Boyarin, Daniel. 1993. *Carnal Israel: Reading Sex in Talmudic Culture*. Berkeley: University of California Press.
———. 1994. *A Radical Jew: Paul and the Politics of Identity*. Berkeley and Los Angeles: University of California Press.
Brahm, Gabriel, Jr., and Mark Driscoll. 1995. *Prosthetic Territories: Politics and Hypertechnologies*. Politics and Culture Series, no. 3. Boulder, Colo.: Westview Press.
Braidotti, Rosi. 1994. *Nomadic Subjects: Embodiment and Sexual Difference in Contemporary Feminist Theory*. New York: Columbia University Press,
Burrus, Virginia. 2000. *"Begotten, Not Made": Conceiving Manhood in Late Antiquity*. Stanford: Stanford University Press.
Bush, Corlann Gee. 1983. "Women and the Assessment of Technology: To Think, to Be, to Unthink, to Free." In Joan Rothschild, ed., *Machina Ex Dea*, pp. 151–70. New York : Pergamon Press.
Gray, Chris Hables, and Steven Mentor. 1995. "The Cyborg Body Politic and the New World Order." In Gabriel Brahm, Jr., and Mark Driscoll, eds., *Prosthetic Territories: Politics and Hypertechnologies*, pp. 204–18. Politics and Culture Series, no. 3. Boulder, Colo.: Westview Press.
Grosz, Elizabeth. *Volatile Bodies: Toward a Corporeal Feminism*. Bloomington: Indiana University Press, 1994.
Haraway, Donna. 1991a. "Cyborgs at Large: Interview with Donna Haraway," with an introduction by Constance Penley and Andrew Ross; and a postscript, "The Actors Are Cyborg, Nature Is Coyote, and the Geography Is Elsewhere," by Haraway. In Constance Penley and Andrew Ross, eds., *Technoculture*, pp. 1–20. Cultural Politics Series, vol. 3. Minneapolis.: University of Minnesota Press.
———. 1991b. *Simians, Cyborgs, and Women: The Reinvention of Nature*. New York: Routledge.
———. 1992a. "Ecce Homo, Ain't (Ar'n't) I a Woman, and Inappropriate/d Others: The Human in a Post-Humanist Landscape." In Judith Butler and Joan W. Scott, eds., *Feminists Theorize the Political*, pp. 86–100. New York: Routledge.
———. 1992b. "The Promise of Monsters: A Regnerative Politics for Inappropriate/d Others." In Lawrence Grossberg, Cary Nelson, and Paula A. Treichler, eds., *Cultural Studies*, pp. 295–337. New York: Routledge.
———.   1997.   *Modest_Witness@Second_Millennium.FemaleMan _Meets_OncoMouse*[tm]*: Feminism and Technoscience*. New York: Routledge.
Hillyer, Barbara. 1993. *Feminism and Disability*. Norman: University of Oklahoma Press.
Hockenberry, John. 1995. *Moving Violations: War Zones, Wheelchairs, and Declarations of Independence*. New York: Hyperion.

Kaufman-Osborn, Timothy V. 1997. *Creatures of Prometheus: Gender and the Politics of Technology.* Lanham, Md.: Rowman and Littlefield.

Keller, Catherine. 1996. *Apocalypse Now and Then: A Feminist Guide to the End of the World.* Boston: Beacon.

———. 1998. "No More Sea: The Lost Chaos of the Eschaton." Paper presented at "Christianity and Ecology" conference, Boston, April.

Linton, Simi. 1998. *Claiming Disability: Knowledge and Identity.* New York: New York University Press.

Melville, Herman. 1961. *Moby Dick.* New York: Signet Classic/New American Library.

Mitchell, David T., and Sharon L. Snyder, eds. 1997. Introduction to *The Body and Physical Difference: Discourses of Disability.* Ann Arbor: University of Michigan Press.

Moltmann, Jürgen. 1992. *The Spirit of Life: A Universal Affirmation.* Minneapolis: Fortress.

Noble, David F. 1998. *The Religion of Technology: The Divinity of Man and the Spirit of Invention.* New York: Alfred A. Knopf.

Rothschild, Joan, ed. 1983. *Machina Ex Dea: Feminist Perspectives on Technology.* New York: Pergamon Press.

Soper, Kate. 1996. "Nature/'nature.'" In George Robertson et al., eds., *FutureNatural: nature/science/culture.* New York: Routledge.

Wendell, Susan. 1996. *The Rejected Body: Feminist Philosophical Reflections on Disability.* New York: Routledge.

Yuan, David D. 1997. "Disfigurement and Reconstruction in Oliver Wendell Holmes's 'The Human Wheel, Its Spokes and Felloes.'" In David T. Mitchell and Sharon L. Snyder, eds., *The Body and Physical Difference: Discourses of Disability.* Ann Arbor: University of Michigan.

Williams, Terry Tempest. 1992. *Refuge: An Unnatural History of Family and Place.* New York: Vintage/Random House.

Sharon Betcher *received her Ph.D. from Drew University in Madison, New Jersey. After working as a teaching associate at the School of Theology at Drew University, Sharon is now assistant professor of theology at Vancouver School of Theology in Vancouver, B.C.*

Wild Bodies/Technobodies

Susan Hawthorne

Bodies have become the focus of a host of theoretical discussions among feminists in recent years, and whatever one's position the body has become an icon for ideological scripting. This is nowhere more so than in those areas where conflict occurs between opposing ideological forces. The conflict between the localizing knowledge systems of indigenous peoples and the homogenizing and universalizing systems of those engaged in the Human Genome Project provides one example of conflict over the body through a difference in ideological position. For women, the primary site of conflict is around notions of bodily experience. This conflict is exemplified in the paradoxical messages conveyed to girls and women around sexuality, independence, physical strength, and beauty. Theorists such as Donna Haraway (1991) have proposed liberation through the cyborg;[1] Sandy Stone (1995) suggests that prosthetic experience will get you there; and others are suggesting an increasing disconnection from the body through experiences in cyber- and virtual worlds.

But women already experience disconnection of the self through rape, abuse, and economic exploitation. For many women in poorer countries who work in the export processing zones, disconnection is already rife; their wages will continue only so long as they remain lower and more exploitative than those of another competing poor nation. Disconnection is also a feature of cyberprostitution. Mobile men, men who have surplus cash and the mobility provided by fast international travel, can now network among themselves and find out how to cheat even more effectively the women whose bodies they buy for sexual pleasure.

Big business, global business, and a trend toward homogenization are some of the forces at the root of these disjunctures. Advances in information technologies and biotechnologies have increased the pace of globalization and have increased the likelihood of everyone being affected by these cultural shifts. In this essay I propose a different way of conceptualizing the body, using the idea of the "wild body" as a site of resistance to the homogenizing forces of global capital and global culture.

Global Technobodies

The global technobody is something that has come into being in the past decade. It is a body that has lost all identifying markers, that is, markers that might link it to a particular time, locale, culture, or even individual. Like the global market that it imitates it can be found anywhere, everywhere, even where there is no there there—that is, in atopia, a no place that exists all across the globe.

The forces that have brought this bodiless body into being are the combined forces of information technology, biotechnology, and globalization. Globalization is the process by which individual nation-states enter the global market. To become a full player in this market, countries give up their sovereignty to the international bankers and bureaucracies represented by the International Monetary Fund (IMF), the World Bank, and the World Trade Organization (WTO). The process of globalization involves an orientation toward export, at the expense of the domestic market. It creates homogenized products and processes, which best suit the needs of the wealthy and powerful sectors of the global market.

What connection does this have with bodies? Just as countries are asked to surrender their sovereignty, so too are individuals asked to surrender their identities. These identities of class, sex, ethnicity, ability, age, sexual orientation and so on—hard fought for over the past four decades and more—have suddenly become fluid and permeable. Instead of our diverse identities having meaning, we are asked to let go, to become ambiguous, bodiless, selfless. But for what?

Instead of looking to the well-being of women and men in what I call the diversity group (those who are *not* male, wealthy, white, mobile, and young), we are asked to concentrate our attention on "out there." In a move similar to globalization and orientation toward export, the individual is asked—through manipulative ideologies arising from global advertising and media hype around science and technology—to cease paying attention to their inner selves. Attention to the self creates awareness, bodily intelligence, self-knowledge. We used to call it consciousness-raising in the early days of the women's liberation movement. We focus instead on out there, begin to think of ourselves as exportable. By extending ourselves into cyberspace, we effectively "export" ourselves into the global economy. The domestic (the self) is no longer of any importance. It's boring. It doesn't make enough money. It isn't exotic in any way.

When we give up our identities, we do so at our peril. We give them up to the powerful elites who run the Human Genome Project or the Human Genome Diversity Project (also known as the Vampire Project by some indigenous peoples). We give them up in order to become homogenized products, clones, designer babies with plenty of R&D (research and development) in their genes(is). After they've had their go we won't any longer be black, or lesbian, or poor (unless they design us that way), or disabled, or even aging, or possibly even female.[2] Most likely, some will have to remain female—but for what purpose? Uppity, thrill-seeking females will certainly be done away with. People like you and me.

We log on and plug in, and away we go, we know not where but it's out there and exciting. But whose out there are we traversing? Do we know anything of where we come from? Do we know our local environment? Do we know our flesh-and-blood friends? Do we know ourselves?

The globalized body is a dissipated and atomized body, fragile and vulnerable, not located in any real place, not connected to any real people. It is disengaged and impoverished. The globalized body is so extended it has no depth, no inner resources on which to draw, and if they get it right it has no culture either, other than the loud American scream that pervades the earth.

The ideal globalized technobody is so lacking in content that it can be rented out, leased, downloaded, stolen, and sold without any ill-effects.

The technobody has been romanticized by some cyberculture theorists, including the much quoted Donna Haraway, who claimed in her Cyborg Manifesto that "the machine is us" (1991, 180) without seriously considering how such a claim might begin to be manifested within less than a decade. The postmodern body of cyberculture ranges from the "meat" and "wetware" metaphors to glimmering virtual surfaces without weight or mass. And, I could add, without heart.

The strategy of disconnection from the self suggested by transsexual cybertheorist Sandy Stone (1995) is to "become one's prosthesis," but "choosing" the prosthetic and identic change of gender as Sandy Stone has makes for an experience very different from that described by Audre Lorde, who refuses the prosthetic breast after a mastectomy; or by Vivian Sobchack, whose "prosthetic experience" makes her critical of decontextualizing flesh into insensate signs or digitizing it into cyberspace (Sobchack 1995, 209). Sobchack's experience is an interesting one. A film theorist by profession, after undergoing major surgery on her thigh for cancer followed by a leg amputation she challenged Baudrillard and others for their romanticization of the novel and film *Crash*. She goes so far as to wish him "a car crash or two and a little pain" (207) to remind him what the body feels like *in extremis*. The corporeal cybertheorists seem to have lost their connection with their own bodily experience, as though they are experiencing an intellectual form of locked-in syndrome, such as that described by Jean-Dominique Bauby in his marvelous book *The Diving Bell and the Butterfly.* Indeed, an experience such as this might just bring them to their senses. Disconnective cyperhype might not be a problem were it just an entertainment for the bored elites. The problem is, it leads to reinventions of ersatz bodies, many of which are hyped as the "latest scientific breakthrough." They are, one suspects, the latest in that interminable search for immortality that is reflected in so many religions centered on the disembodied male god.

We already have Kyoko Date, a virtual teenager marketed to the Japanese adolescent male as a girlfriend "who will never grow old" and "always do as she's told" (Kunii 1996, 75). Then there's Webbie, the virtual New York model who has a body no woman could live up to, whose thighs have that impossibly long, never-ending look. Great for modeling clothes, but who could wear them? We'll all fall short of the ideal and shop (on the Internet) endlessly for the elusive garment that will make us feel good. And in case you're thinking I'm only having a go at men's products, there's also Lara Croft, who has a body that reminds me of a Meccano set, with its mechanistic muscles and curves.

These are just some of the things that are possible now. Hans Moravec's vision of the future is even more frightening. He writes of a postbiological age in which we will leave behind those sluggish and damageable organic bodies. For Moravec, rescuing the mind from "the limitation of a mortal body" (1988, 5) will allow for ever faster exchange of information. And of course, these disembodied "mind children" will be commodified, they'll be copied and sold, patented and leased for some thrilling experience, and as Renate Klein (1999, 205) indicates, there'll be a burgeoning "mind industry" of young and fresh cloned minds. This might sound like science fiction, but much of reproductive science has sounded like that over the past twenty years, and Moravec is a scientist, not a novelist. Moravec's vision will nicely do away with women's bodies altogether. What reproductive technology hasn't quite achieved, information technology will.

Much of the language surrounding these bodies is a language of transgression, disruption, hybridity. The excitement conveyed by these transgressions sometimes becomes a sexualized theoretical excitement. Zachary Nataf (1997, 188) writes about creating a "proliferation of new erotogenic zones" through "cutting and stitching" the flesh. One wonders why anyone would want to do such a thing. The ideology of transgression is one that is promulgated in the economies of free marketeers. It is pushed by those interested in crossing the "carbon/silicon divide," crossing boundaries between organisms and machines, or crossing the boundaries between different kinds of organisms, such as occurs with genetically modified organisms. But transgression is not always exciting or even productive, as crossing the boundary between herbivores and carnivores showed with its outcome of mad cow disease.

Preglobal Bodies

Within the ideology of the global market, the leasing and stealing and dislocating of bodies is a daily event and not worthy of headlines. The bodies of underpaid workers (mostly women) in export processing zones (including the maquiladoras of Mexico) are there to be used while wages remain at heartbreakingly low rates. The multinational will simply move on when the costs go up. The international money controllers have total mobility and will rent whatever bodies are on offer. Refugees from countries destroyed by the economic rationalist policies of the IMF are shunted from one refugee camp to another. Somali women in refugee camps speak of fearing rape by bandits when they go in search of firewood. And when fuel and food are in short supply they are "forced to have sex with male camp guards" (Hynes 1999, 200).

Just as the colonizers of earlier centuries stole land and resources from the indigenous inhabitants, transnationals are now mining the knowledge and living resources of indigenous and colonized peoples. Bioprospecting is the latest form of capitalist banditry.[3] The U.S. company W. R. Grace has patented the active ingredients of the neem tree from India, and the search is on in many other places for the lucrative drug that will cure cancer, or the common cold, or menopause.[4]

The preglobal body responds to these abuses, and suffers the indignities of them. The preglobal body, colonized by the dominant groups, has been rented and stolen. Slavery and body theft persist in different forms around the world, from Africa to the Americas, Vanuatu to Australia. Slavery's recent forms include the stealing of Aboriginal and Native American children, justified on the grounds of assimilationist policies, or the "exporting" of East Timorese children to Indonesia to be "educated." Ghanaian novelist Ama Ata Aidoo perceptively notes the purpose of scholarships and the education system of the colonizers:

> *Post-graduate awards.*
> *Graduate awards.*
> *It doesn't matter*
> *What you call it.*

But did I hear you say
Awards?
Awards?
Awards?

What
Dainty name to describe
This
Most merciless
Most formalised

Open.
Thorough,
Spy system of all time:

For a few pennies now and a
Doctoral degree later,
Tell us about
Your people
Your history
Your mind.
Your mind.
Your mind. (1977, 86)

Forced marriage, rape, prostitution, abuse of all kinds are other ways of renting or leasing the bodies of women and children. They are part of what Kevin Bales refers to as "the new slavery" (1999, 1). The new slavery is intimately connected to the global economy as people are dispossessed economically, as they are moved from their ancestral lands or travel to urban centers for economic reasons. Many of these "new slaves" are young women who are sent to urban centers to earn money for their families; some end up in sweatshops, such as the maquiladoras in export processing zones, and others end up in prostitution. Whatever their work, they are the "disposable people" (Bales 1999). Women may be "the last colony" (Mies and Bennholdt-Thomsen 1988), but the process of colonization has by no means ceased, even in this misnamed postcolonial, postfeminist, postmodern world.

In the allegedly disembodied world of cyberspace, mobile men can procure women wherever they are. The World Sex Guide homepage has a header: "Where do you want to fuck today?" (Hughes 1999, 159). Like the colonizers acquiring cheap land, and like the bioprospectors of the 1990s, mobile men want to pick up women wherever they are.

They can even find out about the local conditions, and like the other prospectors, they can report back to their colleagues over the Internet.

Women's bodies are being globalized via the Internet, with some women becoming global stars. Donna Hughes describes a woman called "Honey," whom a number of men have returned to visit in a named brothel, and about whom individuals have now begun "keeping a special Web site . . . for men to post their experiences of buying this one woman" (Hughes 1999, 161). Hughes points out: "This economic and electronic globalization has meant that women are increasingly 'commodities' to be bought, sold, traded and consumed" (158). And not only in domestic markets. Women are also export commodities, as trafficked brides (168ff.), as a cash crop (167), and as a means of potentially generating income to pay foreign debt (Lee 1991, cited in Hughes 1999, 167) at the recommendation of the United Nations, the World Bank, and the International Labor Organization (ILO). Governments have not been slow in recognizing this; as Janice Raymond points out, in 1998 Belize "recognized prostitution . . . [as] a gender-specific form of migrant labor that serves the same economic functions for women as agricultural work offers to men, and often for better pay" (1998, 2).

The global economy has many faces. In poor countries exploitation is relatively explicit. What remains constant is a process of homogenization. In poor countries this is achieved through a dehumanizing process of objectification, which suggests that all poor people are the same and can be subjected to the same exploitative systems. The Western capitalized body is subjected to the homogenizing influence of globalized fashion (and this applies to both men and women). Each season a new look appropriated from an exotic and marginal culture is presented as if it had been the fashion designers' original idea, rather than one drawn from long cultural traditions. The muumuu of the 1960s was the first such fashion to have an effect on me; in the first decade of the twenty-first century, reflecting perhaps the bioprospectors' interests, one is more likely to find the fashions of indigenous peoples on the racks.[5] An interesting parallel of this process can be found in the world of population control and reproductive technologies. As Renate Klein (1989, 268–72) argues, the provision of in-vitro fertilization (IVF) as a "choice" for privileged women in the West is "a prelude . . . to the technological takeover of the reproduction of those millions of people" (269) in poor countries who are perceived as "reckless breeders." The eventual goal, Klein argues, is control of who is born. She suggests that sterilization of poor women will occur, and IVF will then be used to select a few "worthy ones" (269), thereby ensuring quality control. And, I would argue, a new level of sameness. Diversity will be out.

Many feminist theorists have commented on the power of the body icon for women in Western cultures, as well as in countries with very different cultural paradigms.[6] Bordo, for example, calls it an "unbearable weight" and refers to "the pervasiveness of certain cultural images and ideology" (1992, 8) in relation to the body. Some theorists have even celebrated the fact that the body is capable of producing "fragmentation, fracturings, dislocations" (Grosz 1994, 13).

It is this latter theoretical move that worries me. Knowledge of the local is important. It is what has created thousands of diverse human cultures. It is local conditions that create biological diversity in plants and animals. The human body is similar. "Our Bodies, Ourselves," claimed the Boston Women's Health Collective ([1973, 1984], 1992) and it was a prescient call, for women did become active around our bodies, and it became political to recognize and accept our differences.[7] In recent years, research on the effects of abuse and sexual violation has provided new insights. Lepa Mladjenovitch (Copelan 1994, 202), writing about the experience of rape in war, describes this as being "homeless in her own body." This phrase, which describes dislocation from the self, is an important clue. Just as the local is important in issues around land and biodiversity, the personal, the connection with the body, the place, the space, is important close to home: in the way in which we perceive the body, the way we use it, the way we inhabit ourselves. Do we really want to create personalized "export processing zones" whether in the immaterial or material world?

Dislocations are a signal that something is wrong. And they are a signal in many contexts. Being "homeless in the body" is a signal of psychic dissociation. Geographical displacement through exile or refugee status is a signal of dispossession and colonization. In its latest incarnation, the colonization is related to globalization and the dominance of market forces. The displacement of the psyche in Alternate World Syndrome (AWS) (Heim 1995) caused by spending long stretches of time in virtual reality (VR), is a signal that something is wrong.[8] Dissociation, and dislocation of the self, is not unusual for those who are afflicted by anorexia nervosa or various mental disorders in which the self loses its moorings or encounters "an inner world which is extremely hostile" (Jeffs 1998, 38).[9]

The current fad for the experience of bodilessness through cyberspace is one move toward an experience of the globalized body on the part of some elite Western women. To extend is to spread out;

extending into other peoples' territories has been precisely the method of the colonizer, the harasser, the stalker, the rapist. And as Renate Klein (1996) has pointed out, the technodocs of reproductive technology have colonized women's bodies, extending their control to eggs, ovaries, fallopian tubes, and the uterus. The dislocations of reproductive technologies and of the cyber- or virtual body have much in common.[10]

I suggest that a corporeal feminism, which takes up extension and dislocation as a positive attribute, has major problems. Corporeal feminism with a thinly spread body (a cyberanorexia?) or without the body, is like the seed that can produce only sterile seeds,[11] or the knowledge stolen from indigenous people, now without context and reproduced in the laboratories of pharmaceutical companies for sale around the world.

Bodilessness in cyberspace is the ultimate in export, an extreme experience commodified and sold to those who have everything. To risk losing our autonomy, losing our connection with the real, solid body—however limited—is too much to risk, and it plays into the hands of the globalizers.[12]

The technologies that lead to extensions of corporality are more of the same. They are colonizing, commodifying, homogenizing, flattening the diversity of bodies and selves. They dislocate us from our locales and from our selves. In the atopic zone of cyberspace women are rendered a gray sameness that ignores much of what we have struggled for over the past thirty years.

Wild Bodies

I want to propose an alternative vision of bodies and what might be possible. I use the term *wild bodies* here to represent the notion of not interfered with by man—and I mean man. Wild types are the vital resource for continuing generational health in any population, be it plant, microbial, or human. The wild element is that element in a culture that keeps the culture healthy by challenging assumptions, power blocs, and institutions. Most radical political forces play this kind of role in moving the culture forward, although their visions are rarely fully realized.

Global culture is currently engaged in trespassing on people's bodies—think of the sampling of indigenous cell lines by pharmaceutical companies; think of the so-called women's health products for menstruation, fertility, and menopause invented over the past half century; think of the designer babies, the trade in organs and bodies that is growing year by year; think of the genetically modified organisms you are ingesting through food or absorbing through tampons.

Wild bodies are bodies in revolt against these homogenizing forces.

Indigenous peoples are challenging the right of the Human Genome Diversity Project to sample their cells and to commercialize them for the profit of transnationals. As Debra Harry, a Paiute from Nevada and an advocate for indigenous peoples, says: "Now it's colonialism on a molecular level. . . . For us, genes are our ancestry, our heredity and our future generations. They are not to be tampered with" (Horvitz 1996, 34). For indigenous cultures in which the body and the land are conceptually the same (Bell 1998), bioprospecting, development, and tourism also represent an attack on the body.

Radical feminists challenged the biotechnologists in the early 1980s for the way in which women's bodies were being colonized in the name of reproductive freedom, and they highlighted the eugenic basis of this research. In spite of these efforts, the designer babies previously found only in fiction have now become a reality. The ideology of the Nazi doctors is reincarnated in these contemporary bodily interventions. It is clear that no wild bodies—children with detectable disabilities—will be born to those using these techniques.[13]

Health care in the mainstream favors a homogenized model body, usually male and white, or female. The homogenized model of the body—a male body—means that heart attack in women is underdiagnosed, that AIDS research ignores the specificities of HIV's manifestation in women, that lesbians have no special health needs. A context-sensitive health care system would avoid these false generalizations and take note of the individual histories and environments influencing the state of health.

Most important of all to this alternate vision are the principles that life is more surprising than we can ever imagine, that the wild element is critical to survival, and that diversity and context is integral to the continuing existence of all life forms.

I want to finish with an example of wild bodies drawn from my own experience. The wild bodies are a group of women in Melbourne, Australia. These are the women who are members of the Performing Older Women's Circus (POW). They are women over forty who have decided to learn circus skills at an age when most people in the culture would consider it either impossible or, at best, foolhardy. I want to use this group as an exemplar because these women break rules.

Think for a minute of your image of the female circus performer: usually she is young, athletic, slim, and not suffering from any physical disability. Then imagine a woman who suffered polio at the age of eight, joins POW at age fifty-three, and learns to walk on stilts at age fifty-four. Or imagine a woman in her late sixties who has had two knee operations with disastrous results, is about to go into hospital again, and during the three-night season crawls from the door of the theater to her place at the keyboards; she is admitted to hospital the next day. Imagine a woman who has three children and has just had a mastectomy; in the show she walks on stilts and falls intentionally, arms across her chest. Imagine a woman in her late forties with epilepsy learning aerials, using the trapeze as her major art form in the show.

These women and others are among the members of POW. Two members have died from cancer since the group was formed in late 1994.[14] Without a sense of the context of these women, any outsider would say we were crazy to participate in such a group at *our* age. And this is precisely my point, the context. Melbourne, where POW is based, is also home to Circus Oz, the National Institute for Circus Arts, and the Women's Circus. A six-week project for women over forty, run as an experiment by Jean Taylor, a member of the Women's Circus, resulted in the formation of POW. When she joins—and the only requirements are that she be over forty and prepared to work safely and have fun—each woman is introduced to the various skills as they arise in classes. Our main focus most weeks is acrobalance, which involves two or more women creating balances using only their bodies. Handstands on thighs, standing on shoulders, inverted balances of various kinds, as well as group pyramids are among some of the possibilities. We have also maintained a small but committed aerials class over the past three years working on trapeze, cloud swing, rope, and tissue. The very existence of POW is a challenge to societal norms— even feminist norms—about what it means to be an aging woman.

Over the six years that POW has existed, we have created six major shows and an equal number of small, sometimes almost spontaneous, shows. Around sixty women have participated and have learned skills such as juggling, clowning, acrobatics and acrobalance, aerials, stick manipulation, stilts, and performance, as well as skills in scripting, rigging, lighting, and sound.

One of the purposes of POW is to challenge assumptions about aging and disability; it is that wild element that won't go away. But we also want to create a connection, create the means for women to say to themselves, "I could do that." We do this by subverting our message with humor, or by including elements that anyone could do. Our content is also driven by this desire, and most of our shows have incorporated something to do with women and aging.

The sense I want to convey through this example is that of resistance. Resistance to the forces of homogenization that are so strong. They create the preconditions for doing things that are bad for us, both individually and collectively.

I argued early in this essay that the paradoxical images portrayed of women feed into a sense of disconnection from the self, a dislocation of the emotional and physical life. The experience of the women in POW is a reconnecting of these forces. The development of trust is as integral to training as is the development of strength. Each woman participates in whatever way best suits her needs and wishes. In this way, POW encourages the recognition of differences, allowing for the various diverse needs of members.

Globalization, with its push toward homogenization and stress on the importance of market forces, is completely contrary to the principles of POW. Established so that older women could learn new skills and have fun, POW does not include among its aims any reference to economic viability.

Among the hype of the producers of virtual reality are such fantasies as virtual gyms and VR applications for sport and fitness. Such VR applications are elitist (with the starting price for a VR home installation at around US$250,000) and escapist and represent packaged entertainment for the mainly male market.[15]

Disconnection, globalization, and the hype surrounding cybertechnologies are distractions from ourselves, our environment, our communities, and the limitations of the real world and our own mortality. Diversity of cultures and biodiversity in the natural world are the sustainable elements. Immortality, homogenization, reductionist biotechnologies, and the rush for profit—at the expense of the poorest and most vulnerable—represent short-term, unsustainable futures. What we need is a vision of ourselves that enhances collective diversity, takes account of our contexts and our environments, and allows the wild element to flourish.

NOTES

I am indebted to Renate Klein for the term *technobodies* (1999, 203) and for many discussions about technobodies and biotechnology. The concept of wild bodies is drawn from my dissertation in progress, "Wild Politics: Feminism, Globalization, and Bio/diversity." This essay is based on a paper presented at the twenty-first annual conference of the National Women's Studies Association, Simmons College, Boston, 18 June 2000.

1. Liberation implies an overturning of systematic power relations. The problem with cyberliberation is that it replicates existing social relations or masks them in ways that simply do not challenge the system.
2. For an imaginative story about this possibility, see O'Brien 1991, 150–58.

3. Indeed, the term *prospector* has some interesting resonances. A prospector is one who makes a claim, and the word is associated with claiming parcels of land, ore bodies, or goods with prospects. A prospectus is an account showing the forthcoming likely profits of a venture as a means of obtaining support. As a noun, a prospect is a view of the landscape from any position; and when applied to time, it is a view that looks toward the future.

4. A number of countries targeted for bioprospecting because of their biodiversity are also important locations of cultural diversity. Moran (1999, 250) has identified the following countries as sites of highest biological and cultural diversity: Indonesia, India, Australia, Mexico, Zaire, and Brazil.

5. For more on globalized corporate fashion drives, see N. Klein 2000.

6. Female genital mutilation has been an important field of study in recent years, provoking a great deal of discussion among feminists. See, for example, Dirie 1998; Dorkenoo 1994; Rioja and Manresa 1999.

7. My own experience of acceptance was a turning point in my view of myself as someone who had hidden an invisible disability for many years.

8. Michael Heim (1995, 67) describes the symptoms of AWS, after three hours in VR: "[The body experiences] an acute form of body amnesia which can become chronic Alternate World Disorder (AWD). Frequent virtuality can lead to ruptures of the kinaesthetic from the visual senses of self-identity."

9. The literature in the fields of anorexia and psychiatric disabilities is wide-ranging and controversial. Bordo's (1992) discussion on hunger, anorexia nervosa, and the slender body draws out many of the issues, while McLellan (1995) looks at the intersection between feminism and psychotherapy, then extends this analysis in McLellan 1999. The poetry of Sandy Jeffs gives an insight into the experience of madness (2000) while in her nonfiction she explains her approach (1998).

10. In her afterword to *Infertility*, R. Klein (1989) had already made the connection between the availability of in vitro fertilization for wealthy Western women and similarly intrusive population control techniques for Third World women.

11. Seeds containing the so-called terminator gene developed by Monsanto, and now cancelled due to reduced sharemarket prices.

12. I am not suggesting a conspiracy theory here, although it is tempting. Rather I am pointing to the fact that those in favor of globalization have parallel interests, not competing ones, as the rhetoric would suggest.

13. See R. Klein 1989; Raymond 1995; Corea 1985 for analysis of these issues.

14. For the story of one of these women, see Taylor 2000. For further information on POW, see Hawthorne 1999b and 2001; and on the Women's Circus, see Liebmann et al. 1997.

15. For more on cyberfitness, see Hawthorne 1999b.

REFERENCES

Aidoo, Ama Ata. 1977. *Our Sister Killjoy: or, Reflections from a Black-Eyed Squint.* London: Longman.

Bales, Kevin. 2000. *Disposable People: New Slavery in the Global Economy.* Berkeley: University of California Press.

Bauby, Jean-Dominique. 1997. *The Diving Bell and the Butterfly.* Translated by Jeremy Leggatt. New York: Knopf.

Bell, Diane. 1998. *Ngarrindjeri Wurruwarrin: A World That Is, Was, and Will Be.* Melbourne: Spinifex Press.

Bordo, Susan. 1992. *Unbearable Weight: Feminism, Western Culture, and the Body.* Berkeley: University of California Press.

Boston Women's Health Collective. (1973, 1984) 1992. *Our Bodies, Ourselves.* New York: Simon and Schuster.

Copelan, Rhonda. 1994. "Surfacing Gender: Reconceptualizing Crimes Against Women in Time of War." In *Mass Rape: The War Against Women in Bosnia-Herzegovina,* ed. Alexandra Stiglmayer. Lincoln: University of Nebraska Press.

Corea, Gena. 1985. *The Mother Machine: Reproductive Technologies from Artificial Insemination to Artificial Wombs.* New York: Harper & Row.

Dirie, Waris. 1998. *Desert Flower: The Extraordinary Life of a Desert Nomad.* London: Virago.

Dorkenoo, Efua. 1994. *Cutting the Rose: Female Genital Mutilation—the Practice and Its Prevention.* London: Minority Rights Publications.

Grosz, Elizabeth. 1994. *Volatile Bodies: Toward a Corporeal Feminism.* Sydney: Allen & Unwin.

Haraway, Donna. 1991. "A Cyborg Manifesto." In *Simians, Cyborgs, and Women: The Reinvention of Nature.* New York: Routledge.

Hawthorne, Susan. 1999a. "Connectivity: Cultural Practices of the Powerful or Subversion from the Margins?" In Susan Hawthorne and Renate Klein, eds., *CyberFeminism: Connectivity, Critique, and Creativity.* Melbourne: Spinifex Press.

———. 1999b. "Cyborgs, Virtual Bodies, and Organic Bodies: Theoretical Feminist Responses." In Susan Hawthorne and Renate Klein, eds., *Cyborgs, Virtual Bodies, and Organic Bodies: Theoretical Feminist Responses.* Melbourne: Spinifex Press.

———. Forthcoming, 2001. "Older Women Performing Circus." In Laura Lengel, ed., *Intercultural Communication and Creative Practice: Women, Performance and Civic Discourse in Global Contexts.* Seattle: Greenwood Press.

Heim, Michael. 1995. "The Design of Virtual Reality." In *Body and Society: Cyberspace/Cyberbodies/Cyberpunk: Cultures of Technological Embodiment* 1 (3–4): 65–77.

Horvitz, Leslie Alan. 1996. "'Vampire Project' Raises Issue of Patents for Humans." *Insight on the News* 12, no. 27 (July 22).

Hughes, Donna. 1999. "The Internet and the Global Prostitution Industry." In Susan Hawthorne and Renate Klein, eds., *CyberFeminism: Connectivity, Critique, and Creativity.* Melbourne: Spinifex Press.

Hynes, H. Patricia. 1999. "Consumption: North American Perspectives." In Jael Silliman and Ynestra King, eds., *Dangerous Intersections: Feminist Perspectives on Population, Environment, and Development.* Cambridge, Mass.: South End Press.

Jeffs, Sandy. 1998. "Madness, Language, and Reclaiming Meaning." *Australian Quarterly* (May–June): 36–38.
———. 2000. *Poems from the Madhouse.* Melbourne: Spinifex Press.
Klein, Naomi. 2000. *No Logo.* London: Flamingo.
Klein, Renate. 1989. *Infertility: Women Speak Out about Their Experiences of Reproductive Medicine.* Sydney and London: Unwin Hyman.
———. 1996. "(Dead) Bodies Floating in Cyberspace." In Diane Bell and Renate Klein, eds., *Radically Speaking: Feminism Reclaimed.* Melbourne: Spinifex Press; London: Zed Books.
———. 1999. "The Politics of CyberFeminism: If I'm a Cyborg Rather Than a Goddess Will Patriarchy Go Away?" In Susan Hawthorne and Renate Klein, eds., *CyberFeminism: Connectivity, Critique, and Creativity.* Melbourne: Spinifex Press.
Kunii, Irene M. 1996. "The Ideal Dream Girl." *Time,* August 26, 75.
Liebmann, Adrienne, Jen Jordan, Louise Radcliffe-Bown, Patricia Sykes, and Jean Taylor. 1997. *Women's Circus: Leaping off the Edge.* Melbourne: Spinifex Press.
Lorde, Audre. 1980. *The Cancer Journals.* San Francisco: Spinsters Ink.
McLellan, Betty. 1995. *Beyond Psychoppression: A Feminist Alternative Therapy.* Melbourne: Spinifex Press.
———. 1999. "The Prostitution of Psychotherapy: A Feminist Critique." *British Journal of Guidance and Counselling* 27 (3): 325–37.
Mies, Maria, Veronika Bennholdt-Thomsen, and Claudia von Werlhof. 1988. *Women: The Last Colony.* London: Zed Books.
Moran, Katy. 1999. "Toward Compensation: Returning Benefits from Ethnobotanical Drug Discovery to Native Peoples." In Virginia Nazarea, ed., *Ethnoecology: Situated Knowledge/Located Lives.* Tucson: University of Arizona Press.
Moravec, Hans. 1988. *Mind Children: The Future of Robot and Human Intelligence.* Cambridge: Harvard University Press.
Nataf, Zachary I. 1997. "skin-flicks." In Sue Golding, ed., *The Eight Technologies of Otherness.* New York: Routledge.
Nwapa, Flora. 1986. *Cassava Song and Rice Song.* Lagos: Tana Press.
O'Brien, Mary. 1991. "Elly." In Susan Hawthorne and Renate Klein, eds., *Angels of Power and Other Reproductive Creations.* Melbourne: Spinifex Press.
Raymond, Janice G. 1995. *Women as Wombs: Reproductive Technology and the Battle over Women's Freedom.* Melbourne: Spinifex Press.
———. 1998. *Legitimating Prostitution as Sex Work: UN Labor Organization (ILO) Calls for Recognition of the Sex Industry.* Amherst, Mass.: Coalition Against Trafficking in Women.
Rioja, Isabel Ramos, and Kim Manresa. 1999. *The Day Kadi Lost Part of Her Life.* Translated by Nikki Anderson. Melbourne: Spinifex Press.
Sobchack, Vivian. 1995. "Beating the Meat/Surviving the Text, or How to Get Out of This Century Alive." *Body and Society* 1 (3–4): 205–14.
Stone, Allucquère Rosanne (Sandy). 1995. *The War of Desire and Technology at the Close of the Mechanical Age.* Cambridge: MIT Press.
Taylor, Jean. 2000. *The C-Word: A Story about Cancer.* Melbourne: Spinifex Press.

Susan Hawthorne *is completing her Ph.D. in the Department of Politics at the University of Melbourne. Her thesis, "Wild Politics: Feminism, Globalization, and Bio/Diversity," looks at a broad range of issues, including the colonization of scholarship, intellectual property rights, economics, and ecology within a feminist framework. She is the author/editor of ten books, the latest of which is* Cyberfeminism: Connectivity, Critique, and Creativity. *She is also a poet, novelist, and circus performer. She teaches in the Department of Communication, Language, and Cultural Studies at Victoria University, Melbourne.*

Breaking the Code

Women Confront the Promises and the Perils of High Technology

Stephen Newton

> *She was not created by the bronze tool alone, and the machine alone will not abolish her.*
>
> —Simone de Beauvoir, *The Second Sex*

The new economy, fueled for the most part by expanded Internet usage and electronic commerce, has been rapidly outstripping the supply of qualified workers. By 2006, according to U.S. Department of Commerce projections, not only will 50 percent of all U.S. workers be women, but also 44 percent of the U.S. workforce will be employed by industries that are engaged in producing or using information technology products and services.[1] This unprecedented demand for essential technology workers such as system analysts, computer scientists and programmers, as well as the untold numbers of newly created and emerging information technology (IT) occupations indicates that the timing may be ideal for more women to enter the fields of computing, the Internet, and high technology.

Although the future may look bright, women who might otherwise pursue technology as a career are still daunted by pervasive societal stereotypes and deep-rooted educational prejudices that favor a *male's-only* admission to science and technology. In her 1986 book *The Science Question in Feminism,* Sandra Harding writes, "Women have been more systematically excluded from doing serious science than from performing any other social activity except, perhaps, frontline warfare."[2] Although it appears that progress in changing these entrenched perceptions has been slow since Harding's observation more than fifteen years ago, there are nevertheless a number of very successful women currently working in the technological trenches. As a new-media designer and Web site developer who works closely with computer "geeks" every day, I decided to interview some of these women to discover how they had overcome the challenges of "breaking the code" to work side by side with their male counterparts.

Gail Williams, executive director for The WELL, an influential online community (www.well.com), candidly described for me her own academic frustrations while in college. "When I went to college in the 1970s, the gender division around computers and engineering was ferocious. I took some mostly male science classes, but didn't even briefly consider that computers might be fascinating, even though I wanted to break gender barriers in some scientific field. The disturbing news is that the numbers are only slightly better now."

Although she says that she doesn't have a theory as to why more progress has not been made, she offers, "It could be that either a reality or a perception of geekiness concerning math and computer obsession in high school is part of the problem. I sort of hate that theory, but it resonates with my long-ago experience. I needed to be too cool for punch cards, even though I was good at math." On a more constructive note, Williams adds, "We do need classroom teachers who can mediate in situations where kids compete for shared computer access, and boys want the access more. This is one place where throwing money or technology at the problem can be helpful. Computer time for girls is still not a sure thing even in affluent areas."

Whether or not more computer access for girls can be guaranteed, it may not be the only solution. The existing gender gap as well as the prevailing notion that high technology is still a field dominated by males contributes to doubts many women express about their own abilities to master the skills necessary.

I asked Ellen Ullman, experienced software engineer and author of *Close to the Machine: Technophilia and Its Discontents,*[3] for her suggestions on how women could begin to narrow the gap and overcome barriers. She responded by telling me that women need to develop a completely different attitude when faced with the challenges of new technology. "The main pedagogical strategy to alter the technology gender gap would be to stop worrying about making women *comfortable* with technology. This came to me when a young woman once wrote to ask me how I'd stopped being intimidated by computers. I stared at the question for a while, then laughed, and had to answer her honestly: I've *never* gotten over being intimidated by computers. Every new machine, operating environment, library, and language presents a formidable challenge. I often feel very stupid and frustrated at first. But the only way forward is to use that feeling of stupidity as a motivator. A lot of things in highly technical professions get accomplished because the practitioner is trying to avoid being humiliated!"

Ullman believes that the majority of women have been taught to withdraw helplessly when confronted by challenges. "I don't mean to be glib," she cautions. "I think boys and men are taught to use discomfort as a motivator—to find a way to get comfortable in a situation, to find some kind of mastery. Whereas too often girls and women are taught to withdraw at discomfort, I think we should tell girls and women potentially interested in technology that the work is hard—but the good, interesting kind of hard, one with great internal rewards."

Nevertheless, women who do survive the educational gauntlet may still have to face an oppressive "masculine" technological environment once they are actually in the workplace. Ullman describes what she refers to as the typical "cultural milieu" in which most technology workers find themselves: "That culture is a kind of perpetual guy adolescence: offices full of toys staffed overwhelmingly by young men without lives (no significant others, wives, or children) or by older men who spend most of their time at work (not spending much with their significant others, wives, or children). I'm drawing broadly here; not every man in the computing professions is like this. But the dominant office culture encourages everyone to more or less live at work; and if you feel the need to play, well, hey, here are some toys."

Most of the women I interviewed who are currently working in high technology seem to agree that Ullman's workplace description fits. Deb Agarwal is a computer scientist at Lawrence Berkeley National Laboratory, where she is working to provide the complex remote-control and monitoring mechanisms needed for researchers to collaborate on scientific experiments directly from their own sites. "I think one major factor to encourage women would be to reduce the perception that computer science is the field for 'unwashed' males with no social skills," she explains. "Although there are plenty of these types of programmers, they are a smaller minority than most people perceive."

Drawing from her own experiences, she believes that women who have persisted despite the obstacles have already made significant contributions. "Women have played a key role in the development of many of the computer technologies. Their contributions may often be forgotten, but women are definitely out there helping to make history."

If technology and the new high-tech workplace intimidate some women, the increased connectivity available through digital communications offers them another option: working from home. Seemingly, telecommuting is an attractive alternative that allows women the flexibility to spend more time working at home rather than in the office. However, I spoke with some women who saw telecommuting from another, less favorable perspective.

Ellen Ullman points out what she believes are some downsides for women who choose to telecommute. "Letting women work from home is a way for companies not to deal with the issue of home life—to utterly dismiss what was first discussed as a social and political question and turn it into something that has been *solved* by technology. First, the physical office remains the real power center. Women (and men) whose only solution to the needs of young children is to work from home are necessarily banished from all the formal and informal office meetings in which fundamental governance decisions get made. Second, companies now have little incentive to work out job sharing, formal flextime, part-time, etc.—remember those?—all the arrangements that were being negotiated in the 1980s that allowed women to have time *away* from work responsibilities. Finally, I think technology has given women with families, still left with the bulk of the child-rearing responsibilities, the worst of both worlds: They are out of the decision-making loops; and yet they are expected, despite home responsibilities, to be *at work* all the time, as productive as thirty-year-old bachelors."

Despite the real and perceived obstacles women clearly face in the digital age, it may well be a paradox that technology itself offers an unexpected source of support in the form of online communities designed by and for women. These comprehensive Web sites offer career advice, technical training, and resources as well as access to mentors such as Ellen Ullman, Deb Agarwal, and numerous other technologically proficient women who offer inspiration and leadership online.

In January 1995, Aliza Sherman founded the first woman-owned Internet marketing and online publishing company, Cybergrrl, Inc., building the first women's Web site (www.cybergrrl.com) and the first searchable directory of women's sites (www.femina.com). A few months later she founded Webgrrls International (www.webgrrls.com), the first real-world global Internet networking group for women. She is also the author of *Cybergrrl: A Woman's Guide to the World Wide Web*[4] and *Cybergrrl at Work: Tips and Inspiration for the Professional You*.[5] Sherman has devoted herself to building communities on- and offline with the sole aim of helping other women integrate technology into their lives. Her latest venture is as cofounder of Eviva.net (www.eviva.net), the Web's first bilingual online network and marketplace for Hispanic women. Although she admitted during our conversation that women in the United States are more fortunate than women elsewhere, she warns women not to sit back and let men enable them to continue the role of helpless user. "There are still a lot of barriers, a lot of issues regarding education and the fact that so few women are coming out of college with a technology curriculum; or worse, are dropping out because no one is paying attention to their particular needs or interests. They begin to feel isolated, that there is no relevance to technology in their lives. There must be a change."

Sherman feels strongly that to effect any significant change, women must participate in the creation of technology. "There's nothing mysterious about doing it—just do it—there is no right or wrong way. The more you philosophize, pontificate, and overresearch, focus-group, study, the less you'll get done and the more likely you are to fail." In her second book, *Cybergrrl at Work,* Sherman focuses on how women can use the Internet for their careers and businesses. She also includes advice on transitioning careers, starting new businesses, and working at home.

As more women turn to the Internet as a resource, they eventually will face additional issues, the most sobering for the digital age being freedom and privacy. Jennifer Granick, a San Francisco criminal defense lawyer whose specialty is defending hackers and crackers[6]— or any individuals who have been charged with computer crimes— deals with those issues on a daily basis. Working *with* but not *inside* the world of technology, Granick saw the potential for her specialty early. "I have a geeky nature but I'm not a technical person," she says. "By 1992 I was on the Internet and enthralled by it. As a criminal defense attorney, I realized right away that it was uncharted territory and there were all kinds of new complicated legal issues being raised."

Granick's own educational experiences seem to reflect those of most women who, although they enjoyed science, were not exactly encouraged to pursue it as a career choice. "When I was growing up I remember liking science and thought about pursuing it as a career. I even had a kid's chemistry set with a toy microscope. I took a lot of math including calculus in high school and wanted to continue when I went to college. After the first two classes, I was confused and realized I just didn't care. The result was that my political science classes seemed far more interesting by comparison and I never took another math course."

As one of the very few criminal defense attorneys whose job it is to understand technology and interpret it from a legal standpoint, Granick admits that although she is not intimidated by it, she sees it as a double-edged sword. "I wouldn't say that I am intimidated by technology, but more by the fact that if I don't understand the issues, my client may go to prison. I have technical experts—a bunch of guys— that I can bring in that do understand it and can explain it to me so that I can understand it and explain it to the prosecutor. In the general sense I definitely fear technology. I have a love-hate relationship with it. I think that it's because I see technology as a powerful thing.

We use it for whatever it can do without a great deal of moral questioning about it. There seems to be a trend to get something bigger, better, faster and deploy it and not ask whether it really helps us after all."

Granick is a frequent speaker at hacker conferences, where she talks about Fourth and Fifth Amendment rights and what can and cannot be done within the law and how hackers can stay out of trouble. She believes that the prevalent use of most technology, especially the Internet, is removing the public's Fourth Amendment rights along with their privacy, as information is placed in the hands of third parties, from whom it can be accessed with much less effort than having to show a search warrant. "Although I believe that the Internet should allow us to be as free if not freer than we are in our real lives, I am not a policy person. My job is to defend people who have been accused of computer crimes. I do hope that in some way the work that I do contributes to future policies."

Granick may be typical of women who, although they are not creating technology, are confronting it, working with it, and contributing in a positive way to important issues surrounding it that may shape its development and use for many years.

For Anita Brown, founder and CEO of Black Geeks Online (www. blackgeeks.com), the Internet was a catalyst that rekindled her former 1960s activist spirit and placed her center stage as Miss DC—the impassioned, no-nonsense voice of the African American technical community. Brown created Black Geeks Online in her living room in 1996 with eighteen participants. Since then, the Web-based nonprofit community has grown to more than twenty-five thousand members and become an essential resource for extending technology to the unconnected urban communities. *Heads-Up,* Brown's thrice-weekly email bulletin, has established Black Geeks Online as a reliable source for education and employment opportunities, technology policy, IT trends and alerts, and success stories of IT business owners and community technology leaders.

"I came online kicking and screaming," the fifty-seven-year-old grandmother and information griot recalls. "Like many folks my age who had used PCs for desktop publishing or mundane work, I was untrusting of this 'info superhighway.' But once I discovered this was a collection of communities—people—it was all over."

In addition to her online efforts, Brown has organized another way to narrow the technology gap. "We take technology right into the 'hood,' with music blasting and folks in T-shirts and jeans, not dressed like corporate execs," Brown says, describing her Taking IT to the Streets program; a sort of mobile information technology workshop that travels to the people living on the fringes of technology.

Voicing her concerns about the digital divide at Harvard University's "Internet and Society 2000" conference, Brown stressed that the solution to the gap between technology haves and have-nots should not be to simply throw money at the problem. "My main concern . . . is that all this equipment and money is being handed out in a vacuum. They're putting computers in the schools without talking to the parents or the community. None of this money is going to train people. They're just creating new consumers, and the last thing poor people need to do is to find a new electronic mall."

Brown was recently selected as one of the top twenty-five women on the Web by San Francisco Women on the Web (SFWoW), a San Francisco–based association of professional women involved in the Internet. Mary Choy, the chairperson of the selection committee, said of Brown, "She isn't your typical CEO [Brown dropped out of college after six months and spent several decades as a civil service secretary], but she has made a difference by helping other women get over their fear of the Internet."

Speaking for her own generation, Brown says, "Parents and grandparents may start out just sending email to their children at college. And before you know it, they're participating in Oprah's message boards, comparing financial investments at COBI.com or swapping photos and family history at their own family Web site."

When I asked Anita Brown what she considered the necessary career qualities women needed to become active participants and not passive users, the self-proclaimed "technorealist" offered advice seasoned with her own life experience and her warmly contagious optimism. "If you're going to look for a job in this arena, do your homework," she advises. "There are unparalleled opportunities for people who do their homework. Talk to people, find a mentor, take classes." She cautions, however, that: "You have to have a propensity for IT to be successful at it."

Echoing Anita Brown's advice, Deb Agarwal claims that women also need self-esteem in order to pursue a career in technology. "One of the major qualities is self-confidence. It is not so much that she needs to be boisterous and aggressive but that she will need to have a basic confidence in her own abilities. It also really helps to be able to think logically. Problem-solving ability is critical to the technical fields, and logical reasoning capabilities really help with the problem-solving capabilities. Most of the real-life technical problems do not present themselves as nice equations. It really helps if she is level-headed and does not anger too easily."

Aliza Sherman suggests that women who are creative, pay attention to detail, love learning, and have an ability to work under pressure in less-than-ideal environments are more likely to succeed in a technological career.

According to Ellen Ullman, a good programmer has the imagination of an architect and the persistent, no-fear-of-getting-hands-dirty nature of a master plumber. Her description embodies an attitude that surfaces whenever Ullman talks about women and technology. "In general you can't walk around in the world saying, 'I'm a woman, I'm a woman, I'm a woman.' What makes you good at what you do is that you are really engaged in it. To a certain extent the more you're engaged the better you are at it and the more people tend to put up with your eccentricities, among them being a female."

Be fully engaged; don't think about it, "just do it"; don't be overwhelmed by technological problems, but tackle them instead; and most of all: believe in yourself are all strongly encouraging mantras for women breaking the code and entering the technological world.

Sheer numbers alone, Ullman urges, may create the sea change necessary to overcome the barriers and the trepidation that prevent so many women from taking an active part in shaping the future of technology. "I can't say enough to encourage women to enter these professions," Ullman emphasizes. "The need for able personnel is so great that a woman with the talents and abilities to work with technology can have an engaged, interesting, secure, and very well paid working life. It's only guys with water guns, after all; they won't kill us. The more of us there are, the more things will change. I'm hoping for a tipping point."

If the demands of our increasingly complex, information-hungry, global economy continue to outstrip our supply of technologists, the powerful cyber-engine of e-commerce may well contribute to Ullman's notion of a tipping point by re-creating the workplace, transforming it into a productive and impassioned community free of gender bias.

NOTES

This essay features interviews that were conducted from April through June 2000.

1. *The Emerging Digital Economy II* (Washington, D.C.: U.S. Department of Commerce, 1999).
2. Sandra Harding, *The Science Question in Feminism* (New York: Cornell University Press, 1986), 35.
3. Ellen Ullman, *Close to the Machine: Technophilia and Its Discontents* (San Francisco: City Lights Books, 1997).
4. Aliza Sherman, *Cybergrrl: A Woman's Guide to the World Wide Web* (New York: Ballantine, 1998).

5. Aliza Sherman, *Cybergrrl at Work: Tips and Inspiration for the Professional You* (New York: Penguin Putnam, 2000).
6. A hacker is a person who understands and uses computer technology. A cracker refers to a computer vandal.

Stephen Newton *is a new-media consultant and writer specializing in online communications and content management. He is currently completing work on his first novel and exploring the form of the "eZine," or online magazine.*

Pink Collars on the Internet

Roadblocks to the Information Superhighway

Mary E. Virnoche

In their seminal work on women, children, and poverty in the United States, Stallard, Ehrenreich, and Sklar (1983, 18) coined the term "pink collar ghetto." They acknowledged the increasing paid labor force participation of women. Yet they brought to light the structural inequities women face in occupational sectors into which they are segregated.

Almost twenty years later, women's work still does not pay as well as men's work. And with the influx of information technologies, workplace inequities are taking new shapes and forms. Today "doing good work" in the service sector necessitates a matrix of telecommunications support: phones, FAX machines, voice mail, computers, and Internet access. Women are structurally disadvantaged when their workplaces are technologically inadequate.

Nonprofit and human service organizations are gendered work environments. In the organizations that I have studied, women occupy a majority of the staff positions. These organizational settings are highly subject to trickle-down technology practices: staff members often accept donations of older computer technology, creating difficult if not impossible workplace environments and service delivery issues. Furthermore, the clientele in human services are largely members of low- to no-income groups. The technological roadblocks encountered by workers in human service organizations have communications-equity implications not only for women who work in these settings, but also for the groups that they serve. In this essay I consider the experiences of staff members and their clients with computer and Internet technology and explore ways in which organizations can improve workers' access to technology and achieve greater equity for both workers and clients.

Background

The One-Stop Career Network (OSCN) Internet project was a community outreach technology initiative undertaken by the Boulder

Community Network (BCN).[1] The project was aligned with BCN's mission of assuring public access to the Internet through community training, technical assistance, and the maintenance of a community Web site. One-Stop targeted human service organizations, many of which operated on shoestring budgets with a skeleton staff. They also faced never-ending threats of program closure. These organizations provided a broad range of employment- and training-related services ranging from job and rehabilitation services to education, childcare, and mental health resources.

The overall goal of the One-Stop project was to streamline employment and training resources and processes in Boulder County through the use of Internet technologies. The project was developed in response to government demands for more efficient and less expensive service delivery mechanisms. Staff members from thirteen agencies working with employment and training were part of a pre-grant body known as the One-Stop Consortium. These agencies became grant partners and most actively participated in both the planning and implementation of the project. Seventy-six percent (108) of those organization staff members identified by their supervisors as involved with the One-Stop grant project were women.

Methods

This essay is based on field research data collected between 1994 and 1998, during which time I was employed as the research coordinator for BCN. I was a participant observer (Adler and Adler 1987) during my tenure with BCN, presenting myself as a researcher and a staff person. On a day-to-day basis, other staff, community members, and volunteers interacted with me based on my dominant organizational hat for the day: volunteer coordinator, trainer, administrator, technical troubleshooter, or receptionist. Throughout my years in the field, I kept an archive of emails and personal notes about observations and interactions. In addition, I conducted semistructured interviews with volunteers, community members, and staff from organizations for which BCN provided assistance. These data provide the empirical basis for this essay.

Technology Diffusion

Prior to the 1980s, the diffusion research held a largely functional perspective: different groups and cultures adopt new technologies when they find a use for them. The classic diffusion work assumed that the human actor was a passive recipient of technology (Rogers 1962).

There was little of the attention to how actors shape and transform technology that I found in later technology research (Bijker 1994; Fischer 1988; Ling 1999; Virnoche 1998). Technology was always seen as good, and this assumption led to late adopters being categorized as having the low social status of uneducated and poor. Even Ogburns's (1951) classic description of "cultural lag" largely skips over the culture embedded in the technology itself that may or may not lend itself to adoption by different groups of people.

More recent research on technology diffusion takes a much more critical perspective on technology and its use. This body of literature tends to focus on power and equity related to technology and how it is adopted or imposed upon different groups of people. It provides a glimpse of the actors and social factors behind and within the technology (Douglas and Isherwood 1979; Ling 1999; Silverstone 1994) and brings the social component of the artifact and its contexts back into the discussion.

Roadblocks to the Information Superhighway

In an organizational environment, "media choice" is a misnomer (Fulk and Boyd 1991). While individuals bring to their workplace beliefs about technology, they must negotiate any technology within the given constraints and opportunities of their specific work environment. Understanding barriers to technology use in the human service sector must go beyond simply considering the technological skills of the actors. In addition, we must also understand the ideological and social position of organizational staff members and their clients, as well as the structural specifics of their work environments.

The Individual and the Technology: Perception, Time, and Place

Participants in the study discussed here presented a slightly different outlook toward technology than had been reported of human service employees in other research. Lie (1997, 22) wrote that "social workers find the computer suited for several purposes, but these are tasks which are neither considered central to their profession nor representative of their skills." In my research related to the One-Stop Career Network, participants did not polarize their relationship to technology as did Lie's participants.

One-Stop participants were usually specific about their concerns with Internet technology use. They reported concerns about confidentiality and user mistakes. They described organizational cultures that valued homegrown methods of dealing with their bureaucracies and paperwork. While staff members were generally in favor of integrating Internet technology into their workplace, there was some evidence that they remained uncertain exactly how they would use the technology. Finally, life situations of staff members and clients presented barriers to technology use.

Concerns for Confidentiality

Concerns about confidentiality affected attitudes about sharing information over the Internet. In a work environment where staff deal with many sensitive issues related to their clientele, it is not surprising that an electronic mode of information exchange was suspect.

Agency staff who dealt with vulnerable populations were particularly concerned about a common online client-intake form that was being discussed in early planning meetings. The form was to be used by all agencies that supported an individual in the employment process and provided services such as training, childcare assistance, and counseling. At one consortium meeting, a mental health agency staff member expressed concern about her clients being linked via online forms to her agency. According to Rhonda: "For some clients, it is obvious [that they have a disability]. For others it is not and they don't want our [agency] name associated with disseminating information about them to companies."

Rhonda went on to explain that while it might be positive to have one's name and application associated with a minority job service, the same was not true of an association with a mental health–related agency. Gideon, a technology champion who worked for a central employment agency, became frustrated with the discussion and expressed his belief that "confidentiality issues have always been a way to avoid cooperating." He felt that the employment agencies were too territorial and that technology paranoia had just become another smoke screen for avoiding cooperation.

Yet even staff with more technical experience had concerns about technology and confidentiality. Kathy was a longtime computer user and Internet advocate and had even been a technology instructor at one point in her life. But as the lead caseworker for a special project for the education and employment of single parents, she had concerns: "We do a lot of voice mail stuff. We leave a message and say, 'This is what is going on and this is what I need to know.' And it could be put in writing. But my initial impression is, 'Who's watching?' If it's voice mail, I trust more that it's confidential than if it's on the Internet."

In the preceding examples, the role of technology shifted depending on a staff member's organizational position. Gideon was a champion for pushing the use of new Internet technologies and was his office's technology expert. Rhonda and Kathy provided direct client services that often included the discussion of sensitive issues. They were more cautious about technology use, as it posed a threat to their gatekeeping of client information. At least one of Gideon's goals was making things "easier" by getting everyone on board with Internet technologies. The bureaucracy of human services welcomed the assumed efficiency of new Internet technologies. Yet the women staff who provided direct services found themselves putting up their own roadblocks for what they perceived to be in the best interests of clients—particularly those in vulnerable positions. Staff members' beliefs about confidentiality threats influenced the extent to which they were willing to incorporate Internet communications into their daily work practices.

Fear of Mistakes and Misunderstandings

Several of those interviewed latched on to the potential volatility of email communications. They were particularly concerned because of what they perceived as unique workplace environments that were highly territorial and politically charged. While it is likely that all workplaces have elements of territory and politics at play, at least the staff interviewed here felt that their workplaces were high on a continuum of dealing with these issues.

Kathy, the lead caseworker who had expressed concerns about privacy, was also concerned about online misunderstandings: "But I'm a little hesitant [for human services] just because of the politics and the interaction with people around the city and the county and how everything works around here. I think on little things it would work very well. But on some things, you couldn't use it at all." The critical component influencing technology use was that staff members "believed" that their work environments were highly volatile.

Other research has documented that employees prefer in-person contact to computer-mediated communications for ambiguous, socially sensitive, and intellectually difficult interactions (Culnan and Markus 1987; Rice 1987). Because of their organizational positions, and also because of communication preferences, women may be more likely to voice caution about how and when to use mediated communication. It is women who are more likely to provide direct client services; and they incorporate more nonverbal cues in interpreting conversation (Belenky et al. 1986). These factors and others may help

explain why women may be more cautious about some uses of electronic communication.

Affinity for the Old and Familiar

Some staff insisted that the "old way" of doing things was sometimes
just better. The battle over the "Red Book" was an ongoing issue that
epitomized the tensions between old and new. The Red Book, a directory of service agencies in the county, had been produced by an
umbrella nonprofit organization that divided its funding among many
agencies. Prior to the One-Stop online project, funding had been cut
for the paper publication, last produced in 1993; the old Red Book
information was revitalized when it was put online in 1995. The One-
Stop project provided a mechanism for the information to be updated
and expanded. Even though the defunct paper directory had only
been updated every two years, many staff voiced preference for their
old penciled and tattered Red Books over the new online resource.
That was certainly how Nancy felt.

Nancy was the director of an employment resource agency primarily targeting women. While she used computers, she also revealed that
she still tallied her reporting statistics manually with pencil and paper.
She was also one of a number of voices that I heard over the years
lamenting the loss of the paper copy of the Red Book:

Nancy: Sometimes it's not totally practical to have everything on computers. It is nice to also have a hard copy. Computers are great
sometimes—but sometimes they just make the process slower.
Sometimes it's just nice to pull a page out of a binder, Xerox it,
and hand it to a client. . . . It was a big mistake to quit publishing
[the Red Book].

Researcher: Now you know that some people would say, "Well, it's online."

Nancy: Pfff [laughs]. We don't have the number of computers needed
to use it online. The systems that we have don't work well. It's just
not convenient.

Researcher: What if you had a room full of computers that worked well and one
on each desk?

Nancy: [Laughs.] Well, I just don't see that happening. But even if that
were the case, still, many clients aren't comfortable with computers. And we are worried about really drawing off staff time to do
support on computers.

There were several reasons for the resistance to the online Red Book.
First, there was the reason of practicality. Without computers on every
desk, it was inconvenient to go to a computer and look up resources.

Second, even when Nancy was asked to hypothesize computers on every desk, the established routine of pulling a page, copying it, and handing it to a client still seemed easier to her. She was familiar with that tangible routine. In addition, she was afraid of a drain on staff time as clients required assistance to use the Internet. Reports from other staff members substantiated this third concern: frontline staff members were often swamped by requests for technical assistance with the Internet and other computing tools.

Part of the "old and familiar" roadblock can be understood as an element of "cultural lag." It will just take a little time for human service staff to become accustomed to Internet-based methods of providing and processing information. Yet there is also an element of rationality in the decision to stick with paper, pencils, and photocopying machines. Given the lack of sufficient computing technology and technical support, the old ways often really were faster and more reliable.

Understanding How It All Fits Together

"They just don't get it," sighed organizers leading early One-Stop meetings. Organizers felt that it was difficult to get their colleagues to understand how the Internet could be helpful to their organization. Of course these pre-grant meetings took place between 1994 and 1996; most people in the country did not "get it" at the time. Nonetheless, the notion remained that the human service and nonprofit world had an "understanding problem" when it came to technology.

Matt, the director of a job services program for the developmentally disabled, shared his observations of colleagues and the Internet. While he considered himself technologically savvy and ahead of the curve, he was more than disappointed with the attitudes and aptitudes of his peers:

> This is a world that has separated technology from the job that they do. . . . This is an audience that is not yet online, but the organizations that are serving them are slowly getting there. People in social services don't do well with technology. The free training is great and encouraging. Many say, "I'm a people person. I don't do technology." But we need to be able to communicate as quickly as the business community does.

Despite Matt's observations, I did not encounter any staff members who fit neatly into this picture of "not doing" technology. As was found in the preceding sections, participants discussed quite thoughtfully when and how they liked to use the technology, as well as those situations in which they were more cautious about using it. But that's not to say there did not remain some understanding problems. The Internet can be difficult to "get your arms around," as some might say. Some staff members, such as Rhonda, a mental health counselor, remained unsure of how her organization's needs related to the technology. "I felt that we should be a part of this. But I'm not sure how it will be used. We're not sure how to sell it to clients. How to use it. It still feels like it's at the beginning stages."

Staff members such as Rhonda were frustrating to the technology experts, Matt among them. There was a certain disdain in Matt's voice when he expressed his frustration with the understanding problems of his colleagues. Matt was so convinced that the technology was the answer that he was unwilling to entertain anything but a full commitment to transforming organizations through technology. Ironically, those so thoroughly engrossed with the technology were sometimes not able to translate effectively their appreciation for it to a level that could be helpful for their colleagues. In some cases, negative reactions to the impatience of the experts may have contributed overall barriers to technology use.

The Dance of Time and Place

Busy lives, little discretionary activity time, and the relative location of an Internet computer each directly influenced the likelihood of staff and clients to use the Internet. Particularly for new Internet users, sitting down at an Internet-connected computer required large blocks of time. This was time that many staff members did not feel they had available.

Internet technology and the norms established around its use encourage experienced users to think about their Internet-use time in frequent short spurts. Seasoned users pop in and out of their email boxes many times throughout the day. With a few minutes to spare before a meeting, they may also click onto a frequented news Web site to check on a developing story. Yet in part because new users in this study had not yet established an Internet routine, the prospect of sitting down before an Internet-connected computer seemed all consuming.

This need for large segments of time to "do the Internet" was identified by Peggy, who worked as an administrative assistant at an employment service for people with disabilities. Peggy was relatively new to her position, which encompassed many different tasks from administrative support to marketing and grant writing. When Peggy came on the job, she was handed the "Internet folder" and told that she would need to check an email account and be involved with the One-Stop group. She figured out how to read the email on her own, but could not figure out how to write or send messages. Peggy said: "It's really frustrating for me because I don't have the time or anybody to show me how to do it. . . . I don't have enough time to just play. . . . I need to sit down and do it. Time. I know that libraries have it and that you can just go and do that. But it means just sitting down uninterrupted." For Peggy and others, having focused time to "play" with the computer was particularly important for the early learning phase.

Time and the location of a computer interact to either facilitate or hinder technology use. Even if a user has a block of time available, she may not physically be able to travel to the location of a computer. For many staff members, the day revolved around a desk, phone calls, and visits from clients. If Internet access was not available on a staff member's desk, she was not going to use it.

The interaction of time and place was also salient for the clients of many of the human service agencies who participated in this project. Kathy was a caseworker for a women's training and employment program. While she was adept in the technology, she had observed real problems with the ability of her clients to use the Internet and other computing tools. Kathy discussed the particular time dilemmas of many of the single, low-income mothers who were her clients. She said, "The time that most people have that they can sit down is the middle of the night or early in the morning when the kids are still asleep. Or before school or after they've done their homework. A lot of people come in the middle of the night and do their papers."

Those participating in the program for which Kathy was a caseworker had to be single and have at least one child younger than thirteen living in the home. Ironically, the computer labs were at least theoretically off limits to children. The factors of time and location became interwoven as clients juggled their education and family as well as other demands on their time. Kathy continued: "Childcare is a major thing for most of our folks. Then they either have to pay somebody or swap or whatever. And finding the time to come sit in the lab is really hard. . . . Transportation, childcare, financial stability. Those are all issues. . . . Most of the people who have asked [about the Internet] have not pursued it. Very few people have really gone on with that. [If they did pursue it], they weren't particularly successful in what they were pursuing."

In addition to personal time constraints, Kathy's clients were also faced with limited lab hours in the community-shared computer facilities. The computing equipment was relatively expensive, so the labs were kept under lock and key. As a result, they were not available at times when some mothers could have most easily worked in them.

While we could easily list a number of remedies to the dilemmas described here, there remains a significant underlying issue. Low-income users of technology are confronted with a more complicated path in negotiating technology. The barriers that they face are not exclusively attached to the technology. For the low-income would-be technology user, the everyday nuances of life present substantial road-blocks.

Institutional and Structural Factors

Work environments are embedded in a host of institutional and structural factors that contribute to how staff and clients use technology. The technology itself, workplace routines, technical support networks, and financial factors all affect the technological environment. Yet even amid these powerful "givens," staff and clients often adapt and negotiate to make the best of the situation.

Technological Barriers and the Construction of the Computer Problem

Almost all participants mentioned technical difficulties in using computers and the Internet. The technology and the barriers it created were "real" in every sense that a problem can be real. Staff waited for slow connections to the Internet. Computers were unpredictable. Equipment was incompatible. Yet there were also important social elements in the construction of the "computer problem." These social explanations for the computer problems added mortar to already substantial technological barriers.

The Slow Computer

The speed of someone's Internet connection affects how, when, and if she uses the Internet. Most Internet users have strong feelings about the relative speed of their connection. They are thrilled with "fast" connections and exasperated by "slow" connections. The human service agencies participating in the project usually had low bandwidth, and thus, slower connectivity.

The belief that an Internet connection is "too slow" is culturally embedded. Perceived speed of a a connection is constructed in relation to other Internet sessions as well as to other media experiences. We have become hyper–time sensitive. Any waiting is considered too much.

Minnie was a receptionist for a job service agency for the mentally challenged. She watched the front desk and was always pleased to be given new opportunities to test her skills, such as researching an equipment order. Minnie was frank about the fact that it seemed just about everyone in her agency had a slow computer. She didn't know much else about them except that they were slow. As we met in a small conference room just to the back of the reception area, a coworker walked into the room to pour a cup of coffee. Minnie leaned back in her chair so she could speak to both her coworker and me: "I don't know what kind of computer I got. Everyone here almost has a slow computer. What kind of slow computer do we have here?" Minnie and her coworker laughed.

Staff could not necessarily tell me which kind of computer or modem they had in their office. Many were hard-pressed to tell me whether they used a 386, 486, or Pentium processor, or to distinguish between a 14.4 or 28.8 modem. These terms did not necessarily mean anything to them. But they knew whether their computers were slow or not. And that perceived dichotomy directly affected the likelihood of a computer being used for Internet purposes.

Emily, a receptionist at a women-focused employment agency, was not willing to wait for her Web access. "I get irritated when the Internet's really slow and takes a long time. Like at home my modem's pretty powerful. Unless it's a bad time, I don't really have that problem. But here, it's frustrating. . . . Actually we just got a computer that is a little faster. Before it was such hell to use it here anyway. I never did. . . . It was so miserably slow that really nobody would do that." For Emily, her fast connectivity at home influenced her workplace Internet use. She resisted using the Internet at work because she had much faster and less frustrating Internet sessions at home, where she did not have to wait for images and information to appear on her computer screen.

Emily's experience of the slow computer does not end in her own work patterns. Because Emily felt that the computers in her office were so slow, she also coached clients not to use the technology. Her agency charged by the hour for computer use, and she felt that it was a waste of the clients' time and money to use such slow computers. She would say to those asking about Internet use, "You might as well go somewhere else because our computer can't support it." In that way, Emily's own technological roadblocks were passed on to clients.

The Crazed Computer

Not understanding, or feeling unable to control, the odd functioning of a computer added frustration and barriers to computer use. Since many clients were already wary of computers, staff did not like it when computers were not working smoothly. Crazed computer problems made for difficult technology-related sessions between staff and clients, as well as for staff themselves.

Even for staff members such as Barb who were generally comfortable working with computers, erratic computer behavior was a real strain. Barb was a counseling and social work intern in a program for single parents. For months Barb had been frustrated with a "possessed" community computer. Among other problems, she said, fonts and type sizes in documents on which she was working changed for no apparent reason. This ongoing struggle with the computer was a real discouragement for her in her technology work with clients.

Other staff reported similar frustrations with malfunctioning computers. Emily, the receptionist from the women's employment agency, associated at least part of their problems with viruses. "We used to have a lot of virus problems here before our virus software was updated. And that was awful. Like I hated computers during that. . . . Sometimes the computers used to freeze up because our network isn't as advanced here. And that was really frustrating. I guess I get frustrated when things happen that I can't control."

Amid the technological malfunctions, there developed a social struggle to make sense of what was happening. Emily had a need to remove blame for her frustrations from the computer. She hated the computer when she could not control it. At the same time, she absolved it of fault by pinpointing the dilemma in the virus. This compartmentalizing of the computer problem allowed Emily to love her machine and hate its invaders, which were beyond her control. This construction gives the computer agency and then absolves it of fault for the frustrations experienced in its presence.

The fear of the computer-generated invader may create resistance to opening up internal networks to problems of the Internet. This was the case for the five-person computer staff who worked at a mental health agency. According to Rhonda, a clinician with the agency: "Our computer department—they don't want some computers with Internet. They are concerned about contamination and viruses coming into the network. They want separate workstations for Internet access. They are not excited about the Internet. They want to keep it [the intranet] clean and closed."

At least in Rhonda's case, her internal computing department was blocking Internet access as one means of minimizing virus contamination. For the department, isolating the computing systems allowed for greater control over system integrity. Yet greater control came at the expense of staff and client access to online services.

The Technological Shambles

Mismatched and antiquated hardware and software created difficult technological work environments. In addition to making many computing-related tasks impossible, the technological shambles in many organizations also generated a great deal of frustration. In that sense, the emotional baggage of struggling with the technology fueled the overall practical barriers.

Kathy was a caseworker at an assistance program for single parents and had also been a computer instructor. "I get frustrated with the quality of hardware and software that we have right now. . . . I use email a lot. [I should say] I used to use email a lot. I don't now. I can't get in most of the time. . . . Since I'm not dependent on budgetary direction and communication with the main office, I'm on a low-priority list [for technology upgrades]."

Because of her technological environment, Kathy had not even tried to look at the Web during the past year. She went on to provide more specific examples of the problems that her mismatched and old systems created:

> We have an old database. It's dBase 3. It's not just old, but it's for programmers. And I'm figuring out what to do with it, but it's really cumbersome and really awkward. And we don't have documentation on it. I love database stuff. And I love working with that kind of stuff. And my frustration is, one: I don't really have the time to do that. But to just be able to print out a report takes a long time to figure it out. I like it but it's frustrating with the equipment that we have at this point. . . . . Another thing that has been frustrating is the hardware in the computer lab and the software. Windows is on the machines. But the WordPerfect is not the Windows version. So it's like the old 5.1 or something. And then clients get stuck in different modes and don't know how to get out. And it's just another thing for them to figure out.

So while the technological shambles is difficult and frustrating for the staff, the environment also affects Kathy's clients. With the clients already hesitant in many cases about dealing with computer technologies and facing many other personal roadblocks, the makeshift computer facilities in some cases made them even more wary of the technology. Their fears are confirmed as they stare at unfamiliar screen displays and means for maneuvering through software programs. Their community lab provided odd matches of software and hardware.

Nancy, from the women's employment center, relayed similar experiences in her agency. She described a laundry list of technical problems that seemed like a black hole to her. "Networks break down all the time. We need a new printer. The wiring is old. We are not even renting out computers anymore. . . . We are going through *hell* with our computers. We are burned out and angry. If [this Internet project] works, there need to be upgrades in hardware and in systems."

The women's-center dilemma was only exacerbated by BCN's Internet work with them. The center was brought into the project early on. The staff was trained. An organization Web site was developed. Yet bureaucratic issues left them unaided in their most desired need: "upgrades on hardware and systems." So as the project drew to a close, the women's center was left without full participation in the project. Their slow connectivity and old systems meant that few people would in the near future spend time at their facility accessing online employment information.

As articulated by Kathy and Nancy, mismatched and piecemeal computing systems directly influenced their own and their clients' use of computing and Internet resources. As a result of her frustrations with the system, Kathy did not even try to get online anymore. Nancy's hope for a better system through the Internet project dead-ended with the inability of the project to provide anything but used computers. Each of the agencies received some type of assistance from the community network, but there was always more that was needed.

Workplace Routines

Routine is an important element in the operation of work environments. Organizational norms and expectations about workday activities influence how and when people interact and accomplish their work. For many of the organizations that participated in this project, Internet communications had not yet become a part of the daily office routine. For example, staff frequently checked and responded to voice mail, yet there were few organizational expectations for tasks related to Internet communications.

Establishing new patterns of interaction was something that Patty, a project leader, struggled with for many months during the initial stages of the project. Each of the thirteen agencies that made up the One-Stop Consortium was provided with an email address and Internet access. Yet as Patty checked logs to determine who had received her communications about the project, she complained that many of the participants were still not checking their email.

At a consortium meeting four months into the project, Patty made one of many pleas for staff to check their email. Patty planted the seed for what she believed to be a reasonable workplace routine: "Check your email once a day." Patty promised that email was *the* mechanism by which staff would find out about project progress and other important information. In framing the email routine as the only portal to important information, Patty reinforced a broader cultural expectation regarding Internet communication: "If you're not online, you're missing out." For better or worse, and sometimes with an element of coercion, work environments become microcosms of the processes transforming societal communication practices.

In addition to reading and responding to email messages, there is a set of other routines that accompany the emailing task. One of those routines includes the process of collecting and maintaining information about networks of people with whom messages are exchanged. This information collection process is also more commonly known as "keeping up your address book."

Staff members working on the One Stop project were still piecing together their Internet routines. Reading email was one issue. Knowing addresses of others to whom they wanted to send a message was another. At one consortium meeting, Nancy, from the women's employment agency, requested a list of email addresses. She could read her email, but did not know how to address messages to others.

Patty and other project leaders assumed that staff knew to record addresses from incoming messages into their online email address book. Many of the addresses that Patty herself sent out included many agency staff names. Yet for Nancy and the others who nodded in agreement with her request for a paper email address list, this Internet culture routine had not yet become their own workplace practice.

The degree of Internet integration in an office can also be measured by staff and organizational reliance on the Web. Web use includes everything from Web surfing to maintaining an organization Web site. Web surfing is a passive activity compared to Web site maintenance or even emailing. Yet in comparison with email, Web sites created by an organization have a longer life, and they are available to a broader audience—anyone who can access the Internet. Organizational Web sites can become a significant portal for public and interorganizational information sharing. They can also, however, be graveyards for outdated and inaccurate information.

The minority-employment agency was one of few agencies that had made its Web presence and Internet use an organizational priority. The director, Tony, explained that he had committed both time and financial resources to making Internet communications and the Web central to how his small agency did business. He was optimistic that the new modes of connecting employers and employees would greatly improve his agency's capacity to facilitate good matches.

One tangible outcome of the One-Stop project was the development of organizational Web pages for each of the project participants. While most staff members were pleased to have Web pages for their organizations, Web site maintenance was not a central organizational priority. For many staff, maintaining a Web site was just one more "to do" item on the bottom of a long list. Few staff members were interested in the day-to-day building and maintenance of an online resource. Organization expectations were low or nonexistent in regard to their Web sites.

These lags in workplace culture serve to illustrate the role that routine plays in facilitating or hindering the use of Internet technology. As technology ambassadors introduce new routines, there are bound to be chasms between new-user assumed and real knowledge. In an example given earlier, Nancy felt that it was reasonable to request a paper list of email addresses. Patty, the technology expert, was frustrated because she felt that everyone should already have one another's addresses. The staff members had been receiving email from her for months and each message included these addresses. These disjunctions between assumed and real knowledge and practices aggravated parties on both ends of the technology-learning continuum. Even when new users begin with positive attitudes about integrating technology, they may become frustrated with the technology and process if too many assumptions are made about "commonsense" technology practices. If that is the case, then ironically the technology ambassadors themselves become the roadblocks to technology use.

Technical Support: Getting and Providing Help

The availability of help networks was a critical variable in staff and client use of Internet technologies. Human service agencies were likely to rely upon informal networks for technical assistance. When the informal help networks fell short in meeting staff and client needs, the intensity of the roadblocks to the Internet increased.

Staff members did not like being alone with a computer with no one to turn to for help. Even when some technical assistance was available by phone, they felt that it was not the same as having an in-house technical assistant. Without immediate on-site assistance, work was often disrupted for extended periods, and staff became frustrated with their technological situation.

Almost every staff member could quickly name a person to whom they turned when they ran into computer problems. Yet these "technology companions" did not necessarily have better computing skills than the person asking for help. Regardless of the technical knowledge of the staff called to the scene of a technology problem, staff members felt that two heads were better than one. As one female staff member at a community center said, "At least we can try to figure it out together. You're not alone looking at a book and trying to figure out what to do." With a technology companion at one's side, there was some degree of emotional safety in facing the cold resistance of the monster on one's desk.

The practice of relying on another person for moral and technical computer support was a problem for some organizations. Some agency staff were concerned that providing ongoing informal staff and client technology assistance was draining away valuable human resource time. For example, at the women's employment center, Emily, the receptionist, juggled many responsibilities. In addition to carrying out the many administrative tasks that were a part of her job, Emily now found herself assisting walk-in clients in the computer lab. Both Emily and her supervisor were particularly concerned about clients with high computer-assistance needs taking her time away from other organizational priorities:

> A few too many [clients] really have no idea. Our job is simply to answer certain questions. We don't sit down [with them.] As you know the phone is ringing. Like the phone can be ringing and I am helping a person on a computer. So it doesn't really work well to have to help those people. There definitely are people who are just getting by typing their resumes. We try to assist them as much as we can in the time frame that we have. But if someone was really illiterate on it—we would not sit there and help them learn. Most people perhaps that end up using it have some skills. They wouldn't use it if they had none because we would send them away.

There were other employment centers that did provide some basic computer assistance for job seekers. Yet even at these centers that were more oriented toward technology training, staff members were concerned about where they themselves could turn for day-to-day technical training and suggestions. According to Peggy: "It's really frustrating for me because I don't have the time or anybody to show me how to do it." With no particular malfunction to face, Peggy just wanted someone who could help her make use of the technology that was sitting on her desk.

Money: Financial Barriers to Internet Technology

Financial resources also played a role in creating barriers to technology access and use. The technological equipment, as well as the training and ongoing technical support, had a monetary cost. This price tag was more easily financed by some human service organizations than others.

Each organization operated on its own budget. For a few agencies, this entailed engaging in discussions about purchasing the latest in office computing systems. For most others it meant dealing with donations of computers with 386 and 486 processors at a time when the industry was several generations ahead. Software and particularly Web content continued to be created for the latest "most powerful" systems. Even though a 386 may have been functional for an organization's stand-alone word processing programs, its use for Web browsing became frustrating at best, as described earlier in this essay. In addition, even twenty dollars per month for Internet access charges was too much for some small agencies and nonprofits, as well as individuals. As Kathy explained, the financial constraints did make working with the technology more difficult:

> There is certain software that they use at the [main employment office]. I would like to have our lab upgraded to so that [clients] could walk into any of these places and see something that is similar. But our WordPerfect is ancient. . . . In the past, there wasn't even anybody who had time to even look at it and do anything with it. And now it's more budgetary. How do we get systems? [Our board president] has gotten some donations. [One company] donated some 386s that we are hoping to send home with people to their houses. And then [another company] is probably going to be donating some 486s. And then hopefully we can upgrade the lab and get some machines out to people. And the same with Internet access. We have a couple clients that are going to take classes on the Internet—via Internet. And they need access from home. So how do they get access without having to pay twenty dollars a month? So [our board president] is pursuing that. Miracle worker Patty.

While barriers to technology cannot be simply boiled down to financial resources, finances are an important element in the overall matrix of moving Internet technologies into the norm for staff and client use. The lack of financial resources leads to a more piecemeal approach to integrating Internet and other computer technologies. Many organizations rely on technology grants and donations of used equipment and services. They become techno-panhandlers hoping to collect enough technical capital to stay wired a little longer.

Discussion

In this essay I have presented some roadblocks that were experienced by human service staff members and clients involved in the One-Stop Career Network Internet project. It has become clear that individual perceptions of technology, as well as institutional and structural factors, contribute to a difficult negotiation of new information technology. Staff and clients have been unveiled as active participants in adapting, integrating, and rejecting information technology.

This work supports current research in the technological-diffusion literature that contextualizes the use or rejection of technology (Antonelli 1990; Punie et al. 1994; Wolf 1998). As opposed to early diffusion literature that discussed "late adapters" as poorly educated, this research looks more closely at the intricacies of roadblocks and passages in the use of Internet technologies. Power struggles surface between artifact and actor, as well as between actor and the structure and culture that fuel and stifle the diffusion of Internet technologies. In many instances, rejection of the technology is the rational choice, given the context in which staff members are asked to function. The rejection of technology as a reasonable choice is counter to much of the diffusion literature for which adoption is normative.

This research also suggests that women in particular may be facing another type of technology-driven workplace inequity. Most of the staff members in the organizations studied were women. Most staff members worked daily in a technological pink collar ghetto. Earlier work that discusses the pink collar ghetto (Stallard, Ehrenreich, and Sklar 1983, 18) focused on pay inequities in women-dominated occupations such as clerical work, food service, nursing, and teaching. The One-Stop research extends that concept to include new forms of workplace social capital such as technology access and assistance. And because human service and nonprofit organizations largely serve lower-income groups, these workplace inequities are passed on to clients already on the "wrong side" of the digital divide (NTIA 1999).

A newer cultural message for women is that they are just as adept with technology as are men. Yet once again, women find themselves facing contradictions. They ask, "If we can do this, why am I always so frustrated?" Perhaps one answer is that women are more likely than men to be asked to function in the messiest of new technology environments.

The people served by human service staff members also look to them for help with the technology. Yet clients encounter technology ambassadors whose own experiences with the technology are mixed at best. As in the case of the employment- and training-assistance program for single mothers, the face of technology in the environment of these technology ambassadors looks nothing like that depicted in the media. This troublesome computing environment sets up staff members and their clients for an outsider's relationship with information technology.

Beyond the scope of this research was the investigation of male-dominated human service fields such as corrections. My theoretical assumption would be that male-dominated areas of human services would fare better than female-dominated sectors. In the case of corrections, the field carries male-dominated occupational power along with the financial and political clout of a culture bent on criminal-justice solutions to social woes. More research is needed on a range of occupational sectors to provide perspective on the extent and types of technological inequities.

While this essay was about barriers to access, in all fairness I must mention the waves of excitement among organizations that are slowly coming online. In particular, staff members who have tasted Internet access at home or in other work settings set their sights on the transformative potential of information technologies. After all, their jobs are largely about communicating and sharing information. The extent to which technology will live up to their expectations is yet to be seen.

Finally, this research also provides insights into how human service organizations can better plug into the technological matrix. As they do so, they might consider this shortlist of "lessons learned" in the field:

1. Social barriers to accepting technology are more than just cultural lag. Consider the roots of these concerns and whether technology is necessarily an appropriate tool for a particular organizational context.
2. Sometimes, no computer is the best computer. Trickle-down technology practices can leave organizations lost in an antiquated technological jungle that no one can figure out.

3. Sometimes the old way really is better.
4. There is safety in numbers. Encouraging "technological companions" in the workplace can go a long way toward easing the pains of technology transitions.
5. Socially constructed or not, slow connectivity is a drag. Organizations owe it to themselves to aggregate their demand so they can afford equitable access to high-bandwidth connectivity.
6. Technology plans are not just for techies. Organizations with the least technology savvy should put the most thought into their technology planning. A plan provides a protective coating against finding oneself surrounded by technology that one never really wanted nor needed.
7. Everyday life can put the brakes on any technology plan that has not taken into consideration the lives of the people it is intended to serve.
8. *Time-saving information technologies* is an oxymoron. Information begets more information. Where one phone call in earlier days may have sufficed, now you'll have twenty email messages.
9. Information technology generates a need for more rather than fewer staff members. Someone needs to manage the technology itself and help all those who do not have the interest or need to become technical experts.

As a point of public policy, it is irresponsible to slash human- and social-service budgets and assume that technology can now streamline the process. This blind faith in the computer is part of a larger fetishism of technology. It is fueled by a multibillion-dollar international computer industry adept at infusing computers into every facet of life. The Internet and related computer technologies create a need for people at many levels as much as they create a need for artifacts. In organizations where the technology is made available without these supports, staff and clients will be stranded. They will be structurally disadvantaged in facing the powerful impact of information technology and a society that increasingly demands proficiency around its use.

NOTE

1. The One-Stop Career Network (OSCN) Internet project and this research were partially funded by the Department of Commerce National Telecommunication and Information Administration (NTIA) Telecommunications and Information Infrastructure Assistance Program (TIIAP). The Boulder Community Network (BCN) was itself a grant-initiated university TIIAP project that in 1998 became a 501 c. 3. nonprofit organization. BCN remained housed on the university campus during the time in which this research was conducted.

REFERENCES

Adler, Patricia A., and Peter Adler. 1987. *Membership Roles in Field Research.* Beverly Hills, Calif.: Sage.

Antonelli, Cristiano. 1990. "Induced Adoption and Externalities in the Regional Diffusion of Information Technology." *Regional Studies* 24: 31–40.

Belenky, Mary Field, Blythe McVicker Clincy, Nancy Rule Goldberger, and Jill Mattuck Tarule. 1986. *Women's Ways of Knowing: The Development of Self, Voice, and Mind.* New York: Basic Books.

Bijker, Wiebe E. 1994. *Of Bicycles, Bakelites, and Bulbs: Toward a Theory of Socio-technical Change.* Cambridge: MIT Press.

Culnan, M. J., and M. L. Markus. 1987. "Information Technologies." In F. M. Jablin, L. L. Putnam, K. H. Roberts, and L. W. Porter, eds., *Handbook of Organizational Communications*, pp. 420–43. Newbury Park, Calif.: Sage.

Douglas, M., and B. Isherwood. 1979. *The World of Goods: Towards an Anthropology of Consumption of Goods.* London: Routledge.

Fischer, Claude. 1988. "Gender and the Residential Telephone, 1890–1940: Technologies of Sociability." *Technology and Culture* 29: 32–61.

Fulk, J., and B Boyd. 1991. "Emerging Theories of Communication in Organizations." *Journal of Management* 17: 407–46.

Lie, Merete. 1997. "Technology and Gender versus Technology and Work: Social Work and Computers." *Acta Sociologica* 40: 123–41.

Ling, Rich. 1999. "A Short Note on the Use of Mobile Telephony in the 'Hyper-Coordination' of Teen Activities." Kjeller, Norway: Telenor FoU.

NTIA (National Telecommunications and Information Administration). 1999. "Falling Through the Net: Defining the Digital Divide." Washington, D.C.: U.S. Department of Commerce.

Ogburn, William F. 1951. "Cultural Lag as Theory." *Sociology and Social Research* 41: 167–74.

Punie, Yves, Alexa Veller, Pascal Verhoest, and Jean Claude Burgelman. 1994. "The Diffusion of Telecommunications Innovations from the Users' Point of View: The Case of Small-Scale Professional Users." *Technologies de l'Information et Société* 6: 219–47.

Rice, R. 1987. "Computer-Mediated Communication and Organizational Innovation." *Journal of Communication* 37: 65–95.

Rogers, Everett. 1962. *Diffusion of Innovations.* New York: Free Press.

Silverstone, R. 1994. *Television and Everyday Life.* London: Routledge.

Stallard, Karin, Barbara Ehrenreich, and Holly Sklar. 1983. *Poverty in the American Dream: Women and Children First.* Boston: South End Press.

Virnoche, Mary E. 1998. "The Seamless Web and Communications Equity: The Shaping of a Community Network." *Science, Technology, and Human Values* 23: 199–220.

Wolf, Christof. 1998. *Going Virtual: The World Wide Web as a Market Place for Religious Organizations.* Cologne, Germany: Research Institute of Sociology, University of Cologne.

Mary E. Virnoche *is an assistant professor of sociology at Humboldt State University in Arcata, California. She writes and has published about technology, gender, and communications equity. Her most recent grants have supported research on the intersection of technology, arts, and K–12 education.*

Listening to Our Side

Computer Training Issues of Middle-Age and Older Women

Dolores Fidishun

Those who work in libraries are faced with the rapid changes involved in information retrieval today. It is noted in the literature that influxes of new technologies, most necessitating some form of computer use, require constant training on automated systems for all employees (Bryant 1999; Krissoff and Konrad 1998). According to the American Library Association (Office of Personnel Resources 1991) the majority of the staff members of libraries are female. Therefore, it is important that we examine how women feel about computer training and technology as well as that we discover women's preferred methods of computer training.

Computer trainers in libraries have reported that some middle-age and older women who work in libraries are reluctant to learn computer skills. These women are not using or retaining skills learned after training or are leaving their positions before computer training takes place rather than learning to use new technology (Gist, Rosen, and Schwoerer 1988; Rodger 1994). There are, however, other middle-age and older female employees who embrace new technology and effectively learn new computer skills. The purpose of the research discussed in this essay is to identify factors that encourage or inhibit a middle-age or older woman library worker's acceptance and retention of computer training.

The Research Problem

An understanding of middle-age and older women's attitudes, beliefs, experiences, personality, and socialization, their adaptation to change, and other issues with regard to computers and computer training will be valuable in helping library administrators and others understand their attitudes toward computers and computer efficacy. These established attitudes may affect the priorities that the women set in their lives. If the learning of computer skills is not important to them, the women may not be motivated to become proficient in what is taught during computer training. Moseley and Dessinger (1994) have cited motivational studies of adult learners that suggest that they are more highly motivated when learning meaningful material. Knowles (1980) in his theory of andragogy, which emphasizes teaching in ways that meet the needs of adult learners, states that adults want to apply knowledge and skills to living more effectively tomorrow. If middle-age and older women view the introduction of computers to their job as not important to the scheme of their lives, or if they believe that they are unable to learn computer skills, they may not be willing to follow through with learning. Therefore, it was important to learn, using symbolic interactionism—a point of view that looks at how people act on the basis of the meaning that objects have for them (Woods 1992)— what meanings and values these women ascribe to the interactions involved in computer training and to see if there are differences in the library employee's view of technology implementation and computer training compared with the view of library administration.

Review of the Literature

Technology and Libraries

Today's libraries are being affected by rapid advances in technology. Dan Marmion (1998) states emphatically that the biggest technological challenge for libraries is "the challenge of preparing our employees to use technology" because, as he stresses, "computers, connectivity, and electronic information are playing an increasingly important role in what we do as librarians" (216). The impact of technology on libraries is felt not only by librarians but also by support staff. This recognition of the changes involved in technical implementation within the library world was heralded earlier by Conroy (1982), who felt that as rapid advances take place, decisions about the implementation of new technology should include staff development as a response to the need for "new skills, new attitudes and an ability to deal with change itself" (93). The great need for staff development in the rapidly changing library makes it important to use the most efficient and effective training techniques possible. As systems evolve it will be even more important to balance the need for rapid training with the human factors involved in system implementation. Only by listening to the needs and priorities of those being trained can library administrators achieve this needed balance and find the most effective training methods.

Computer Anxiety

Although there seems to be no reason related to intelligence or memory that explains why middle-age and older adults cannot or will not learn computer technology, computer anxiety has been mentioned as a reason for some of the resistance to computer technology. Maurer and Simonson (1993–94) describe components of computer anxiety as "apprehension about or fear of computers, and even reticence to use them" (205).

Researchers have found that computer anxiety may be a result of inexperience or negative experiences with computers (Morgan, Morgan, and Hall 2000; Maurer and Simonson 1993–94; Jay and Willis 1992) or of the socialization that an individual has undergone with regard to sex roles (Boyd 1994). Jo Sanders explains that women believe that they cannot deal with machines; therefore they feel that they cannot operate a computer (Boyd 1994). Many middle-age and older women were socialized in traditional ways with regard to gender roles (Filene 1974). This may affect their computer efficacy (Lewis 1987). Asking women about their socialization and attitudes toward gender roles and computers may help establish reasons why they may accept or reject computer training.

Workplace Computer Training

Computer anxiety is only one of the issues that affect computer training. A study by Urs Gattiker (1988) of on-the-job computer training shows that attitudes toward computers and training do influence an individual's ability to effectively use technology. Gattiker investigated how an individual's perception of her/his career success might be related to her/his beliefs about a computer-based technology. In his study, Gattiker found that feelings of job success and general career success were related to the respondent's beliefs about computer-based technology. He also mentioned that people's success constructs are influenced by their environment, which includes peers, friends, and family. These concepts are reflective of the theories posed in symbolic interactionism.

Socialization

In the early nineteenth century in the United States, women's roles were centered in the home and were interpreted as mostly interpersonal. Those women who worked outside the home usually did so in domestic positions. At the beginning of the Industrial Revolution, most women continued to work at home or in sales or clerical positions. Those women who worked in factories did so in low skill positions. Women in professions were few in number. In the early twentieth century, middle-class women began entering professions, but only those that were considered feminine, such as nursing, teaching, and social work. These required the feminine qualities of "nurturance, empathy and motherliness" (Denmark, Neilson, and Scholl 1993, 244). Although women did work at defense jobs during World War II, it was expected that they would once again take up their more domestic roles when the war ended. The result was the postwar baby boom of the 1950s and the reinforcement of women's traditional roles. The 1960s and 1970s led to new definitions for the roles of women, but those who had been born before and during the 1930s and 1940s had already established their view of gender roles (Denmark, Neilson, and Scholl 1993). In addition, Soloman (Denmark, Neilson, and Scholl 1993) concludes that "gender role behavior does not change throughout life unless there is a conscious effort to do so" (463).

Lupton (1993) states that "certain tasks, accomplished with certain tools, have become associated with women's work, while others traditionally have been assigned to men" (7). She further comments that a person sees herself as a woman in part through the material objects and images that surround her each day. Thus, women view their roles as oriented toward practical uses of technology. Washing machines, telephones, and other "household appliances" became the traditional mechanical domain of women, utilized for purposes allowing them to fulfill their duties as homemakers. Homemakers learned to operate the appliances but not to repair them or to feel comfortable understanding how they worked (Rothschild 1983). When these appliances needed to be repaired, women traditionally have called upon husbands or repair*men* to have them fixed. The generation of women whose culture this study is intended to explore was particularly socialized to this attitude toward machinery. This generation also may envision computers as the large mainframes that were once the province of the military and the factory. Consequently these women may view computers as machines that need to be built and repaired rather than as utilitarian devices. As Lubar (1993) explains, in the 1960s computers were considered "outside of most people's experience, and still intimidating, complex machines" (318). If women have had little experience with machines it may affect their comfort with computers; as Morgan, Morgan, and Hall (2000) state, "Individuals with little previous experience with mechanical devices tended to have negative attitudes toward computers" (73).

In addition, societal attitudes toward computing technology are primarily masculine (Margolis, Fisher, and Miller 1999/2000; Wyer and Adam 1999/2000). The concept of the computer as a machine, belonging in a generally accepted masculine domain, is an unquestioned truth to many. Edwards (1990) remarks that "computers do not simply embody masculinity; they are culturally constructed as masculine mental objects" (125). The computer is also viewed as a machine used by mathematicians and scientists, a group identified by both men and women as male (Lewis 1987). This concept is still propagated by the primarily male contingent within the computer industry. In fact, even the small, but important, contingent of women who helped to develop computers are barely mentioned in works on the history of computing.

Methodology

Referrals of study participants were solicited from library directors, department heads, and trainers, as well as interviewees. Participants were women who are, or were, employed in libraries in institutions of higher education. Using snowball sampling, I asked participants whom else I should interview. I then interviewed the person whom they suggested and at the end of each interview asked who else they felt would have an interesting perspective on computers and computer training. This process continued until the research was complete. To avoid sampling bias, I interviewed women of different ages as well as those who work in different library environments, whether college or university libraries. In addition, participants were from different departments within the library, such as technical and public services areas. Twelve women were interviewed for the study, one each age 42, 43, 52, 54, 57, and 60; and two each age 50 and 64. Two other women would not give an exact age; one was older than 60 and the other older than 70. These women represented academic libraries located in eastern and middle Pennsylvania. Four of the women were librarians: two reference librarians, one documents librarian, and one cataloger. Eight of the women were support staff: one from microforms, two reserve, two administrative, two periodicals, and one reference/interlibrary loan. The institutions that they represented included two private college libraries, two state-owned university libraries, four state-affiliated university libraries, and three community college libraries; one woman had retired from a state-affiliated university. The women were from several ethnic groups: one was African American, one was European, and ten were European Americans. Their comfort with computer training can be described as three very resistant, three very successful, and the other six across the spectrum between these two ends. Access to the participants was facilitated through the library colleagues or the interviewee who recommended them.

The Interview Process

Before each woman was interviewed, she was asked to fill out a questionnaire. Items on the questionnaire included demographics and background information about when the women were trained on computers. Requests for critical incidents regarding positive and negative computer training experiences were also included.

The data-gathering portion of this study consisted of an in-depth interview with each of the participants. A pilot interview was conducted to test both the questions that would be used as well as the interview format. An in-depth interview worked well, as the women could tell their story in a continuous manner without interruption. Interviews lasted from about one and a half hours to three hours.

Interviews were loosely structured and highly interactive. Initial questions in the interview were used to establish background information about the woman, her life, and her family. These questions began with life experiences that may have contributed to the women's socialization to gender roles, their attitudes toward change, their feelings about machinery and power, and other issues that emerged as the interviews progressed. Further questions revolved around current computer attitudes and training experiences, including positive and negative critical incidents from their computer training or experiences with technology. Other types of issues addressed included the interviewee's expectations of the system; her view of its relationship to her work; her perception of locus of control during training and implementation of the system; effectiveness of training methods; and some of the woman's perceptions of support from family, friends, and coworkers during the training period and beyond. Interviews focused on how each person constructed herself as a woman, how she constructed that role in relation to technology, and how, or if, each interviewee imputed meaning to the use of technology. In addition, I tried to evaluate each woman's sense of power during the use and implementation of technology.

Interviews were audiotaped and notes were transcribed for later evaluation. Following the suggestion of Strauss and Corbin (1990), sections of the audiotapes were transcribed as needed. Notes taken at the interview included specific notations of nonverbal cues and emotional responses.

Data from the interviews and questionnaires were coded using a thematic content analysis to look for beliefs, behaviors, personality factors, and attitudes on the part of the women that may have affected their interactions with computer technology and training. Conceptual analysis and interpretation proceeded from this point as I analyzed contextual clues and meanings, as well as notations from my interview notes about unspoken messages, to draw conclusions about the informants' perspectives on computers and their lives.

Validity Issues

In the qualitative perspective, the researcher needs to be concerned with the trustworthiness of the results; do the results ring true? I had to be aware of biases in interpretation of the data. As a younger woman who has accepted computers as a basic part of life, I needed to view the women's ideas of computers through their eyes. I kept a journal during the study to allow me to continuously evaluate my understanding of the research as it was conducted. This journal also serves to document each research decision and the rationale behind it.

As another way to help minimize these biases, I used triangulation, bringing more than one source of data to bear on a single point (Marshall and Rossman 1989). In the case of this study of middle-age and older women, triangulation was achieved by the use of the reporting of critical incidents on paper as well as through conversation in the interview and the participation of a second researcher who also assessed the findings of the study. My interpretations of the texts of the interviews and the reporting of computer attitudes were compared dialogically with another researcher well versed in technology implementation and training as well as in women's issues.

Analysis of Data

In the process of analyzing my conversations with the twelve women, I was able to associate themes with the constituent texts of each woman's interview. In the following passages, the women's names have been changed to protect their identities.

We Think We Are Training, But . . .

Administrators throughout the country are spending hours planning and executing training programs as they implement new technology. What I found when I spoke to the twelve women was that most of their learning was done by what Leah referred to as "the seat of the pants." Many of the women interviewed said that although they had been to formal training sessions conducted in their libraries or at the local library network, most of the actual training they had received was what they could learn on their own. This was especially true when the first round of online systems and almost all CD-ROM systems were installed. This brief exchange with Claudia at the beginning of her interview set the stage for similar dialog with many of the women:

Dolores: What was the first library computer system you were trained on?
Claudia: [The online catalog].
Dolores: How were you trained on it?
Claudia: They just gave us a manual and you worked the manual.

The tendency for staff to learn by the seat of their pants has not disappeared now that libraries plan more formal training. Instead, it becomes an important supplement to this formal training. Learning on the job still remains the most frequently mentioned method of learning new technology. Many times formal efforts do not work. As Leah explained, she is unable to take advantage of her college's new mentoring system as as much as she would like:

> Prior to a month ago it was always by the "seat of my pants" or if I chose to take a formal course such as the online course after I got my degree. But as of a month ago there have been many more opportunities for informal training, I'll call it, and I think the college is doing a great job to cover many different learning aspects and many different ways to learn the new computers but it is real early on. They have an array of times to sign up for specific workshops and . . . of them are at 11:00 . . . when the classes end, where every faculty member is theoretically free, however, the library becomes crowded at that time so it is difficult for me to get a piece of that.

Margaret describes the usual form that her training takes when she is learning a new system or dealing with a computer problem:

> Now I think it sort of is a disadvantage, I work the two-to-ten shift. Believe me, everybody goes home at 5:30. There is the girl in circulation and there is one reference librarian and there's myself. Even when the system that we just got, what, two months ago or something, they had people from the computer department here for about two weeks day, night, whatever. After the two weeks, hey, you fly on your own. Always on Saturday, you fly on your own! If they can't get the computers on over there, huh! Once in a while if it's really drastic

the reference librarian would call somebody from the computer [center] at home to ask them what to do.

So although library administrators may be conscientiously trying to train their staffs, especially those who work evenings and weekends, we do not always do the thorough job we had planned. Vera was adamant about how she had learned much of her computer skills: "Most of [the] things I've learned I learned by practicing on my own. You ask your basic questions and then you proceed on your own and by playing around. You have to try by trial and error, otherwise you never learn." For some, learning on their own is actually the preferred method, allowing them to adapt the training to their needs.

My colleagues and I had noticed that some of the middle-age and older women whom we trained seemed to understand how to use the computer system at the time of training but did not retain the computer skills that they had learned. It appears that even when there were formal classes, several women did not have time or did not make time to practice their skills when they returned to their desks. They felt that this lack of practice inhibited retention of what they learned. Johanna stated: "A lot of it you learn or, you know, you go to class, and you kind of understand it and you learn it, but then you come back to the office and you have no way to apply it and then you lose it. You have to use it all the time."

Since much of these women's computer learning seems to be taking place on their own or after training classes are over, the role of mentor has become extremely important. Almost every women interviewed found that she was greatly helped by the presence of a mentor, trainer, colleague, or other person who took the time to answer questions on the level that the woman asking them could understand. Several women spoke of mentors who were colleagues. Ruth says that "mainly I like someone to show me and I pick up on it. After one or two times I'll pick it up a little bit faster."

When asked about her best computer training experience, Lillian spoke of a librarian who helped her learn the computers that she would work with to process interlibrary loan requests:

> I think the Technical Services librarian, she was just wonderful! She really was! She was very encouraging and would come out, and usually the problems I was having were with the computer and she would just come out and explain how I had gotten into the predicament and show me, and she really never did interlibrary loan but she knew a lot about computers.

Empowerment

Whether or not women felt comfortable with computers, they appeared to have little or no input into the selection of the technology their library introduced. I wondered about the issues that Sandra Harding (1991) had posed about "the distinctive features of women's situation in a gender-stratified society" (119). For the most part, the women interviewed were not in positions, either in the library or society, that would grant them the power to individually choose or shape library technologies or to initiate change in such matters. Most women had no input at all into how computer systems operated. Even those who said that they did reported that their suggestions had limited effect. Joan discussed a new online system that her library would be choosing. She said that although there would be some input, their library was only one of fourteen that would share the system. She wondered how much influence any one person could have. In the final analysis, none of the women felt that they had much control over the system they were to use; however, a number of them emphasized a point expressed by Margaret: "If you want to have a job, you have to learn it; computers are here to stay."

Leah explained her feelings about the perceived power of librarians as she described her role in technology implementation:

Dolores: Do you feel that you are being listened to or is it an uphill battle?
Leah: I guess I feel I am being listened to because they, the group, not all the powers that be, but the Internet committee, understands that I know more than they thought I knew. However, and I'll say this for the record, I usually am very careful about what I bring up at the meeting and I would prefer to email the chairman and hopefully she'll be my mouthpiece. It's a she . . . and her just saying, "I think we should be doing this . . ." I'd rather it come from her because I don't know how it is going to be perceived coming from me and so maybe that's a little bit of how I think others would be.

Although the women felt that they had very little formal power over technology in general and the choice of which technology would be used, most of them stated that they wanted or needed to continue working and so found it essential to feel that they were capable of using the technology. They had to empower themselves so that they could feel that they had some control over their computer environment. Most of the women interviewed had been socialized to women's roles by the 1950s, when a woman's purpose was more traditionally defined. Computer technology was something they never could have imagined. Almost all the women admitted to having been uncomfortable with computers in the beginning. In order to empower themselves to acquire computer skills when the time came to learn how to use the technology, they had needed to look beyond the way women were defined, a definition that they had lived with for most of their lives. Some women had done this more successfully than others. Those who were most successful seemed to be the women who had encountered much transition and change in their lives. Joan reminisced about her initial reaction:

> I can remember maybe early seventies, like '73, '74, sort of being like petrified of all this computer stuff that I would have to learn. Thinking like, this isn't what I got into libraries for. You know, I'll never learn it, but I was really starting to go through some training, and at that time we were starting to talk about indexes coming online. I would say I was apprehensive about it and then all of a sudden, I think I just realized that whatever I . . . I guess what it was that, initially I thought I had to prepare myself to take the course or to have a real long learning curve in terms of trying to do my job well or even adequately. Then somehow I just figured, well, there was no sense getting uptight about it, whatever I have to learn I'll learn when I learn it and that's really the way it came out. But I do remember a period when I really felt anxious and that my profession was changing.

Lillian expressed a similar sentiment: "I do recall I was very nervous initially not ever having used a computer. You wonder, can you ever do it? And now you look back and think it was not that difficult at all but I didn't know that then."

Those women who were most strongly resistant to computers tended to be those who had led more traditional lives. Change was not a powerful factor in their life histories. They were also less self-reliant than those who were comfortable with computers. The resistant women were less likely to empower themselves in dealing with computers and often relied on a supervisor or others to help push them into technology.

Johanna described how her supervisor motivates her to learn technology:

> I have a supervisor that pushes, in a nice way. She pushes in a nice way. When I had to write a program, she thought I should put it in my evaluation. Well, then when the evaluation came around the next time and the program wasn't written . . . "Now, I really think that this

needs to be tended to." And when I sat down to do it was fun! I enjoyed
it, and I got it all done but it was just I needed that extra push, for
someone to say this really needs [to be] done. And now I don't have
any qualms about sitting down and changing stuff on Q & A but it's,
you just have to say . . . I guess the big word is intimidation.

Along with the women's feelings of self-reliance is the fact that some
of the resistant women appeared to lack confidence in their ability to
perform computer skills. Ruth was convinced that she could not work
on computers, yet she proudly showed me spreadsheets that she had
developed on Excel. When I asked her if she knew more than she
thought she did, she said that her supervisor kept telling her, "You
know more than you realize." Johanna told me several times that she
was intimidated by computers but if she just sits down and works on
them she learns what she needs to know and then wonders, "Why do
I feel that way?" Finally, Loretta said that she was "not smart enough
to make that thing work," yet she did word processing on her computer all the time.

Even the most self-confident women felt uncomfortable with their
computer knowledge. Leah told me how her knowledge of computers
had evolved and then added:

> I came to another revelation several months ago, that I know a fair
> amount about computers and [the] Internet. I know a lot about cer-
> tain pockets, but there is still some general things I don't get the drift
> about. But I thought on the learning curve, in the scheme of things,
> with the professors that are here, that I was low man [*sic*] and indeed,
> I think I'm much further along than I realized. It was hard for me to
> get the perspective, do I know more or less than the average person?
> And I think I'm further up than I gave myself credit for.

People Versus Machines

The women interviewed tended to view the computer in different ways.
Many saw them as tools that could assist them with their work whereas
others felt that they were intimidating machines without any connection with humanity. In Margaret's case there was intense evidence of
a perceived lack of humanness of the computer:

> I'm a human being concerned about other human beings because
> that's what I was put on this earth for, not to play with little machines!
> I see that there is no going back, I mean computers are here.
> Computers are going to be more advanced, it's like the car, or the

radio went into television and airplanes are now jets. On the other hand the atomic bomb saves a lot of people but it killed a lot of people too! The technology, I don't think we should all be cave people but I feel we are losing your identification for sure with the computer. I mean, anymore, you're not even a person, you're a number, because the number fits better into the computer.

Others, like Ruth, look at computers more pragmatically. She spoke for those women:

> I think that computers are very useful but they told us that they would get these computers and it would lessen the manpower, well, they don't see what I do. You need more people. You need more people with computers. And I don't feel that it saved any on the paperwork because we waste paper in our printers sometimes. For one sheet it prints on you might lose two, two sheets of paper. I don't think we save on paper but I think there are a lot of advantages to them.

Margaret's other comment described the feeling that some women had about computers, feeling, and communication:

> [I object to,] I think the inhumanness [*sic*] of it. I say, my objection to the whole thing is it *does not have a soul!* I can work with people. I can love them, I can hate them, I can . . . but not the computer. I don't want to curl up in bed with a handheld computer to read at night.

Even though she has a positive feeling about computers, Isabel understands the lack of the human element inherent in dealing with a computer: "Well you certainly don't develop an interpersonal relationship with computers. Then sometimes you feel as though you should. In trying to look back and analyze my reaction to it there were times when I felt like kicking the stupid thing."

Another factor that reflects the antagonism between people and computers is the importance of attitudes of supervisors and trainers. Ruth's initial message from her supervisor did little to help her learn computers:

> I started in cataloging. . . . They didn't have computers here. . . . They got them six years later. They said they were getting computers and my supervisor at the time said that I could never be able to learn computers. " Voilà," she said, I could never learn computers. So I came over to accounting, they had a bookkeeping machine and I

didn't know if I could learn it or not and I came over to accounting
and I've been here ever since.

Trainers' attitudes are also important to women who see the computer
as a machine that they cannot conquer. Ruth complained that in training "they are talking over my head." Virginia was annoyed by a trainer
who "could not talk in noncomp [noncomputer] language."

When trainers relate to women as human beings, the women tend
to be more successful in learning. In spite of her lack of comfort with
computers, Johanna praised the trainers who work at her library, claiming that "they are really good because they don't make you feel bad if
you don't understand something and they start with the basics and
they're just real good. They're very good at not making you feel bad,
or you know, getting it through to you on layman's terms."

From the comments of these women, it appears that computer trainers need to make training more human by paying attention to adult-
learning principles. This includes understanding that adults require
individualized learning and teaching strategies and that there is a need
for recognition of the adult's previous experiences (Knowles 1990).

From the other side of training, Leah explains why she thinks she
can be a good teacher:

> I also think that because I came by this knowledge by the "seat of my
> pants" and because I initially lacked some self-confidence that I think
> I could be an excellent teacher because I understand "the dumb
> question." Or maybe because I was a teacher by trade and had those
> innate skills, because I think I can teach anybody tennis as well as
> computers. But that's my perception and maybe my students don't
> feel that way.

People Servers Versus Information Providers

Finally, the women's perception of library work emerged as an indi-
cator of computer comfort. Those who saw libraries as *people servers* and
those who understood libraries as *information providers* looked at the
need to learn computers in different ways. The priorities established
in each of these contexts served to facilitate things such as the amount
of time women spent practicing with the technology.

Many of the resistant women are people servers. They are much
more dedicated to assisting others than they are to relating to new
technology. There is a powerful emphasis on the human side of library
work. They do not see technology as a better way to help patrons, just

an extra responsibility that is added on to the job. Johanna explained it best when she stated that computers are not a priority:

> My supervisor tells us to take time and it's our fault if we don't take the time and we don't use it. But you are so programmed in your work schedule. I hate to let something go that I'm responsible for to sit at the computer. Now, she will understand [if I let something else go to practice my computer skills]. It's my fault if I don't play around with the computer and get it going. So she has no problem with me applying things to the computer but I have a personal problem because I want to take care of the things on my desk. And that might be called intimidation or procrastination too.

Jessica says,

> I sort of feel guilty taking the time to go sit here and really play with this thing and it doesn't seem like you are really doing a whole lot of work. You're pushing buttons and moving the little mouse around and moving the screens around and this really doesn't seem like a lot of work.

Women like Vera who are more comfortable with computers see their role differently. They see themselves as information providers. Vera feels that

> there is a time when you have to be on the floor and help your students but if you don't play and learn some basic tricks you'll fall so far behind that the world will spin so fast that you won't be able to catch up with it. That is why I say, we do spend, most of us, time at home working. We do have to practice and learn new tricks every day so that we can better assist them. It is good enough that we are out there helping them but there comes a difficult set or a question out of the ordinary that in the past you could not resolve with the print material but you can do it now with First Search or DIALOG or OCLC or Uncover. So I feel it is equally important. Now how you are going to manage it, it's your own trick. It is very important that one takes the time to practice and play around. It should be balanced. You should give the time to try new things, especially with the Internet. You can learn a new thing every day and you go back the next day and it won't be there.

Leah summed up the way of thinking for those who see a new version of libraries as information providers:

[Computers] are here to stay and everybody better learn them. They make some of our work a lot easier and some more difficult and it is going to take a new way of thinking because computers are not simply the print media on a screen. It took me a long time to realize that. The revelation came when my daughter was working on a CD-ROM for a chemistry professor and it was not taking the textbook and putting it on CD-ROM and you can flip the pages. It was to be interactive and it was a whole new mode. Computers are the same thing, you don't just take the print index and put it on the computer.

Discussion

The ability to learn by the seat of their pants may reflect women's ability to do what Turkle and Papert (1990) suggest that women do well. They shape a program or technology to their best use, creating a final product—in this case, the woman's knowledge of the computer system—based on the what she needs to know to use the program.

Given the prevalence of seat-of-the-pants learning, it was logical that there would be a strong positive influence in training when a woman had a mentor, a person to whom she could go to ask questions and get help, not only during training but also afterward. The person may have been a trainer, but in most cases was a colleague or peer who was non-judgmental and could answer questions at the level of the woman's computer knowledge. This interaction with people—in many instances, that between one woman and another—appeared over and over in the women's conversations. Not only did the mentoring relationships make women feel more comfortable learning technology, but these women also utilized what Malcolm Knowles (1990) calls the "richest resources for learning, the learners themselves." Knowles talks of an "emphasis on peer-helping activities" (59), an adult-education concept that points up how the women in the study learned best.

Empowerment

Whether they were librarians or support staff, most women interviewed felt that they did not have much power in the selection of technology. A few indicated that they may have been consulted regarding their comments on a new online catalog or on which database is needed, but most of the decisions were not in their hands. They realized that there was nothing they could do about this, so they did what they needed to do to perform their job. Most said that they either needed or wanted to work, and since the technology was part of the job, they had to learn how to use the computer.

A woman's ability to empower herself to learn to use a computer became a key factor in her success. Women did demonstrate differences in their ability to decide to learn computers on their own. The most successful women were those who sometime in their life found themselves in situations that necessitated changing their definition of themselves as women. These were women who had gone through life-changing experiences such as divorce, separation, widowhood, or having a husband who traveled extensively.

Those women who were most resistant to technology were those who had led the most traditional lives, change not having been a significant element in their life histories. They were also less self-reliant than those who were comfortable with computers. These women were more passive in their attitude toward life, often relying on family or friends to push them to do things. They tended to be in more comfortable, traditional situations with regard to family and job and had not taken as many risks as their more self-reliant sisters. The resistant women had not been forced by circumstances to go beyond what they believed were their capabilities.

Several of the women did finally learn the new technology, but persisted in being unsure of their skills even when reassured by others that they were doing well. Ruth commented that her boss kept telling her that "you know more than you realize." When asked why she did not realize how much she knew about computers, she admitted that she lacked self-confidence. One explanation for the women's inability to believe that they knew how to use computers is the finding of some researchers that women who have a more traditional view of themselves have lower self-esteem (Anderson 1993). The reflections of traditional women's roles versus a broader view of an individual woman's capabilities fits with the symbolic interactionist perspective. Resistant women do not see computer technology as a priority in their lives; therefore, they may not respond to training in the same way as someone who considers it important. In fact, the resistant women may not truly associate themselves with computers at all. The resistant women see themselves as associated with people and not computers. From the standpoint of andragogy (Knowles 1980), adults want to apply knowledge and skills to living more effectively tomorrow. If the perspective of these women is that family and people are what makes life better, learning a new computer system may not be that important to them.

People Versus Machines

A further major issue was the contrast of people versus machines. Resistant women viewed the computer as a soulless machine. They were trying to emotionally connect to the computer. Those women who were more comfortable with computers viewed the computer as a tool. They saw it as something to be used to assist them to do their job.

Another part of the phenomenon of people versus machine was the way in which trainers treated the women they trained. This concept follows Sherry Turkle and Seymour Papert's (1990) conjecture that typically computer experts have been so indoctrinated with the planner's or black-box approach to programming and technology that they cannot relate to others, including women who are more sculptors or simply users of computers. It also illustrates a key concept from Knowles's (1990, 60) theory of andragogy: "in any situation in which adults' experience is ignored or devalued, they perceive this as not rejecting just their experience, but them as persons."

Finally, in almost all cases, the connection of having another person who could respond to a woman's questions was important for the human connection. Women felt that the mentor cared enough about them to help them understand a difficult subject or develop skills. Thus mentors were important in training.

People Servers Versus Information Providers

The knowledge that technology is a necessary part of library work was echoed by both resistant and accepting women. There is, however, a changing view of what library service is all about. The more resistant women tended to be people servers. These women focused on the service they gave to people.

The women who were resistant saw practicing computer skills as playing with the computer, something to be done after all the patrons were served and the work on their desk was cleared. To them the priority was the need to personally help patrons. They saw people, not the computer, as important.

By contrast, information providers viewed computers as essential to helping patrons locate information. As Harris (1992) suggests, the new roles for librarians, and in many cases library staff, will be more along the lines of teaching and consulting than the direct service seen by the more traditional women interviewed.

Through all the interviews, the women exhibited what Nancy Hartsock (1987) describes as the female construction of self, that is, the "valuation of concrete, everyday life, sense of a variety of connectednesses and continuities both with other persons and with the natural world" (170). Regardless of the women's level of comfort with computers, there was a very prominent emphasis on their identity as human beings and on how much the human interface makes a difference for most people. In the context of reviewing the findings from a symbolic interactionist and feminist standpoint, the female themes of nurturance and mentoring emerged strongly from the whole group.

There was one exception to the literature that I found extremely glaring. In speaking with the women, I did find beliefs about what Anderson (1993) describes as gender roles, expectations for behavior and attitudes that the culture defines as appropriate for men and women. However, Soloman (Denmark, Neilson, and Scholl 1993) had expected that these roles would be formed early in life and remain static. In the cases of several of the women interviewed, their ideas of gender roles changed in adulthood as they encountered transforming experiences such as divorce or traveling husbands. This coincides with the findings of Aslanian and Brickell (1980) that adults undergoing life-changing experiences realize that they will need to learn something new if they want to successfully make necessary transitions. In these cases, the women learned to be more self-reliant than they had originally been. This, in turn, affected their ability to learn computers.

Implications for Practice

The results of the present study may be used by academic library and other administrators and trainers who wish to consider possible causes for the success or failure of their training programs. The factors that the twelve women spoke about in their interviews seem likely to be reflected in training situations at other places of employment. Thus, administrators and trainers may want to observe the types of training offered in their own institutions. There may be less formal training happening than they realize, and there may be a need to encourage already occurring mentoring relationships. They also may want to question whether there is enough time for trainees to practice what they have learned after training is completed.

Administrators and trainers should also realize that some women are more traditionally oriented than others. Those in charge of training may need to be reminded of the importance of human interaction and that they thus need to have more patience and be much more aware of the individual needs of the people they train. By being more cognizant of the principles of adult learning, those in charge of training may find their instruction to be more effective. Included in these principles is the impact of collaborative learning and the recognition of women's life experience. Also to be considered is evaluating the responsiveness of trainers to individual differences and checking the pace of the instruction. More opportunity for trainees to ask questions of someone knowledgeable in the software after they have had time to work with the package may also be important.

Although these issues are important ones and may serve as catalysts for thoughts about individual training situations, it should be remembered that this study was qualitative in nature; therefore, none of the findings can be generalized to any group other than the twelve women interviewed. There will be circumstances, however, in which some of the ideas in the study can serve as a place from which to start discussions about successful training methods and situations.

Recommendations for Future Research

On the basis of the findings set out here, several issues should be explored further. A follow-up study should test whether the finding that a woman's self-reliance relates in an important way to her success in computer training would apply to the general population of all middle-age and older women. A quantitative study of some group of indicators of self-reliance compared with attitudes toward computers and computer training seems to be an obvious first step. Further studies of this phenomenon could introduce measures that might increase the women's self-reliance as a means of testing women's attitudes toward computer training as a woman becomes more self-reliant.

Studies should be done analyzing the effects of mentoring on middle-age and older women in computer training. It would be important to test whether the findings of the significance of mentoring for these women could be generalized to a larger population. Qualitative research could elicit the factors important to such a mentoring relationship.

Further studies could extend findings to other groups who will need to be trained on computers, including younger women and men of all ages. It would also be valuable to look at comparative training issues for younger and older women, since in most cases, in any single session, institutions are training a group of women who are of mixed ages.

All these studies could be conducted with groups outside of a library population; many women with whom I spoke during the development of this study indicated that they had the same kinds of trepidation about computers although they did not work in libraries.

Conclusion

As I listened to this group of twelve women, it was evident to me that they were conscientious about their jobs, but that some of them were having difficulty adapting to the computer environment that their libraries valued. The amount of self-reliance developed by an individual woman seemed to have a major impact on her comfort with computers. The lack of time available in which to practice new computer skills also emerged as a dominant issue with both reluctant and enthusiastic women indicating that there are many other priorities to balance and that finding time to reinforce skills learned can be problematic. This is in spite of the fact that those who made time to practice felt much more comfortable with computers than those who did not.

Many women in this study indicated that formal computer training was nonexistent, especially in their early experiences. The role of mentors emerged as the most positive method of computer training experienced by any of the women. There was a theme of the women being able to ask someone whom they could easily relate to what they needed to know, to go back to their desk and experiment, and then to ask more questions. Important traits of these mentors were the ability to speak about computers at the level of the person they were assisting and the ability to be nonjudgmental as that person learned through trial and error.

The women in this study also demonstrated their resiliency as they strove to keep up with a constantly changing technology that is here to stay. The definition of library work has changed dramatically. Some of the women have been more comfortable with the implementation of technology than others, but my final finding is that all care about their jobs, even if some do not feel comfortable with the technology required to do the work.

REFERENCES

Anderson, M. L. 1993. *Thinking about Women: Sociological Perspectives on Sex and Gender.* New York: Macmillan.

Aslanian, C. B., and H. M. Brickell. 1980. *Americans in Transition: Life Changes as Reasons for Adult Learning.* New York: College Entrance Examination Board.

Boyd, Robert S. 1994. "Electronic Age Brings Anxiety to Many." *Philadelphia Inquirer,* 6 May, A2.

Bryant, Eric. 1999. "Triumph of the Web." *Library Journal* 124: 4–6.

Conroy, B. 1982. *The Human Element: Staff Development in the Electronic Library.* Philadelphia: Drexel University Press.

Denmark, F. L., K. A. Neilson, and K. Scholl. 1993. "United States of America." In L. L. Adler, ed., *International Handbook of Gender Roles.* Westport, Conn.: Greenwood.

Edwards, Paul N. 1990. "The Army and the Microworld: Computers and the Politics of Gender Identity." *Signs: Journal of Women in Culture and Society* 16: 102–27.

Filene, Peter G. 1974. *Him/Her/Self.* Baltimore: Johns Hopkins University Press.

Gattiker, Urs. 1988. "Computer End-Users: The Impact of Beliefs on Subjective Career Success." In Urs Gattiker and Laurie Larwood, eds., *Managing Technological Development: Strategies and Human Resource Issues,* pp. 161–85. New York: Walter de Gruyter.

Gist, Marilyn, Benson Rosen, and Catherine Schwoerer. 1988. "The Influence of Training Method and Trainee Age on the Acquisition of Computer Skills." *Personnel Psychology* 41: 255–65.

Harding, Sandra. 1991. *Whose Science? Whose Knowledge?* Ithaca: Cornell University Press.

Harris, Roma M. 1992. *Librarianship: The Erosion of a Woman's Profession.* Norwood, N.J.: Ablex.

Hartsock, Nancy. 1987. "The Feminist Standpoint: Developing the Ground for a Specifically Feminist Historical Materialism." In Sandra Harding, ed., *Feminism and Methodology: Social Science Issues,* pp. 157–80. Bloomington: Indiana University Press.

Jay, Gina M., and Sherry L. Willis. (1992). "Influence of Direct Computer Experience on Older Adults' Attitudes Toward Computers." *Journal of Gerontology* 47: 250–57.

Knowles, Malcolm S. 1990. *The Adult Learner: A Neglected Species.* Houston: Gulf.

———. 1980. *The Modern Practice of Adult Education: From Pedagogy to Andagogy.* Chicago: Follett.

Krissoff, Alan, and Lee Konrad. 1998. "Computer Training for Staff and Patrons." *Computers in Libraries* 18: 28–32.

Lewis, Linda H. 1987. "Females and Computers: Fostering Involvement." In Barbara Drygulski Wright, ed., *Women, Work, and Technology: Transformations,* pp. 268–80. Ann Arbor: University of Michigan Press.

Lubar, Steven. 1993. *Infoculture.* New York: Houghton Mifflin.

Lupton, Ellen. 1993. *Mechanical Brides: Women and Machines from Home to Office.* New York: Princeton Architectural Press.

Margolis, Jane, Allan Fisher, and Faye Miller. 1999/2000. "Caring about Connections: Gender and Computing." *IEEE Technology and Society Magazine,* winter.

Marmion, Dan. 1998. "Facing the Challenges: Technology Training in Libraries." *Information Technology and Libraries* 17: 216–18.

Marshall, C., and G. B. Rossman. 1989. *Designing Qualitative Research.* Newbury Park, Calif.: Sage.

Maurer, Matthew M., and Michael R Simonson. 1993–94. "The Reduction of Computer Anxiety: Its Relation to Relaxation Training, Previous Computer Coursework, Achievement, and the Need for Cognition." *Journal of Research on Computing in Education* 26: 205–69.

Morgan, Konrad, Madeleine Morgan, and John Hall. 2000. "Psychological Developments in High Technology Teaching and Learning Environments." *British Journal of Educational Technology* 31: 71–19.

Moseley, J. L., and J. C. Dessinger. 1994. "Criteria for Evaluating Instructional Products and Programs for Older Learners." *Performance and Instruction* 33: 39–45.

Office of Personnel Resources, American Library Association. 1991. *Academic and Public Librarians: Data by Race, Ethnicity, and Sex.* Chicago: American Library Association.

Rodger, Joey. 1994. *Information Revolution: New Pitfalls, New Possibilities, New Partners.* Paper presented at the Pennsylvania Library Association Conference, September, Harrisburg, Pennsylvania.

Rothschild, Joan. 1983. "Technology, Housework, and Women's Liberation: A Theoretical Analysis." In Joan Rothschild, ed., *Machina ex Dea: Feminist Perspectives on Technology,* pp. 79–93. New York: Pergamon.

Strauss, Anselm, and Juliet Corbin. 1990. *Basics of Qualitative Research: Grounded Theory Procedures and Techniques.* Newbury Park, Calif.: Sage.

Turkle, Sherry, and Seymour Papert. 1990. "Epistemological Pluralism: Styles and Voices Within the Computer Culture." In C. D. Martin and E. Murchie-Beyma, eds., *In Search of Gender Free Paradigms for Computer Science Education.* Eugene, Ore.: International Society for Technology in Education.

Woods, Peter. 1992. "Symbolic Interactionism: Theory and Method." In *The Handbook of Qualitative Research in Education,* ed. Margaret D. LeCompte, Wendy L. Millroy, and Judith Preissle, 337–404. New York: Academic Press.

Wyer, Mary, and Alison Adam. 1999/2000. "Gender and Computer Technologies." *IEEE Technology and Society Magazine,* winter.

Dolores Fidishun *is head librarian at Penn State Great Valley School of Graduate Professional Studies, Malvern, Pennsylvania. She holds an Ed.D. in Leadership in Higher Education from Widener University, a M.S.L.S. from Drexel University, and a M.Ed. in Adult Education from Widener University.*

Filtered Feminisms

Cybersex, E-Commerce, and the Construction of Women's Bodies in Cyberspace

Anna Sampaio and Janni Aragon

Beaver College, a small liberal arts school in the Northeast, recently embarked on a public relations effort with the principal goal of changing the school's name. On its surface, this gesture appears a bit odd, if only because students, staff, and alumni have long expressed pride in their school's offbeat name and because while unusual, the name does its job of attracting and maintaining public attention. However, over the years members of Beaver College have been beleaguered by sexually explicit jokes, as the school's name is also slang for a woman's genitalia. In a recent article in the *Chronicle of Higher Education*, school administrators reported that prospective students were having difficulties accessing the school's main Web page, as it was being blocked by filtering programs that mistook it for a pornographic Web site.[1] By November 2000 a new name, Arcadia University, was chosen.

While this incident shows that these increasingly popular filtering programs are hampering access to important information (an ironic effect, given the Web's success in decentering the base of information and increasing public access to otherwise obscure databases), this incident with Beaver College is a fairly innocuous example of the programs' negative effects. However, for women and others who have traditionally been marginalized from mainstream politics and who've looked to the Web as a source of alternative organizing, as a place where the inherent anonymity of cyberspace allows for greater flexibility in identity and a freedom from the traditional markers of race and gender in spoken word, these filtering programs present a formidable challenge.

As we will demonstrate in this study, the proliferation of these filtering programs has often restricted access to women-centered and feminist-friendly Web sites. While filtering programs have satisfied the needs of parents, educators, and librarians concerned with protecting children from the growing numbers of pornographic and sexually graphic Web pages, they have often cast their net of protection too wide. In this essay we examine how the filtering of women's activism on the Web is compounded by the proliferation of pornography and the commodification of women's bodies in the burgeoning market of e-commerce directed at women. Ultimately, it is our contention that the proliferation of women-directed e-commerce and sexually graphic pornographic sites coupled with the increasing obstacles presented to women's political expression have transformed the once abundant opportunities for feminisms to flourish into a realm of filtered feminisms.

Theory and Representation

Eschewing traditional interpretations of new technologies rooted in the understanding of individuals as rational, coherent, and purposeful, poststructuralists have put forward an alternative interpretation of individuals and subjectivities as "decentered . . . and multiplied in continuous instabilities." Rather than individuals being positioned as absolute entities guided largely by reason/rationality, our subjectivities (and sensibilities) can more accurately be described as a collection of environmental and discursive influences that are at work in a given time and place. The most obvious implication of this is that our identities, our personalities, and our very selves are never "set," but are constantly in the process of being constructed and deconstructed given the changes in environment, people, and stimuli we encounter.

It is from this altered view of subjects and individuals in the world that many political theorists and poststructuralists have examined the impact of new technologies on our lives. In particular, the suggestion that the advent of information systems such as the Internet and email constitute far more than simply a shift in the presentation of information but are instead important processes in the actual construction and deconstruction of subjects has most influenced our understanding of new technologies.[2] Critical theorists such as Mark Poster and Donna Haraway have substituted the traditional view of new technologies as merely extensions of print media, with a focus on the language formations that significantly alter the network of social relations that individuals inhabit and the subjects that are constituted through these networks.[3] In this interpretation, poststructuralists have often viewed new technologies as discursive systems that not only affect, and are affected by, environmental conditions, but that also have the capacity to construct entirely new subjects. As such, traditional perspectives that position new technologies as merely extensions of print media prove inadequate, because they assume the a priori presence of our subjectivities as rational, autonomous, coherent, and purposeful, when in fact, in cyberspace, our subjects are being continuously constructed, multiplied, dispersed, and even deconstructed.

For several feminists, the focus on language and domination inherent in this poststructuralist view helps to specify a new form of power and resistance, one that is grounded in the complex intersection of subjectivities that has permitted particular cultural and intellectual trends to be privileged and to fix women (and other marginalized subjects) in sedentary and essentialized positions. This view also introduces a new critique of pornography as not only objectifying women and promoting hostile environments, but also constructing a limited image of women and their sexuality that is then imposed on them by virtue of its widespread dissemination and reproduction.[4] With regard to cyberspace pornography, this problem has been exacerbated as the sites proliferate and women's sexuality in cyberspace becomes almost entirely captured by graphic images that are uninhibited in their celebration of misogyny and the sexual degradation of women.[5]

However, as we contend in our earlier survey of women's political expression on the Web, cyberspace has also provided new opportunities for resisting cultural, linguistic, and discursive formations—such as those inherent in pornography—that privilege masculinity.[6] The Web's anonymity allows challenges to traditional social and cultural markers such as sex, age, and race, as well as temporal and spatial boundaries that fix the language of everyday life and that are inscribed in both print media and speech.[7] Whereas communication via speech and writing was once wrapped in a cultural context providing clear indications of identity, by reducing communication to a complex code of binary numbers and reproducing information from that code, we have also reconfigured the surrounding cultural context and its signifiers. The types of symbolic indicators that are challenged or even removed in the new technologies are more often those constraining women and racial minorities. These include markers of sex, race, age, and geographical background and of aesthetic appearance, such as weight and size.

The effect of this loss of key cultural signifiers is that new informational technologies challenge the prominence of the autonomous rational masculinized subject embodied in the production and distribution of information. The centrality of the autonomous rational and masculine voice underlying so much of print media can no longer be assumed or accurately asserted in the context of cyberspace, as the anonymity and decentralized nature of communication on the Internet prevents any identity from being "real." Because the very nature of identity is obscured in cyberspace, the existence of hierarchies drawn from subject positions privileged within print and spoken language systems are also challenged. This undermining of the traditional rational male subject position, coupled with the decentering of information and identities, opens up myriad possibilities for women's construction of their own identities that reflects their heterogeneity and the changing salience of gender in their lives. In many ways, the possibilities for women's political expression introduced by the erasure of the previously mentioned gendered characteristics mirror some of the early utopian visions of a genderless society expressed by radical feminists such as Mary Daly and Marge Piercy.[8] That is, as the space of electronic communication becomes largely anonymous, women and men are able to reconstruct themselves online, leading to such outcomes as women logging on as men, or individuals assuming the identity of actors, elected officials, or other public figures. Thus, women as marginalized subjects can and have utilized cyberspace as a site of creative resistance. However, as we demonstrate in the following sections, while the language system of cyberspace introduces this possibility of women being able to engage in public discourse without the trappings of traditional communications, this freedom has been mitigated by the reinscription of traditional gendered roles (and their projection onto women) via such avenues as cyberpornography and e-commerce directed at commodifying women's interests.[9]

In addition to the theoretical possibilities for women introduced by these new technologies, there are other benefits related to access that expand the possibilities of women's expression. Among these are the narrative structure of communication, the availability of women-friendly sites, and a host of new publications written by and for women.

Feminist scholars have detailed the ways in which women's narratives and patterns of communication have been systematically delegitimized by scholarship that emphasizes and rewards objectivity and empirical falsifiability. By contrast, the "text" of online conversations often involves stream of consciousness, inductive reasoning, and the use of lived experience as evidence, thereby validating a type of communication that has generally been defined as "feminine." With these challenges to traditional configurations of language and traditional constructions of subjectivity, women's "narrative" has also been given a renewed sense of legitimacy. The advent of cybercommunication also challenges the structure of grammar and style and the presumption of rationality embedded in print media and speech. The attention given to presentation by way of deliberate (and even unconscious) misspellings and "emoticons" (letters, numbers, and keyboard signs used in email messages to indicate emotions) allows the messenger to become as important as the formal message, calling to mind the famous claim of Marshall McLuhan, "the medium is the message."[10] Hence, the words and symbols transform themselves into "action as resistance," in a distinctive and empowering way.[11] While norms of reason and rationality still abound they are not the same universalizing or bounded rationality prevalent in traditional media. For example, in *Cybergrrl*, Aliza Sherman explores the formation of a fictional character named Cybergrrl, Sherman's own alter ego in cyberspace, who challenges the boundaries of sex-typed norms by her actions as a portal for information and services.[12] In addition, instead of content conforming to a single standard of truth and reason, competing logics and cultural trends are allowed to coexist in cyberspace. This practice results in the proliferation of subcultures and alternative expressions of women that have their own logic, often in conflict with more mainstream expressions of gender, such as that of the Guerrilla Girls (www.guerrillagirls.com) and The Eagle Forum (www.eagleforum.org).[13]

The Internet also affords access to women-related and feminist information that is not always available in the community. The Web sites of Chickclick (www.chickclick.com/), Virtual Sisterhood (www.igc.apc.org/vsister/vsister.html), the ADA Project—Tapping Internet Resources for Women in Computer Science (www.tap.mills.edu/), and the National Organization for Women (www.now.org/) are some of the many that offer pro-girl or feminist visions of women's participation online. These sites have even been referred to as part of a new movement of cyberfeminism or as the "differential mode of oppositional consciousness—a cyber consciousness."[14]

Women who use the Web also transform their bookmarks into their own cyberdatabases. Among sites serving as information clearinghouses by and for women are those of Femina (www.femina.cybergrrl.com); CLNET, in their Chicana Studies page (latino.sscnet.ucla.edu/women/womenHP.html); Feminist.com (www.feminist.com); GeekGirl (www.geekgirl.com); and SisterFriends (www.sisterfriends.com). Through these sites, women may engage in conversations with others in their own towns or across continents virtually any time of the day.

Other women's advocacy sites are set up by activist organizations, centers affiliated with research institutions, and others. Such groups include the Center for Women and Information Technology at the University of Maryland, Baltimore County (www.umbc.edu/cwit/); the Center for the American Woman and Politics (CAWP) (www.rci.rutgers.edu/~cawp/); Women's Environment and Development Organization (www.wedo.org); and the American Association of University Women (www.aauw.org/). Cybercommunication also promises feminist activists and scholars an opportunity to intensify their movement through more efficient ways of disseminating information, quickly and globally, as we saw with the 1995 Fourth World Conference on Women (www.un.org/geninfo/bp/women.html).

Moreover, cyberspace has been an effective medium for undermining the gatekeeping role of traditional print media and opening up new opportunities for the publication and dissemination of women's work and other related interests. Feminist organizations that have made use of these new media in disseminating information include *Ms.* magazine (www.msmagazine.com/), Estronet (www.estronet. com), Bust (www.bust.com), Maxi (www.maximag.com), Heartless Bitches (www.heartlessbitches.com/), Wench (www.wench.com), and W.I.G. (www.wigmag.com).

Finally, certain assumptions about the Internet and its attendant new media require clarification; that is, not everyone owns a computer or has access to these new technologies. While the "language" of cyberspace disrupts traditional symbolic signifiers, as noted earlier, material obstacles remain. As such, the cost of computers; of an Internet-provider account; and of acquiring, installing, and maintaining software still serve to exclude the working class, women, and people of color.

Recent research suggests that the introduction of new technologies has exacerbated traditional racial/ethnic divisions (particularly in the area of access), which are developing into what some see as a "racial ravine," or a "digital divide" between those who have computers and access to new technologies, and those who do not.[15] A July 1999 report issued by the U.S. Department of Commerce documented that from 1997 to 1999 the information and access gap between whites and people of color had widened, and that Blacks and Latinos were the furthest behind in Internet use. More recent studies indicate that the disparities in access also extend to those schools most frequently attended by children of color. Thus, "while 78% of schools in general have computer and Internet access, this is true of only 63% of schools in low income areas or those with at least 50% minority enrollment."[16]

Such studies indicate that despite the theoretical promise and actualization of various possibilities for women in cyberspace, new technologies have in many ways created new obstacles along the traditional divides of race, class, and gender. In what follows, we examine some of the newer obstacles to women's political organizing and expression online presented through the proliferation of cyberpornography, e-commerce, and the recent adaptation of several filtering programs.

Cyber Sex and Pornography

While the Internet provides widespread access to information and databases previously inaccessible to the general public, it has also introduced the sex industry to a new audience. According to various Internet surveys and pundits, cybersex has become pervasive in the United States.[17] Reports from a majority of Web search engines show that most of the searches conducted through their software are requests for sex-related sites. According to Nielsen//NetRatings, the company SexTracker (www.sextracker.com)—a subsidiary of Flying Crocodile, Inc, which provides services and statistical tools for adult Web sites, including an index of more than twenty-four thousand adult Web sites—was seventh among the top ten Web advertisers for the month of February in 2000.[18]

The pornography industry is a multimillion-dollar business allowing professionals and amateurs to "hock" their wares on the Net through such auspicious practices as installing "metatags," or coding that allows manipulations of a Web browser's "Back" button, on unsuspecting surfers. Sex sites are also notorious for capturing a user so that any attempts to close a page result in four or five new pages emerging. Many pornography sites also require enrollment or subscription on their Web pages, which allows the Webmaster to "datamine"; that is, obtain personal information such as the name, telephone number, address, email address, and other demographic information from the user. In short, "the world of adult content on the Internet is an immense tangle of hyperlinks and populism, competition and multi-level marketing."[19] The proliferation of e-sex commerce has led many amateurs to set up their own voyeuristic Web sites and Web cams. The aggressive nature of some of these sites is best exemplified by the policies of organizations such as the Internet Entertainment Group (IEG), which pays its subscribers and subcontractors five dollars for each "raw hit" they post. In sum, sex sells, and according to the IEG Web site (ieg.com), money is being made.[20]

An examination of the many sex-related sites reveals an assumption that there are hypersexualized and sexually available women in all positions, sizes, and ethnic backgrounds. These sites consist largely of downloadable images and text depicting women in a host of contorted positions aimed largely at maximizing the male gaze.[21] And yet, borrowing from the poststructuralist view that the new technologies are not simply the latest manifestation of print media, we maintain that the proliferation of pornographic Web sites does not represent simply another extension of print-media publications such as *Playboy* and *Penthouse.* Cyberspace not only alters the configuration of our subjec-

tivities through the invention of a new language system, it also recon-
figures the terrain in which we express our subjectivity. Cyberspace
offers us a seamless integration of reality and fantasy, substituting the
enduring presence of forward time with a timeless indulgence in our
immediate space. Moreover, new technologies reconfigure this public
space in more personal and intimate ways. Because entrance into these
virtual communities is mediated through our desktops/laptops, which
necessarily isolate us from others, our connection to the realm of
cyberspace is also more personalized and intimate. In the context of
online pornography, it is precisely this shift in our spatial location that
makes the proliferation of cybersex so unique and problematic. In
other words, the spread of pornography in cyberspace also serves to
normalize and personalize these images of women. Sexually graphic
depictions of women come to be seen as commonplace and readily
available for one's personal pleasure. The extent of this availability and
normalization of sexually explicit images is evidenced in the female
characters of popular video games such as Tomb Raider (www.
tombraider.com/). In the game, viewers are hosted by Lara Croft, a
busty, barely dressed, hypersexualized character invoking danger, sex,
and mystery for popular consumption.

Ultimately, the proliferation of cybersex disrupts the potential for
"distortion-free communication," and particularly for feminist expressions of sexuality, as women's bodies are packaged and the various new
media are flooded with this pornographic depiction of women. In the
realm of cyberspace, where information and access become the primary forms of currency, popular understandings of women's bodies
become dominated by sexually explicit or compromising images as the
cybersex industry grows. The costs include not only women's bodies
becoming hypersexualized on the Net, but also this view of women
becoming increasingly accessible and familiar. Thus, it is not surprising that a Nielsen survey conducted in April 1996 found that *Penthouse*
online recorded the highest number of hits among publication sites
on the Web.

Filtering Software

One common response to the cybersex industry has been the manufacture of filtering programs intended to block access to sex-related
and other sites considered unsuitable, particularly for younger audi-
ences. A recent report issued by the Federal Communications
Commission (FCC) suggested that one way to protect children from
these sites was through the use of filtering mechanisms such as those

provided by Net Nanny and CyberPatrol.[22] In the debates surrounding the 1998 Internet School Filtering Bill sponsored by Senator John McCain (Republican, from Arizona) and Ernest Istook (Republican, from Oklahoma), supporters demanded that libraries and public schools be required to install such filtering programs to receive federal funds.[23] Despite the bill's eventual failure, an alternative version was introduced in 2000 as the Children's Internet Protection Act. Under the terms of this bill, Congress would make any elementary school, secondary school, or library ineligible to receive or retain universal service assistance unless it certified to the FCC that it had selected and installed a filtering program designed to "block material deemed harmful to minors." This bill was eventually added as an amendment to the Education and Related Agencies Appropriations Act 2001 and was passed into law. Congress also passed the Safe Schools Internet Act in 2000 as an addition to the Juvenile Justice Act, a bill performing many of the same functions as the Children's Internet Protection Act. Many organizations, among them the American Civil Liberties Union (www.aclu.org), the American Library Association (www.ala.org), Peacefire.org (www.peacefire.org/), and the Electronic Frontier Foundation (www.eff.org), expect these laws to be challenged in court.[24]

In the rush to protect children, many parents and computer programmers have sacrificed information for security and placed undue burdens on constitutionally protected speech. These filtering mechanisms frequently block access to organizations such as NOW, the AIDS Authority, and Planned Parenthood and to information on breast cancer and birth control.[25] Critics of the software, such as Karen G. Schneider, author of *A Practiced Guide to Internet Filters,* maintain that at best these programs are "overbroad, and underinclusive, and at worst bigoted and misleading."[26] In the following section, we examine the effects of four filtering programs: Net Nanny,[27] CyberPatrol,[28] Cybersitter,[29] and We-Blocker,[30] with a particular view to their effect on cyberpornography and on the formation of a cyberfeminism. We are most concerned with how the software programs block access to information for women on the Web.

Methodology and Analysis

Using the software, we conducted searches to ascertain how the programs influence access or mere searching on the Internet. Prior to beginning our searches, we developed a coding sheet with a list of topical areas central to research in women's studies. These included women's bodies/health; reproductive rights; feminist publications online; feminist organizations online; feminist legislation/political groups; lesbian/gay/bisexual/transgender sites; gender equity in education; violence against women; miscellaneous women-friendly or feminist sites; and Christian women or related material. Each of these categories had subcategories that varied from specific names of sites, organizations, or issues. While this is not an exhaustive listing of the many issues that concern feminists (nor are they inclusive of the breadth of sites available on the Net), they did serve as a snapshot of some of the timely, popular, and prominent women-centered topics in which material is available online. This cross-section of categories was tailored to provide a comparative array of ideologies and interests as well as a means to invoke some of the most controversial issues inside and outside women's studies.

We downloaded trial copies of each of the software programs without modifying the program in any way. Net Nanny, CyberPatrol, and We-Blocker allow users to modify their programs—adding additional sites to be blocked and exempting specific Web pages from being filtered. While some may argue that this feature offers parents and users maximum flexibility and prevents sites such as those pertaining to feminist concerns from being blocked unnecessarily, this feature protects merely individual Web pages and not the general themes or topics. By modifying the software, a user could type in the URL for the Gay and Lesbian Advocates and Defenders Web site (www.glad.org/) and obtain access to this information on a topic such as same-sex marriages. However, if the same user did not have the specific URL and merely typed in the topic "same-sex marriage" for a search, even with modifications the computer would likely shut down.

After downloading and installing these programs, we proceeded to conduct topic and site searches using the Infoseek search engine. Infoseek's directory contains more than five hundred thousand pages, and it provides relevance and ranking, narrowing of searches, and related tools in its search results. We conducted the same searches with each software program in order to measure the accessibility of the sites and to compare findings among software.[31]

In conducting our searches we found that while each of the software filtering programs blocked some access to the women-centered/feminist sites we specified, we also found that the mechanisms used to restrict access were not always the same. Information was filtered in two ways: (1) the search topic was accessible but the software only allowed a limited portion of the range of available sites to be shown, or the sites identified by the search engine proved not to be relevant to the search topic; and (2) the search topic was not accessible—either the software blocked access to the topic, the search reported no available sites, or the entire computer shut down (not just the Internet access). These results varied both by topic and by software; of the four we tested We-Blocker provided the greatest level of access, particularly for women's bodies/health–related topics, reproductive rights, and feminist publications. For research purposes germane to women's studies, this would offer the best choice of the software programs; parents, however, might not prefer it, because it would not offer them the extensive filtering of some of the others.

While the first—and most commonly found—level of restrictions we encountered with the filtering software, that of returning only a limited number of sites that were generally not salient to the search, could be interpreted as an insignificant barrier, such restrictions are particularly harmful for Web newcomers or anyone unfamiliar with conducting more sophisticated Internet searches, whether for personal or research purposes. The majority of these filtering software permitted the searches to take place but provided only limited information (measured in the number of sites identified), only partially relevant information (Web sites that used the words in the search but not in the order or with meaning intended), or no relevant sites.

Two notable health-related topics were included in this restricted group: sterilization and "pink ribbon," the latter referring to sites providing information, support, and advocacy regarding breast cancer. In our search we found that Cybersitter identified only 59 pink ribbon sites with only a 10 percent saliency rate (the remaining sites were largely dedicated to fashion).[32] Searches using CyberPatrol and Net Nanny turned up 132 sites, 264 in total, each search yielding a 50 percent saliency rate. By comparison, in a search conducted without filtering software, more than 225,000 hits were marked and there was a 100 percent saliency rate.

For the topic of sterilization, using We-Blocker, approximately 23,000 sites were returned, with a 40 percent saliency rate. By contrast, with CyberPatrol and Net Nanny 686 sites were listed with only 20 percent providing relevant information. Without the use of any filtering software we also came up with approximately 23,000 sites and a slightly better saliency rate of 50 percent. While we can identify notable differences in the availability of information with and without the filtering software, one explanation for the lack of relevant information in the case of sterilization was the ambiguity of the search topic. It encompasses aspects of female sterilization, pet/animal sterilization, and sanitary sterilization, all sites we found when conducting the search.

Vagueness of topic, however, did not explain the heavily restricted access to information regarding violence against women, sexual slavery, rape, and prostitution. Our search for AWARE (Arming Women Against Rape and Endangerment) illustrates the problem for both researchers and survivors of violence. AWARE offers a well-linked Internet site teaching women how to protect themselves against violent crimes, particularly sexual assault and rape, using a variety of means, from self-defense/martial arts to handguns. The site also lists referrals for women who have been assaulted. In our search for this site Cybersitter identified 5,327 matches with a 30 percent saliency rate, whereas CyberPatrol and Net Nanny each identified only 2 matches, neither of which was pertinent to the topic. A search without the filtering software yielded 28.8 million matches, with all the top ten sites providing information or direct links to AWARE.

In a similar vein, access to COYOTE (Call Off Your Old Tired Ethics), a national organization dedicated to sex workers and pro-sex advocacy, was also restricted using the filtering software. We-Blocker identified a number of matches for the search (5.8 million), but achieved only a 30 percent saliency rate. Cybersitter, CyberPatrol, and Net Nanny each identified matches for this search (8, 80, and 1,310, respectively), but virtually none were relevant. The topic of sexual slavery was also restricted, particularly using the We-Blocker and Cybersitter software. We-Blocker gave 1,031 matches with a 20 percent saliency rate, whereas Cybersitter identified 51 sites with only a 10 percent saliency rate. Without filtering software we found approximately 394 sites with a 100 percent saliency rate.

The sites of a number of feminist publications and online feminist organizations were also restricted, including On the Issues, Web by Women for Women, the Center for American Women and Politics (CAWP), Women on the Well, and the National Center for Lesbian Rights. Of particular note was the absence of relevant Web sites on less controversial topics such as equal protection, the gender gap in general elections, *Planned Parenthood v. Casey,* and *Webster v. Reproductive Health Services.* On this last topic, we not only found few relevant Web sites to this landmark Supreme Court decision; in one search, using Cybersitter, two of the top ten sites were for veterinary services.

At the second level of filtering restrictions encountered with this software, the topic was blocked entirely. This was achieved by preventing Netscape, the browser we used, from processing the search request; returning no site matches when the request was processed; or shutting down the computer altogether. Again, we found that many topics concerning violence against women were blocked by these filtering programs. Searches for *sexual harassment, rape,* and *sexual slavery* turned up no matches using CyberPatrol and Net Nanny, and with Net Nanny the computer was shut down when the searches were submitted. Without using the filtering software we found more than 393,000 matches for *sexual harassment* and *sexual slavery* and more than 99,000 for *rape.* While a search for *battered women's shelters* was not blocked using the software, we found that Cybersitter, CyberPatrol, and Net Nanny each turned up fewer than 100 matches as compared to the more than 529,000 matches found without the software. These results are particularly troubling when we consider the implications of such actions for young women or students—those most likely to be using computers with filtering software. If these women needed to find confidential information regarding sensitive topics such as sexual harassment or rape, they would find their access on the Internet entirely blocked; and in many instances they might feel uncomfortable turning to other avenues of support.

Equally troubling is the blocking of political and research sites geared to women, particularly those offering lesbian and queer resources. Both CyberPatrol and Net Nanny blocked the site for the American Association of University Women as well as information on same-sex marriages. In both searches Net Nanny shut down the computer when the search was submitted; Cyber Patrol shut down the computer when we requested information on same-sex marriages. While a search for Sappho/Queer Resources Directory was not entirely blocked by Cyber Patrol or Net Nanny (both turned up two returns), We-Blocker did block this search. Guerrilla Girls (www.guerrillagirls. com), a popular site by "women artists, writers, performers, film makers and arts professionals who fight discrimination," was blocked using We-Blocker and Cybersitter, while Cyber Patrol and Net Nanny returned only 37 matches for the search.

Other notable feminist sites that were not entirely blocked but resulted in only a fraction of the returns made available in searches without the filtering software included those relating to Women on the Well, Chickclick, Hip Mama, breast cancer legislation, birth control, *Roe v. Wade, Webster v. Reproductive Health Services,* and single-sex schools. Interestingly, when searching for Christian-women or related sites, we found that we suffered no computer shut downs or blocking of the subsites.

With some of the filtering software programs we found that a user would be hard pressed to find certain pro-women or political sites. Most of the filtering software programs blocked or inhibited access to many politically related women's sites, sites on same-sex issues, and vio-

lence-against-women sites.[33] The use of the filtering programs and the
data provided from this exercise indicates that while some sexually
explicit sites are blocked, political sites are simultaneously blocked.
This clearly places women's political issues and activism on the same
level as cyberpornography and graphic violence. Moreover, sites that
make reference to women's bodies in nonpornographic forms (i.e.,
sexual harassment) are equally blocked. Thus, while the formation of
the Internet offered women new opportunities for personal and political expression, with the proliferation of the sex industry and the introduction of these filtering programs women's bodies online have been
increasingly marked and restricted. Women's studies advocates and
those concerned with the research capabilities of the Internet also
have cause for concern, as this exercise presents a glimpse of what can
happen daily even with minimal use of filtering programs.

E-Commerce: Marketing to Women

In addition to expanding the scope of the sex industry, the Internet
has opened up a new market for consumers and businesses through
e-commerce.[34] In particular, many survey sites and business articles
note that women are important consumers, often purchasing the "big
ticket" items, such as refrigerators, stoves, and furniture for family
households. According to Nua Internet Surveys results, the gap in
online spending dollars between women and men was decreasing during the last financial quarter of 1999.[35] Nua cited data from
MediaMetrix, a network of advertising and Web trend companies, documenting that "the top most trafficked sites by females in November
1999 were Kbkids.com 73%, iVillage 69%, Women.com 69%, and
Freeshop.com 66%."[36] A year later, in December 2000, these were still
among the top fifty trafficked sites among women.[37]

In response to this evidence, numerous sites catering to women's
consumer interests have emerged, increasing women's representation
as cyberconsumers. Such sites targeted directly at women include
Oxygen.com (www.oxygen.com), Women.com (www. women.com/),
and iVillage (www.ivillage.com). Women.com and iVillage.com are part
of a network consisting of links to themed sites and women's online
magazines ranging from *Cosmopolitan* to *Good Housekeeping*.[38]

The targeting of women as consumers is not restricted to such
lifestyle-laden Web pages but also includes revised marketing strategies among companies such as Harley Davidson and Ford Motor
Company. These companies, which have long targeted male subjects
with promises of bravado, have achieved online commercial success in

large part by marketing their products to women.[39] Recent reports indicate that young women and girls are also part of this new market of e-consumers, with a number of slick sites trying to sell an array of products to them (for example, gurl.com, bolt.com, and cosmogirl. com).[40] In sum, business articles and books abound with suggestions that companies take women as consumers seriously and that the Net needs to be "feminized."[41]

However, this platitude cuts both ways. Women and their dollars should be taken seriously and sites should gear themselves to women, but with the added attention comes the increased objectification of women's experiences. In the pages of Oxygen.com and iVillage.com or in Women 1.0 Opportunity Kit, a program developed by business-man Tom Peters for companies interested in capitalizing on women's dollars, one would be hard-pressed to find pertinent information about the increasing wage gap between working-class and privileged women or about developing living wages for women workers. These sites are largely targeted at maximizing the spending of a small sector of female users, those with disposable income and the Internet savvy to be able to spend it online. In this context, feminism or cybercon-sciousness becomes as irrelevant as most working-class women, who are not part of this consumer culture. Thus, the onset of e-commerce sites directed at women's credit cards is accompanied by the com-modification of women's interests, a process that results in the siphon-ing away of any issues or ideas that are not easily translated into the market. Moreover, while there is an increasing body of Web sites and e-commerce companies owned by women and for women, both the Web sites and the companies marketing to women are still dispropor-tionately controlled by men.[42] Thus, while the gender gap for online consumers may be disappearing, the same cannot easily be said for the ownership of this new media that targets women.

While more research into the effects of e-commerce needs to be conducted, we are particularly troubled by the effects that the prolif-eration of such sites have on the scope of gendered political expres-sions online. In the same way that pornographic sites hypersexualize women, these consumer-based sites commodify women's interests. In this context women's subjectivities online are increasingly constructed as a form of entertainment—either their own or someone else's—to be bought and sold, and the potential for crafting feminist identities that challenge pornography and commodification become increas-ingly marginalized.

Concerns for the Future

While the formation of new technologies provides us with a structure of communications that has already influenced how we express ourselves, how we relate to others, and even changes in our national economy, this media has also introduced a new set of obstacles for traditionally marginalized populations such as women. In this study we have attempted to outline both the possibilities for the formation of a cyberfeminism as well as the restrictions on such activism through the proliferation of cybersex, filtering software, and e-commerce. We are particularly concerned with the way cyberpornography and e-commerce frame women's online subjectivities, and how filtering software marks all women's bodies—regardless of the form or content of their expression—as suspect.

How we deal with the limitations presented by these industries, particularly on a policy level, remains unclear. On one level, attempts to restrict pornographic material through federal law have proven unconstitutional for the chilling effect they impose on protected speech, as was seen in *Reno vs. ACLU,* in 1997. Moreover, because cyberspace is necessarily a globalized media, imposing sanctions such as fining pornographic producers is futile. Even if we were successful in eliminating most of the violent or degrading pornography produced in the United States, this would do nothing to stem the flow of pornography from abroad. As e-commerce continues to grow, and global economies become increasingly dependent on its success—and the absence of regulations—we will undoubtedly see the profitable sex industry grow as well. Finally, while filtering software is one response to this problem, it is clearly inadequate, as it ends up punishing the user and exacting a particularly harsh penalty on women-friendly and feminist sites.

Despite the apparent futility surrounding policy solutions to these problems, there is reason for hope. What makes the Internet unique is the capacity for grassroots activism to emerge and spread virtually anywhere. What is required is increased access to and advocacy for and by women on the Internet at the grassroots level, in academic centers, and in boardrooms. In short, the effort to protect cyberspace communication and feminist expression online cannot be met without it being a shared endeavor. Thus, while much of the Web's capacity for building feminist-friendly online communities has been curtailed with the advent of filtering programs, pornography, and the abundance of e-commerce commodifying women's interest, we are still encouraged by the Internet's relative flexibility, accessibility, and ability to bring diverse groups of women together in previously unimagined ways.

NOTES

1. Nina Willdorf, "Tired of Being the Butt of Jokes, Beaver College Contemplates a Name Change," *Chronicle of Higher Education,* March 2, 2000. Generally speaking, the filtering programs are software which, once installed onto a computer, serve to shield a user from topics the program deems inappropriate, such as overly violent or sexually graphic Web sites. The manner by which topics are filtered and blocked differs among various programs and is discussed in greater detail in this study.

2. For a review of this literature, see Daniel Bell, *The Coming of Postindustrial Society* (New York: Basic Books, 1973) and "The Social Framework of the Information Society," in Tom Forester, ed., *The Microelectronics Revolution* (Oxford: Blackwell, 1980). See also Anthony Giddens, *Social Theory and Modern Sociology* (Stanford: Stanford University Press, 1987); Jurgen Habermas, *Toward a Rational Society,* trans. Jeremy Shapiro (Boston: Beacon, 1970); Robert Markley, "History, Theory, and Virtual Reality," in Robert Markeley ed., *Virtual Realities and Their Discontents* (Baltimore: Johns Hopkins University Press, 1996): and Patricia Wise, "Always Already Virtual: Feminist Politics in Cyberspace," in David Holmes, ed., *Virtual Politics: Identity and Community in Cyberspace* (New York: Routledge, 1997). Authors such as Susan Bordo, *The Flight into Objectivity: Essays on Cartesianism and Culture* (Albany: State University of New York Press, 1987); Sandra Harding, *Whose Science? Whose Knowledge? Thinking from Women's Lives* (New York: Cornell University Press, 1991); and Uma Narayan and Sandra Harding, eds., *Decentering the Center: Philosophy for a Multicultural, Postcolonial, and Feminist World* (Bloomington: Indiana University Press, 2000) have added to this body of literature by asserting that the traditional autonomous rational subject of Cartesian logic is also masculine.

3. Mark Poster, *The Mode of Information: Poststructuralism and Social Context* (Chicago: University of Chicago Press, 1990); Donna Haraway "A Manifesto for Cyborgs: Science, Technology, and Socialist Feminism in the 1980s," in Linda Nicholson, ed., *Feminism/Postmodernism* (New York: Routledge, 1990), 190–233. See also Jean Baudrillard, *Simulations,* trans. Paul Foss et al. (New York: Semiotext(e), 1983); David J. Bolter, *Writing Space: The Computer in the History of Literacy* (Hillsdale, N.J.: Lawrence Erlbaum, 1990); George Landow, *Hypertext: The Convergence of Contemporary Critical Theory and Technology* (Baltimore: Johns Hopkins University Press, 1991).

4. In discussing cybersex, we make a distinction between pornography, the production and distribution of sexually explicit materials designed to emphasize pain, dominance, and violence; and erotica, sexually explicit materials designed to stimulate arousal through love, pleasure, and sensuality. While we understand the need for filtering programs to inhibit the former, there is an equally pressing need to protect the latter in promoting avenues for women's empowerment. See Gloria Steinem, "Erotica and Pornography: The Clear and Present Difference." *Ms.,* November

1978; and Rosemarie Tong, *Women, Sex, and the Law* (Totowa, N.J.: Rowman and Littlefield, 1984).

5. For examples, see Best of Asia, Exotic Tours and Holidays (www.bestof-asia.com/index.html); Video Travel (www.videotravel.net/new-ulti-mate.html); Big Apple Oriental Tours (www.baotours.com/); Love Tours (www.lovetours.com/); Exotic Tours (www.exotic-tours.com/); Prostitution in Thailand: General Information and links (www.worldsexguide. org/Thailand.html); and Max Hardcore (www.maxhardcore.com/). Many of the sex-tour message boards provide examples of the insidious combination of racism and misogyny. For instance, one message asked how to impress Thai bar girls. The first response noted that you had to "feed them, and then your in" [*sic*]. For more discussion of the traffick-ing of women and sex on the Internet, see Donna Hughes, "The Internet and the Global Prostitution Industry," in Susan Hawthorne and Renate Klein, eds., *Cyberfeminism: Connectivity, Critique, and Creativity* (Melbourne: Spinifex Press, 1999); Azy Barak and Storm A. King, "The Two Faces of the Internet: Introduction to the Special Issue on the Internet and Sexuality," *CyberPsychology and Behavior* 3, no. 4 (August 2000): 517–20; and Mary Ann O'Farrell and Lynne Vallone, eds., *Virtual Gender: Fantasies of Subjectivity and Embodiment* (Ann Arbor: University of Michigan Press, 2000).

6. See Anna Sampaio and Janni Aragon, "To Boldly Go (Where No Man Has Gone Before): Women and Politics in Cyberspace," *New Political Science* (fall 1997): 145–67.

7. Mark Poster (1990) illustrates this point by referring to the availability of anonymous email accounts in certain countries, one being Finland. Until recently, Internet users around the world were able to use a source in Finland to obtain a "fake" identity. They could then send electronic mail or post messages on the Internet without fear of revealing their "true" identities. See "Privacy a Hot Issue on the Internet," *Los Angeles Times,* September 8, 1996. A comparable practice exists today through the abun-dance of Web programs such as Hotmail (www.hotmail.com) that offer users email addresses that can be set up with virtually no connection to a user's "real" identity.

8. For an expanded discussion on the abolition of gendered categories and its possibilities for promoting gender equality, see Mary Daly, *Beyond God the Father: Toward a Philosophy of Women's Liberation* (Boston: Beacon Press, 1973); *Gyn/Ecology: The Metaethics of Radical Feminism* (Boston: Beacon Press, 1978); and Marge Piercy, *Woman on the Edge of Time* (New York: Fawcett Crest Books, 1976).

9. Gillian Youngs, "Virtual Voices: Real Lives," in Wendy Harcourt, ed., *Women@Internet: Creating New Cultures in Cyberspace* (New York: Zed Books, 1999), 55–68; Melanie Stewart Millar, *Cracking the Gender Code: Who Rules the Wired World?* (Toronto: Second Story Press, 1998), 25.

10. Marshall McLuhan, *Understanding Media: The Extensions of Man* (New York: McGraw-Hill, 1964).

11. bell hooks, *Yearning: Race, Gender, and Cultural Politics* (Boston: South End Press, 1990), 145.

12. Besides the Cybergrrl pages, there are also links to other cybergrrl-related areas of interest. Webgrrls (www.webgrrls.cybergrrl.com/wnetscape.htm) provides "the women's tech knowledge connection" and the online comic *Adventures of Cybergrrl* (comics.cybergrrl.com/netscape.htm).

13. See Wendy Grossman, *net.wars* (New York: New York University Press, 1997); Janet Price and Margrit Shildrick, eds., *Feminist Theory and the Body: A Reader* (New York: Routledge, 1999); and Madan Sarap, *Post-Structuralism and Postmodernism* (Athens: University of Georgia Press, 1993).

14. See Chela Sandoval, "Cyborg Feminism and the Methodology of the Oppressed," in Chris Hables Gray, *The Cyborg Handbook* (New York: Routledge, 1995); Kristine Blair and Pamela Takayoshi, eds., *Feminist Cyberscapes: Mapping Gendered Academic Spaces.* (Westport, Conn.: Greenwood, 1999); Sadie Plant, *Zeroes + Ones: Digital Women + The New Technoculture* (New York: Doubleday, 1997); Victor J. Vitanza, ed., *CyberReader,* 2d ed. (Boston: Allyn and Bacon, 1999); Beth E. Kolko et al., eds., *Race in Cyberspace* (New York: Routledge, 2000); and Mark Poster, *What's the Matter with the Internet?* (Minneapolis: University of Minnesota Press, 2001).

15. See Ted Bridis, "Racial Gap Seen in Computer, Internet Use," *San Diego Union Tribune,* July 9, 1999, A-9; see also Patricia Horn and Marth Woodall, "'Digital Divide' Widens," *Denver Post,* July 9, 1999.

16. Rebecca L. Eisenberg, "The Trouble with Censorware," *Ms.,* September/October 1998.

17. In *The Domain Matrix,* Sue Ellen Case notes that at the 1993 Comdex trade show in Las Vegas, the most popular booths were typically porn related; see *The Domain Matrix,* (Bloomington: Indiana University Press, 1996). In addition, Nua Internet Surveys (www.nua.ie/surveys/), Nielsen// NetRatings (www.nielsen-netratings.com/), and Naughty Linx (www.naughtylinx.com) (an online index maintained by JMR Creations of Boston) have sporadically posted statistical information about sex-related Web sites. The writer of a recent article posted on Salon.com (www.salon.com/21st/feature/1998/10/cov_20.feature.html) alleged that pornography has been generalized within our homes today, "normalizing" access to sex-related sites and information.

18. See 209.249/142.16/nnpm/owa/Nrpublicreports/topadvertisersmonthly.

19. David Diamond "The Online Sleaze Squeeze: Why It's Happening, Where It Leads," *Business 2.0,* February 1998.

20. The leader of the Internet Entertainment Group (www.ieg.com) empire is Seth Warshavsky. IEG is barely six years old and annually earns more than twenty-five million dollars selling pornography on line. Based on the growth of Warshavsky's business, it appears as if we are witnessing the development of a cyberspace industrial complex.

21. According to a Tiarra Corporation Survey (www.lumyr.com/indexnormal.htm), the profile of the most likely sex-site surfer is a male, 31–40

years old, earning fifty-one thousand to seventy thousand dollars per year, accessing porn from work (58 percent), and most likely from the United States or Japan.

22. As one reporter recently noted, even though the estimated numbers of sexually explicit sites (with estimates putting the total at around seventy-two thousand with thirty-nine new sites emerging daily) add up to less than .05 percent of all Web addresses, "the problem is that porn sites are easy to access—it only takes a double click on a 'hot link,' embedded in unsolicited and ubiquitous commercial e-mail[,] for the offending sites to appear." See Eisenberg, "The Trouble with Censorware."

23. Ibid.

24. In addition to federal legislation promoting the use of filtering software, a number of state legislatures, including those of Arizona, Colorado, Hawaii, Indiana, Michigan, Missouri, Pennsylvania, South Carolina, South Dakota, Washington, and Wisconsin, have debated and in some instances passed filtering policies for schools and public libraries in the past few years. While the federal statutes have yet to be challenged at the Supreme Court, lower court cases have provided promising insights on the topic. In 1998, in a Virginia district court case (*Mainstream Loudoun v. Board of Trustees of the Loudoun County Library* 2F Supp.2d 783 [E.D. Va 1998]), plaintiffs charged that the policy of the Loudoun County library requiring filtering software on all library computers impermissibly blocked access to protected speech, with the filtering out of, among others, the Quaker Home Page and the sites of Zero Population Growth and the American Association of University Women. While the court did not rule on the specific question of undue burden to constitutionally protected speech presented by the filtering software, it did reaffirm the legitimacy of the petitioners' claims in the case.

25. Eisenberg, "The Trouble with Censorware."

26. Ibid.

27. Net Nanny (www.netnanny.com) was the first filtering software program placed on the market, in January 1995. Its Web site carries messages to parents promoting the software, warning of the online risks of pornography, unscrupulous users on the Internet, and pedophiles lurking in chat rooms. It promises parents "peace of mind" as they protect their children through use of the software. Net Nanny offers multiple levels of access and "auditing" based on the user's preference: a warning, a masking of the offending words, a logging of the violation, a shut down of the application, or a combination of these.

28. CyberPatrol (www.cyberpatrol.com) emerged in 1995 as a division of Mattel, Incorporated. Its "CyberLIST" stipulates material to be blocked: violence and profanity (text and pictures); partial nudity (swimsuits and thongs are excepted); full nudity (excluding in museum sites); sexual acts ("text or pictures, phone sex ads, dating services, adult personals, CD-ROMS and videos"); gross depictions (scatological content, autopsy photos); expressions of intolerance (based on race, religion, national origin,

and disability, among others); Satanic/cult material (advocating the devil/evil); material on drugs/drug culture; unlawful militant/extremist political behavior; weapons for unlawful use; sex education, whether about contraception, disease, pregnancy, or boundaries; gambling; questionable/illegal activities (computer hacking, betting, use of 900-prefix phone numbers); and alcohol and tobacco (advocating sale, production, or consumption). "Adults-only" warning banners are automatically added to the CyberLIST. The LIST is compiled by the CyberNOT Oversight Committee, consisting of parents and educators, who claim impartiality in their opinions and review of material.

29. The Santa Barbara–based Cybersitter was released in 1995. Laying claim to the most technologically advanced filtering software on the market, Cybersitter offers three levels of filtering: the material can be blocked; it can be blocked and the attempt to access a "forbidden" site logged; or the adult user can be alerted when access is attempted. Cybersitter also guarantees "to block over 97% of all objectionable content!" See <www.solidoak.com> for more information on this program.

30. We-Blocker (www.weblocker.com) is markedly different from the other filtering programs in one important way: it is free. The different categories blocked by this software are pornography (pictures or text about sex acts; sex crimes; rape; deviant behavior, products, or services; provocative attire or partial nudity); violence (text or pictures promoting gratuitous violence, cult ritual, suicide); drugs and alcohol (use or glamorization of alcohol or tobacco); gambling (promotion of gambling, casinos, betting); hate speech (based on race, ethnicity, religion, gender, or sexual orientation, including by militant and extremist groups); adult subject matter (profane or vulgar language, adult situations, material generally accepted as inappropriate for children); and weaponry (purchase, use, design, manufacture of weapons).

31. When we began this study a few years back, Infoseek was one of the largest search engines and directories of Web sites available. Since that time, Infoseek has been overshadowed by much larger programs including AltaVista and Google. Thus, while we recognize that some of our research is constrained by our use of Infoseek, we find it nonetheless useful and relevant.

32. The saliency rate was determined by examining the first ten sites returned on a search and assigning a percentage to the number of sites that provided the relevant information. Hence if a search had a 10 percent saliency, only one of the top ten sites returned pertained to the topic in the search.

33. Wendy Grossman notes in *net.wars* that in 1996, Cybersitter's database of blocked sites included the National Organization for Women and the Gopher belonging to WELL . For more information about the error rates of censorware programs, see <www.peacefire.org/error-rates/>.

34. "E-commerce sales includes sales of goods and services over the Internet, an extranet, Electronic Data Interchange (EDI), or other online system.

Payment may or may not be made online." See <www.census.gov:80/Press-Release/www/2000/cb00-40.html> for a fuller discussion of e-commerce in the United States.

35. Nua Internet Surveys can be found at <www.nua.ie/surveys/>.

36. For more about this, see </www.nua.ie/surveys/?f=VS&art_id= 905355532&rel=true>.

37. Reported by MediaMetrix (www.us.mediametrix.com/home.jsp).

38. Women.com and iVillage.com merged on June 19, 2001.

39. Tom Peters, *Circle of Innovation: You Can't Shrink Your Way to Greatness* (New York: Vintage Books, 1997).

40. Maura Johnson, "Girl Power for Sale," *Ms.*, April/May 2000.

41. *Business 2.0*, January 2000; *Canadian Retailer*, November/December 1999; *FastCompany*, December 1999.

42. Notable exceptions include Advancing Women and WomenConnect.com. Advancing Women (www.advancingwomen.com/), does have lifestyle-related links, but is not advertiser laden. Its focus is on advancing women in business and has links for Hispanic and international women and for investment information. . Like Advancing Women, WomenConnect.com (www.womenconnect.com/) serves women in business and their needs. There are also countless academic sites and listserv(s) for women in their particular disciplines.

Anna Sampaio *is an assistant professor of political science at the University of Colorado, Denver, where she teaches and researches in gender theory, critical race theory, poststructuralism, and postcolonialism. She recently coedited a book titled* Transnational Transformations: Re-examining the Politics, Processes, and Culture of Latino Communities in the New Millennium *(forthcoming from Rowman and Littlefield) and is expanding her research in the area of cyberfeminism to examine the positions of women of color in new technologies.*

Janni Aragon *is a Ph.D. candidate in political science at the University of California at Riverside. She is currently writing her dissertation, "The Movement into the Academy: Second Wave Feminism and Political Science." Her areas of interest are women and politics, feminist theory, women and tech-nology, social movements, and critical race studies. She can be contacted at jaragon@home.com.*

A URL of Our Own

The Center for Women and Information Technology

Joan Korenman

"Internet Gender Gap Closing," a March 2000 headline proclaims (Chamberlain). "Women Surpass Men as US Web Users," announces another (CyberAtlas). Given the Internet's origins in the Department of Defense, and the fact that as recently as 1994 a survey by Georgia Tech's Graphics, Visualization, and Usability Center reported that more than 94 percent of Web users were male (Pitkow and Recker), the dramatic increase in female Internet users is certainly good news. Nonetheless, the headlines mask some troubling aspects of women's involvement with information technology (IT). Women remain seriously underrepresented in the IT workforce, and they are often not well served as users of information technology.

In light of the intense demand for technically trained workers and the relatively high salaries they can command, one might expect that women would be rushing to prepare themselves for IT careers. Government figures, however, tell a very different story. According to the Bureau of Labor Statistics, women make up 46 percent of the total workforce but only 25 percent of the professional IT workforce (DeVoe 111); only 10 percent of the top IT jobs are held by women (Gibson 112). Moreover, the situation shows little sign of improving. The Office of Technology Policy reports that "the share of all computer science degrees awarded to women in the United States has fallen steadily from a peak of 35.8 percent in 1984, to only 27.5 percent in 1994—the lowest level since 1979" (24).

The Center for Women and Information Technology or CWIT (pronounced see-wit) was established at the University of Maryland, Baltimore County (UMBC), in 1998 to improve the situation for women as both developers and users of information technology. One important part of CWIT's mission is to encourage more women and girls to prepare for careers in the field. Of equal concern to CWIT, however, is the quality of women's experiences as *users* of IT. Although the headlines report that women are flocking to the Internet in unprecedented numbers and have now achieved parity with men, if we look further, we find that the Internet stampede includes relatively few poor women, minority women, or women outside the United States and Canada. These absences bode ill for the future. As more and more of our information comes from online sources, women who are unable or unwilling to use information technology will have little power to shape that information and, in fact, are in danger of becoming the new illiterates, unprepared for the opportunities and challenges of the Information Age.

Even more privileged women may find the information superhighway a rocky road. What kinds of experiences and resources are women—even privileged women—most likely to find on the Internet? Because search engines tend to favor well-financed sites that can advertise extensively and hire people to optimize search engine placement, the women-related sites most likely to appear in a search engine's top hits are commercial ventures such as iVillage (http://www.ivillage.com/) and women.com (http://www.women.com/).[1] Such sites offer a retro, cliché-ridden version of "women's culture" that Francine Prose describes in the *New York Times* as "far below whatever standard still prevails in the most dumbed-down print magazines" (66). For example, iVillage's homepage offers a pull-down menu to help you find what you need. It carries the heading "today I need to," and the first six choices are "find a recipe," "take a break," "find child care," "read my horoscope," "find a gym," and "shop online." While iVillage includes a computing section, a visitor to that section is greeted with "Hey Valentine! Why not get prepared and set up some sweet little e-Valentines for that special someone?" (accessed January 29, 2001). Similarly, women.com's home page prominently displays a feature called "The Men of the Internet 2001." Clicking on it provides more information: "Check out the Men of the Internet, 10 of the hottest, most exciting bachelors you'll meet anywhere. Tell us what you think of these passionate and creative guys. Who's your favorite? Dish about them with others. You can even win a date with him" (accessed January 29, 2001). If a woman tries to locate Web sites offering a broader vision and more substantive resources, she quickly finds that on many search engines, the keywords *women* and *girls* lead straight to pornography (Korenman, 722–24).

Thus, in addition to encouraging more women and girls to prepare for careers in information technology, CWIT seeks to assure that the richness and breadth of women's lives and concerns will be fully represented and readily available on the Internet. At the heart of the center's endeavors are the women-related online resources that it makes available on its Web site (http://www.umbc.edu/cwit/) and on the affiliated UMBC women's studies site now under the center's aegis (http://www.umbc.edu/wmst/external.html). ABCNEWS.com has called the CWIT Web site "the best resource on women and technology on the Web" (Lynch). Even so, perhaps because some women's studies faculty and students still think of technology as quite separate from and possibly even inimical to women's studies, they remain unaware of the CWIT site and the extensive and relevant resources it offers them. It is my intention in this essay to make those resources more widely known.

Some people mistakenly refer to CWIT as the Center for Women *in* Information Technology. While the Center for Women *and* Information Technology is certainly concerned with women who work in IT, the *and* in the Center's name indicates a broader focus on the many relationships between gender and information technology. One resource that reflects that broader focus is the center's very extensive online collection of news articles about women and IT. Updated almost every day, the collection provides links to current articles in a wide variety of newspapers and magazines, primarily in the United States, but also abroad. To be sure, some articles deal with women in the IT workforce and with efforts to increase interest in IT among young girls, but many of the articles will interest anyone concerned with feminist issues. Here are a few recent headlines: "India's Tech Boom Hits Poor Women," "Girl Games: Beyond the Pink Box," "Warner Brothers Bullies Girl over Harry Potter Site," "Japanese Sites for Women Aim for Empowerment," "Novelist Catherine Lim Opens e-Book Chapter," "Wife Cyber-Spies on Husband," and "The Net Feeds Boom in Sex Trade and Slavery." Such news coverage, drawn from well over a hundred different publications, should be of considerable value to feminist researchers in such fields as cultural studies, American studies, women in development, media and communications, and popular culture, among others.

Another CWIT resource of value to feminist researchers is an extensive bibliography of books and special journal issues about women and IT. Although many universities have put their library catalogs online, finding relevant items about women and IT can be difficult, since some titles are listed under "information technology," others under "computing," and still others under "Internet," "cyberspace," or "cyberculture." Moreover, many library catalogs and bibliographies offer little information about a book's contents and worth. By contrast, CWIT's bibliography utilizes the advantages of the online environment. It is updated frequently, and it provides links to information about the books: tables of contents, abstracts, excerpts, reviews, interviews with the author, a book's Web page, and so on. Sometimes, the entire book or journal issue is available online, in which case the bibliography links to the work itself.

Currently, the CWIT bibliography includes approximately one hundred entries, arranged chronologically, the most recent works first. Like the news collection, the books deal with a wide range of feminist issues, as the following sample entries indicate: a special issue, titled *The Internet and Sexuality,* of the journal *CyberPsychology & Behavior;* a book available online titled *Gender and the Information Revolution in Africa;* an edited volume titled *Feminist Cyberscapes: Mapping Gendered Academic Spaces;* a special issue of the journal *Computers and Composition* with the title *Computers, Composition, and Gender;* and a collection of essays titled *CyberFeminism: Connectivity, Critique, and Creativity.* The bibliography is also useful in calling attention to books whose title gives no indication that the volume pays substantial attention to women and IT. One example: *Meeting the Challenge: Innovative Feminist Pedagogies in Action* includes four essays on women's studies and information technology.

Both the news collection and the bibliography focus on the topic of women and information technology. Other sections of the CWIT site address the issue of women and IT in ways that may be even more directly relevant to feminists in and outside academia. One section, "Curricular Resources," should be of particular interest to women's studies faculty members who wish to incorporate information technology into their courses. This section includes three resources: "Women- and Gender-Related Web-Based Syllabi," "Internet Resources on Women," and "Teaching with/about Technology."

The first of these, "Women- and Gender-Related Web-Based Syllabi," is a collection of more than six hundred syllabi, arranged by discipline. It differs from other collections of women-related syllabi in its size, the number of disciplines represented, and the fact that all the syllabi are Web based and many make substantial use of the Internet (such syllabi are specially noted). Some of these syllabi may also include ideas for Web projects and other ways that faculty can make productive use of information technology in their women's studies classes.

Also useful for this purpose is the second item under "Curricular Resources," "Internet Resources on Women." Designed originally as a guide to women-related online material for faculty wishing to include more content on women in their courses, the site can also help women's studies faculty find online academic materials and integrate technology into their courses. The frequently updated site identifies and describes academic email lists and Web sites, organized by discipline. It also notes selected sites that provide useful information about topics such as Internet search tools, Web-site construction, Windows and Macintosh operating systems, the Eudora email program, and other computer-related matters.

At the end of the "Curricular Resources" section are links to several recommended sites where faculty can find more information about teaching with or about technology. Although none of these sites focuses specifically on gender issues, one, the excellent Resource Center for Cyberculture Studies, includes a good deal of material by or about women.

Incorporating information technology into our women- and gender-related courses may help more women become knowledgeable Internet users. It is equally important, however, that women find a rich array of high-quality women-related resources when they go online. CWIT's section "Links to Related Sites" offers frequently updated, annotated, selective listings of women-related sites about science/technology and about cyberculture, as well as a carefully chosen listing of Web sites for girls and young women. The science/technology and cyberculture listings include such offerings as "Gender and Electronic Discourse," "Women and Biology Internet Launch Page," "Java, Women, and the Culture of Computing," "Gender and the Internet Age," and "Virtue and Virtuality: Gender, Law, and Cyberspace." The listing of Web sites for girls and young women helps people distinguish between sites designed *for* girls (which are marked with a big red asterisk), such as Girl Start and Cyber Grrlz, and sites such as Expect the Best from a Girl: That's What You'll Get and Girls Count that are aimed at adults interested in helping girls. "Links to Related Sites" also highlights the handful of columns, periodicals, and academic programs that focus on women and IT. Dianne Lynch's wry and insightful column, "Wired Women," for example, will delight and inform feminist technophiles and technophobes alike.

Because CWIT's concern extends to all women-related online resources, not just those that deal directly with women and information technology, the CWIT site includes a section called "More Resources about Women" that calls attention to some of the highly acclaimed offerings on the UMBC women's studies Web site. These include "Women's Studies/Women's Issues Resource Sites," "Gender-Related Electronic Forums," "Women's Studies Programs, Departments, and Research Centers," and the "WMST-L File Collection."

The award-winning "Women's Studies/Women's Issues Resource Sites" provides annotated links to more than six hundred high-quality women-related Web sites in such topic areas as activism, arts and humanities, business/work, health, higher education, international, religion/spirituality, sexuality, sports/recreation, women of color, and more. They include links to such varied and information-rich sites as Global Reproductive Health Forum, Women and the Holocaust, Coalition Against Trafficking in Women, Lesbian-Centered European Films, Black Women's Health, Information on Sexual Harassment, Karamah: Muslim Women Lawyers for Human Rights, Gender Equity in Sports, Asian American Feminist Resource Site, and A Celebration of Women Writers, to name just a few.

"Gender-Related Electronic Forums" is another much acclaimed resource. It provides frequently updated information about more than six hundred women- and gender-related email discussion forums, or "lists," including a brief description of each list, instructions for joining the list, and a link to the list's Web site, if one exists. Email lists offer an excellent way for people to connect with others who share their interests. "Gender-Related Electronic Forums" can help in locating lists on everything from feminist activism to life as a Black single mother, an Orthodox Jewish lesbian, or a former nun, and from breast cancer to women's basketball to women and gender in the ancient world.

Women's studies faculty and students are the primary audience for two more resources on CWIT's "Other Resources about Women" page. One is "Women's Studies Programs, Departments, and Research Centers," a frequently updated collection of links to more than six hundred programs around the world that have Web pages. Annotation identifies programs offering graduate degrees or certificates. The other is the "WMST-L File Collection." WMST-L is a large, international email forum for discussion of women's studies teaching, research, and program administration. Many of the more than one hundred files in the file collection contain exceptionally useful discussions that women's studies faculty, librarians, graduate students, independent researchers, and others have held on WMST-L over the past ten years, along with some essays, interviews, bibliographies, and other material contributed by WMST-L members. Here are some sample file titles: "Exercises for the First Day of Class"; "Conservative Feminism: An Oxymoron?" "Women's Autobiography"; "Women of Color and the Women's Movement"; "Gender and Teaching Evaluation"; "Teaching about Pornography"; "Feminist Theory: Suggested Readings"; "Research on Welfare Reform"; "Men in Women's Studies Classes"; "'Women's Studies' vs. 'Gender Studies.'" A gold mine for Women's Studies faculty and students, the collection continues to grow.

The past thirty years have witnessed a dramatic outpouring of attention to and materials about women. Women's studies has had impressive success in putting women's experiences, perspectives, and accomplishments into the curriculum and into people's consciousness. But will that success continue as increasing amounts of our information come to us online? Unless women's experiences and perspectives are both fully represented in the electronic world and easy to find, many of the curricular advances of the past thirty years may be lost, and women's lives may once again be rendered invisible. By encouraging women's active involvement with information technology and by making available online an extensive array of high quality resources about women, the Center for Women and Information Technology hopes to ensure that the gains of women's studies will continue and increase.

NOTE

1. Shortly after this essay was completed, iVillage announced that it would acquire women.com. See Michael Silver, "iVillage to Acquire Women. com," Internet.com, online, available: <http://siliconvalley.internet.com/news/article/ 0,2198,3531_580191,00.html>, February 5, 2001.

REFERENCES

Chamberlain, Art. "Internet Gender Gap Closing." *CNEWS*, March 29, 2000. Online. Available: <http://www.canoe.ca/TechNews0003/29_art.html>. February 3, 2001.

[CyberAtlas]. "Women Surpass Men as US Web Users." *CyberAtlas*, August 10, 2000. Online. Available: <http://cyberatlas.internet.com/big_picture/demographics/article/0,,5901_434551,00.html>. February 3, 2001.

DeVoe, Deborah. "Expanding the Pool of IT Workers." *InfoWorld*, May 18, 1998, 111–12.

Gibson, Stan. "The Nonissue Issue: Gender in the IT Field." *PC Week*, October 6, 1997, 112. Online. Available: <http://www.zdnet.com/eweek/opinion/1006/06just.html>. February 3, 2001.

Korenman, Joan. "Women, Women, Everywhere: Looking for a Link." *CyberPsychology and Behavior* 3 (2000): 721–29.

Lynch, Dianne. "Person of the Year." *ABCNEWS.com: Wired Women*, December 28, 1999. Online. Available: <http://abcnews.go.com/sections/tech/wiredwomen/wiredwomen991228.html>. February 3, 2001.

Office of Technology Policy. *America's New Deficit: The Shortage of Information Technology Workers*. Washington, D.C.: U.S. Department of Commerce, 1997. Online. Available: <http://www.ta.doc.gov/reports/itsw/itsw.pdf>. February 4, 2001.

Pitkow, James E., and Margaret M. Recker. *Results from the First World-Wide Web User Survey*. 1994. Online. Available: <http://www.gvu.gatech.edu/user_surveys/survey-01-1994/survey-paper.html>. February 3, 2001.

Prose, Francine. "A Wasteland of One's Own." *New York Times Magazine*, February 13, 2000, 66. Online. Available: <http://www.nytimes.com/library/magazine/home/20000213mag-prose8.html>. February 3, 2001.

Joan Korenman *is professor of English and director of the Center for Women and Information Technology at the University of Maryland, Baltimore County. In 1991, she founded WMST-L, an email discussion forum for women's studies teaching, research, and program administration. She also created and maintains the UMBC women's studies Web site and is the author of the 1997 book* Internet Resources on Women: Using Electronic Media in Curriculum Transformation *and several essays about women and the Internet.*

$E = mc^2$

Dorothy Howe Brooks

Children of the fifties,
we thought atoms were real,
studied molecules, photons, electrons,
marveled at the space
above all things, the space inside all things.
Michelson and Morley set a beam
adrift in the ether, proving beyond proof
the constancy of light.
That above all.
But who would think to square the c?

We thought we could reduce the irreducible,
the atoms we never saw
but believed in, like the bomb.
More energy than mass. Truer,
but not real, not like color, or pain,
not sharp or sticky, not loud—
more like light. Wave or particle?
Energy or mass? A tidal wave
of light. An explosion.
So now we've learned to square the c.

Einstein, for the rest of his days,
sought that elusive principle
that force that is all force:
an equation to put us back together.
But did we need to square the c?

Dorothy Howe Brooks *writes poetry and fiction. Her work has appeared or is forth-coming in numerous literary journals, including* Cumberland Poetry Review, Slant: A Journal of Poetry, REAL: Re Arts and Letters, Sojourner, The Georgia Journal, *and the* Habersham Review, *as well as the anthology* If I Had My Life to Live Over, I Would Pick More Daisies. *She is currently at work on a novel.*

Noise

Carole Cole

7:30 a.m. I awaken to the whine of chain saws
for the fifth straight day, powered by invisible men
with not much left to destroy.
I meditate, work at my desk, eat breakfast
to a gas-driven shriek that brings trees down.

Evening. Across the street Jim begins
his yard ritual. The steady hum of the mower,
the edger like the rend of metal in an 18-car pileup,
the gas-powered whacker, and at last the blower,
each blade of grass chased down.
It's winter. Dark will come soon and drive him inside.

Next door, in his small workshop my neighbor
works alone, his table saw shrieks
with the bite of lumber then settles
to a scream. He can work all night if he wishes
under the electric lights.

Here in my house, the windows are open
to let everything in—the shrieks, and whines,
the screams enter and become part of the buzz
of my mind. Meanwhile, in silence, the world I've built
explodes like the puff of a dandelion blown apart
in a single, thoughtless breath.

Carole Cole received her doctorate in American Studies from Purdue University and currently teaches in the English department at Manatee Community College in Bradenton, Florida. Her poems have appeared in Kalliope, Broomstick, *and* Sarasota Review of Poetry *as well as in the anthology* Florida in Poetry, *published by Pineapple Press. "Noise" previously appeared in vol. 4 (2000) of the* Sarasota Review of Poetry.

Inconstant Data

Judith Rose

Sheep may safely graze
　　　Take this line number 13 and type right over it
　　　Hold down your delete key　　Let's do a mighty fortress
　　　Remember the field terminator
Come sweet death
　　　Some librarians have been using this technique for years
　　　Now press insert
Behind us the halting organ one quavering voice then the whole choir
<u>*A Bulwark never failing*</u>
inserted into the projector then fading like the last transparency
　　　We'll do a little command stacking to make it faster
　　　You haven't made any constant data yet　　Now watch
　　　these characters in the variable field
I am a character in a variable field
the field variable with poppies wild iris miner's lettuce
a sphinx moth shieldbugs orb weavers
　　　And the fixed field
Field rectangular one clean space inside the constant data
　　　This is what you're faced with when you've got
　　　a blank work form
Faced with the blank fixed field white space　　an almost inaudible humming
alabaster sheets of memory surrounding
Fugue in D minor ("The Little")
The little cursors sweetly weep
wander in fixed fields safely graze among minor keys
　　　I hope that you'll think of constant data
　　　for anything you have to repeatedly key in
Solvent extraction of uranium
　　　This save file starts at 1 and goes up to 9999
File the saved among solvents and weeping cursors delete nothing　weed nothing
listen to the high thin singing of thousands and thousands of computers　singing
for a supper of hands
purring torchsongs across phonelines
lying down at last in a variable field
waiting to be blessed

Judith Rose *is assistant professor of English and women's studies at Allegheny College. Her poetry and fiction have appeared in* The Iowa Review, Prairie Schooner, The Virginia Quarterly, *and* The Indiana Review, *among other journals. She has recently published work on the Venetian poet Gaspara Stampa and the Cremonese painter Sofonisba Anguissola, titled "Mirrors of Language, Mirrors of Self: The Conceputalization of Artistic Identity," in the collection* Maternal Measures: Figuring Caregiving in the Early Modern Period.

Electronic Loom

Maria Proitsaki

A portable electronic
loom, imagine, scanning the
evening paper on a new
linen napkin—

A man's myopic
daydreaming a woman's
mounting guilt.

Verified installation of a
biofunctional home: water the
flowers, mop the floor?

Undoubtedly next stage. In
the meantime, far beyond
microwaves and
fiber optics

see how tapping
a few simple spells could
crack you those eggs in an
intelligent saucepan,

optional, almost telepathic,
regulation of the salt.

Then,
you help the broccoli
find its way to the salad
bowl—freshly manicured
fingernails—introduce
the sauce to the spaghetti

(and double click to sharpen
the kettle's tone . . .)

If the fridge rejects your
code, re-con-si-der probable
overconsumption of
margarine.
               Next stage.

Maria Proitsaki *was born in Greece and received her B.A. from Aristotle University of Thessaloniki. She is currently a Ph.D. candidate at Göteborg University, Sweden, and is writing a thesis in which she examines the works of Nikki Giovanni and Rita Dove.*

Will EC 2000 Make Engineering More Female Friendly?

Sue V. Rosser

Engineering and its product, technology, have had a profound impact on society; one has only to compare the life of the average citizen of 1900 with that of the average citizen of 2000 to realize that virtually all of the differences are the result of engineering. Moreover, the impact in the 21st century will undoubtedly be even greater than in the 20th century, and will be felt in every aspect of our lives, from our personal health to our collective governance. Engineers must no longer limit their sense of responsibility to the products and infrastructure we design, but must include the larger effects they have.

—William Wulf, president,
National Academy of Engineering, April 25, 2000

The engineering profession needs the substantial participation of women if we are to make our full contribution to the solution of the technical problems facing our society.

—Sheila Widnall, institute professor,
Massachusetts Institute of Technology, April 26, 2000

In preparation for the dawning of a new century, American engineers initiated a period of evaluation, study, and dialogue to ensure that the curriculum and training they delivered to students would prepare them appropriately for engineering in the twenty-first century. They recognized that the scope and definition of engineering in the century to come would be likely to change dramatically and deliver an impact at least as profound as engineering had had on the twentieth century.

Beliefs in the pervasive power and influence of technology in the twenty-first century caused leaders to call for engineers to expand their roles in terms of ethics and responsibilities beyond the design of products and infrastructure to encompass their larger effects in society (Wulf 2000). Simultaneously, engineering leaders understood the necessity to reach out to nonengineers in two ways: first, engineers needed to diversify the population they attract and retain to reflect the gender and racial diversity in the United States population. Second, engineering schools had to provide means for liberal arts and other nontechnology students to acquire some understanding of engineering processes and of the implications of specific technologies.

Foundations, professional societies, and accrediting agencies undertook studies to assess the status of engineering education and determine desirable changes. Results of the studies found that current accreditation requirements were met by demanding that students pass courses; this yields students who do well in entry-level jobs but serves the students much less well ten years into their careers. The studies suggested liberal learning as a solution to the educational deficiency resulting in this career problem.

More specifically, the National Science Foundation study (1995) *Restructuring Engineering Education: A Focus on Change* drew the following conclusions:

- The whole world has become increasingly integrated and interdependent, yet the current curriculum focuses on disparate fields.
- It is important to teach synthesis and analysis in the engineering curriculum.
- Student capabilities must be enhanced to make connections between what they learn and other areas of knowledge.

In its recommendations for engineering education, the American Society of Engineering Education Task Force (1987) emphasized team-building and collaboration, communication, leadership, global and international linkages, social and environmental connections, and quality. The Board on Engineering Education (National Research Council 1995) focused on fundamentals and elimination of redundancy in curriculum and courses, while integrating fundamentals with design. The board suggests a curriculum that emphasizes teamwork, orients students toward practice, and underlines social and business understanding and context of the profession.

Synthesizing and distilling the results of these studies, the Accreditation Board for Engineering and Technology (ABET) developed Engineering Criteria 2000 (EC 2000), which established effective criteria for evaluation of engineering programs beginning in 1999–2000. Criterion 3 provided the most dramatic change for most engineering curricula:

Criterion 3. Program Outcomes and Assessment

Engineering programs must demonstrate that their graduates have:

(a) an ability to apply knowledge of mathematics, science, and engineering

(b) an ability to design and conduct experiments, as well as to analyze and interpret data

(c) an ability to design a system, component, or process to meet desired needs

(d) an ability to function on multi-disciplinary teams

(e) an ability to identify, formulate, and solve engineering problems

(f) an understanding of professional and ethical responsibility

(g) an ability to communicate effectively

(h) the broad education necessary to understand the impact of engineering solutions in a global and societal context

(i) a recognition of the need for and an ability to engage in lifelong learning

(j) a knowledge of contemporary issues

(k) an ability to use the techniques, skills, and modern engineering tools necessary for engineering practice.

Each program must have an assessment process with documented results. Evidence must be given that the results are applied to the further development and improvement of the program. The assessment process must demonstrate that the outcomes important to the mission of the institution and the objectives of the program, including those listed above, are being measured. Evidence that may be used includes but is not limited to the following: student portfolios, including design projects; nationally-normed subject content examinations; alumni surveys that document professional accomplishments and career development activities; employer surveys; and placement data of graduates. (ABET 1998)

Faculty and administrators in the liberal arts were excited about these criteria, particularly d, f, g, h, i, and j, which we saw as opening new venues for intellectual and pedagogical exchange between engineering/technology and the humanities and social sciences. We envisioned engineering students taking courses in ethics, international affairs, sociology, political science, and communications studies from humanities and social sciences faculty who had revised their courses or developed new courses in which the significance of their discipline for engineering and technology became a central focus. We also hoped or imagined that our colleagues in engineering would develop courses geared toward students majoring in the humanities and social sciences.

EC 2000 opened the door for dialogue between humanities and social sciences and engineering faculty and provided an impetus for this dream scenario to become a reality in some institutions. But in others, only part of the dream came true: humanities and social sciences faculty developed the courses for engineering students, but engineering faculty continued to teach only engineering majors. In some institutions, EC 2000 resulted in students' having less humanities and social sciences than under the old Engineering Criteria. In these institutions, engineering faculty, who had not acquired additional training or expertise in the relevant discipline of the humanities and or social sciences, taught ethics, communication, or social implications within the engineering curriculum in lieu of requiring students to take courses outside of engineering. As a result, EC 2000 decreased intellectual and pedagogical exchanges between engineering and the liberal arts, as well as actual courses taken by students.

As someone who has devoted the bulk of her academic research career to issues of women and science, mathematics, engineering, and technology, I viewed the response to EC 2000 with the double vision that Joan Scott (1988) describes women as having. Wearing only my hat of the dean of liberal arts at a technological institution, I worried about the issues discussed in the preceding paragraph. As a women's studies scholar who had been alternatively pleased and disappointed at seeing many of her ideas for female-friendly science both implemented and distorted as mainstream science reformers adopted them (Rosser 1997), I worried about the impact of EC 2000 on the goal of diversity. Recent studies (Frasier and Ismail 1997; Felder et al. 1995) note that retention of women in undergraduate engineering programs remains a significant problem; this becomes even more important in light of the fact that women who drop out of engineering programs have higher levels of predicted success and higher grades than do male students in this discipline overall. The *Best and Brightest* report revealed that while 82 percent of the A and A+ male students persist in engineering programs for at least four years, only 29 percent of the top female students persist (Commission on Professionals in Science and Technology 1997).

Although the current engineering curriculum failed to attract and retain women in desired numbers, I have experienced enough curriculum reform to recognize that change does not always lead to improvements, especially in diversity. Realizing that EC 2000 might affect diversity either positively or negatively, especially with regard to gender, depending upon the way the criteria were implemented by each institution, I decided to compare ABET criterion 3 with the twenty pedagogical criteria I had laid out for female-friendly science in 1990 (Rosser 1990):

1. Expand the kinds of observations beyond those traditionally carried out in scientific research. Women students may see new data that could make a valuable contribution.

I developed this criterion after considering why female primatologists (Fossey 1983; Goodall 1971; Hrdy 1986) saw "new" data such as female-female interactions when observing primate behaviors, which led to major theoretical changes in the field. Obviously this data had been present all along in primate behaviors, but had been overlooked by the male primatologists, who had focused on male-male and male-female interactions in their observations. Because women may have had different experiences from men and may hold different expectations, they noted different observations.

Accurate perceptions of reality and perceptions of technological use and impact are more likely to be obtained when many individuals with diverse backgrounds and expectations work on a problem. This fits well with criterion 3 a. For example, as Shirley Malcom suggests, the air bag fiasco suffered by the U.S. auto industry, which resulted in the deaths of short people, would have been much less likely had a woman engineer been on the air bag design team (Malcom, personal communication, 1998). Since on the average, women tend to be smaller than men, women on the design team might have recognized that a bag that implicitly used the larger male body as a norm would be flawed when applied to smaller individuals—killing, rather than protecting, children and small women.

Women in engineering should be encouraged to combine their own experiences and observations with their knowledge of mathematics, science, and engineering to applications (criterion 3 a) in creating better technology. Anita Borg, founder of the Institute for Women and Technology housed at Xerox PARC, holds workshops that bring together high-school girls, female college students, and women from nearby communities to brainstorm for two half days about ideas for useful products. The first series of workshops resulted in product ideas such as a small-group digital assistant, which supplies information requested during a meeting, and "visiting walls," virtual, three-dimensional walls that allow people to connect their living spaces over computer networks (Olsen 2000).

2. Increase the numbers of observations and remain longer in the observational stage of the scientific method. This would provide more hands-on experience with various types of equipment in the laboratory.

Since 1990, when I initially made this recommendation, based partially upon data from the 1976–77 National Assessment of Educational Progress (NAEP), the data continue to support the need for girls and women to have more hands-on experience with equipment. The 1997 NAEP documented that girls continue to have significantly fewer science-related experiences than do boys. Hamilton (1998) demonstrates that the relatively large gender differences found on science achievement tests do not appear to result from differences in general or scientific reasoning ability or from teaching practices that favor males. Instead, they reflect differences in experiences outside of school, particularly those that promote visual or spatial reasoning. Perhaps not coincidentally, the persistent gender gap in the math Scholastic Aptitude Test (SAT) results primarily from the difference in the visual- or spatial-reasoning portion. Programs that have been successful in attracting and retaining women in engineering and other equipment-oriented nontraditional fields for women often include a special component for remedial hands-on experience.

Making women feel more comfortable by providing more hands-on experience with equipment corresponds well with ABET criterion 3 b. Because of time constraints, the designing- and conducting-experiments phase carried out in laboratories is frequently shortened, and students are simply given the data for analysis. This practice may be especially detrimental to females who have fewer extracurricular opportunities for hands-on experiences. Focusing on hands-on experiences with equipment in designing and conducting experiments tends to work better when women are paired with women as laboratory partners. Male-female partnerships often result in his working with the equipment while she writes the observations and report. This arrangement improves her clerical skills but does less for her engineering abilities. Similarly, during group work, the roles of individuals on the team need constant monitoring to ensure that women work with the hardware and equipment and do obtain the hands-on experience recommended by ABET criterion 3 b.

3. *As part of the class discussion or the laboratory exercise, incorporate and validate personal experiences women are likely to have had.*
Considerable evidence (Hacker 1981; Wajcman 1983, 1991; Kunda 1992) suggests that the perception of the cultures of engineering and technology as masculine and violent becomes a primary deterrent against increasing the numbers of women and girls entering those professions. The report *Tech-Savvy: Educating Girls in the New Computer Age* (American Association of University Women 2000), reiterated this perception. The commission writing the report made it clear that girls are

"critical of the computer culture, not computer phobic": "Girls find programming classes tedious and dull, computer games too boring, redundant, and violent." The report emphasized that it did not advocate "pink" or "Barbie" software. It found that "girls have clear and strong ideas about what kinds of games they would design: games that feature simulation, strategy, and interaction. These games, in fact, would appeal to a broad range of learners—boys and girls alike" (AAUW 2000).

A "focus on the many design elements and themes that engage a broad range of learners, including both boys and girls, and students who don't identify with the 'computer nerd' stereotype" (AAUW 2000), fits well with ABET criterion 3 d, g, and j. Smoothly functioning multidisciplinary teams (d) rely on individuals who can understand the broader elements and themes that unite the group, as well as those with respect and appreciation for the diverse perspectives individuals can contribute. Engineers taught by instructors who use examples coming from a variety of experiences and backgrounds may be encouraged to think more broadly in the design and creation of technology. Use of examples based upon different experiences also strengthens the ability to communicate effectively (g). When an individual must explain an example, reasoning, or experience to another person who comes from a background where it is not familiar, in order to communicate effectively, the speaker is forced to consider its salient aspects and why it might lead to new or better technology design. Engineers who do not rely on a common background of military and masculinity as a given to underpin all technology and all explanations reflect not only a knowledge of contemporary issues (j) in terms of diversity in the pool of engineers, but also indicate an awareness about the future directions of technology itself.

4. Undertake fewer experiments likely to have applications of direct benefit to the military and propose more experiments to explore problems of social concern.
Studies (Hynes 1995; Nair and Majetich 1995) document that some girls and women articulate that they avoid science, technology, and mathematics because of the destructive ways technology, particularly through its military applications, has been used in our society against the environment and human beings. Exclusive use of examples from the military, seen, for example, in problems involving the calculation of bomb or rocket trajectories and laboratory exercises focused on the design of fighter planes, reinforce the strong link between the military and technology (Wacjman 1991; Hacker 1981) that many women find problematic. In contrast, numerous studies (J. Harding 1985; Kahle 1985; Rosser 1993; Miller et al. 2000) have documented the attraction

of science and technology for females when they can perceive their social usefulness, especially for human beings. For example, Jan Harding's work (1985) demonstrates that girls solve an engineering problem as quickly and as well as boys when it is embedded in a social context of helping people (for example, designing a prosthesis to help an elderly person). For boys, the social context in which a problem is embedded does not seem to matter; the technological fix/problem itself is sufficient. The authors of *Tech-Savvy* (AAUW 2000) underline girls' interest in social uses of computers, noting, "Girls said they use computers to communicate and perform specific tasks."

Refocusing engineering education to emphasize the social usefulness of technology, as opposed to its military applications, also is congruent with ABET criterion 3 h, j, and k. At the millennium, engineering itself has become much less linked with the military and more linked with social and global issues (h) such as biomedicine and the environment, which represent contemporary issues (j) at the beginning of the twenty-first century. This is reflected in federal funding for basic research, in which the Department of Defense budgets have steadily decreased, while those of the National Institutes of Health have increased dramatically. Not surprisingly, engineering has refocused its research and education to fit funding and societal priorities:

> In the decades after World War II, "the Department of Defense," wrote historian of science Stuart Leslie, "became the single biggest patron of American science, particularly engineering and physical sciences" (Hynes 1995, 213).

> MIT has been widely known as a premier defense research and teaching institution, providing a steady stream of military research for the government and graduates for defense contractors. Electronics in labs and classrooms at MIT meant military electronics predominantly (Mitgang 1993, C11).

> With the decline in defense contracts and the national transition to a more civilian economy, the Institute has launched ambitious environmental programs across the social, natural, and engineering sciences and the business school that range from global climate research and cleaner metallurgical processes to industrial ecology and pollution prevention (Hynes 1995, 213).

Information about the environment, biology, medicine, and society has become part of the modern engineering tools necessary for engineering practice (k).

5. Consider problems that have not been considered worthy of scientific investigation because of the field with which the problem has been traditionally associated.

Because science and engineering are considered masculine pursuits in our culture (Fee 1983; Hacker 1981; S. Harding 1986, 1998; Keller 1983, 1985), science and technology done by women are often defined differently. H. Patricia Hynes (1989) documents the redefinition of Ellen Swallow Richard's experiments at MIT in water chemistry, toxicity, and food purity: they were removed from the science of chemistry and placed into home economics. Her male students went on to become leaders in chemistry and founders of ecology; her work, however, was considered unscientific, because it was interdisciplinary research done by a woman (Hynes 1989).

Much of the cutting-edge research in engineering today is interdisciplinary. Biomedical engineering, bioinformatics system designs, and tissue engineering exemplify frontiers of twenty-first-century engineering research. All require even more than "a broad education necessary to understand the impact of engineering solutions in a global and societal context" (h); each demands that engineers have in-depth knowledge of biology, an ability to function on multidisciplinary teams (d), and a use of techniques, skills, and modern engineering tools (k). Since women now receive 52 percent of undergraduate degrees and 48 percent of the Ph.D.s in biology, it is not surprising that these new, interdisciplinary fields that clearly focus on human health attract a higher percentage of women than do most traditional engineering programs. Maria Klawe, professor of computer science at the University of British Columbia, stresses that outreach programs to attract teenage girls to computer science should "emphasize the benefits of applying information technology to social problems such as pollution, the loss of biodiversity, and the need for greater access to health care and education" (Olsen 2000, A47).

6. Formulate hypotheses focusing on gender as a crucial part of the question asked.

Technology in general is usually presented as gender neutral, and engineers often express the belief that gender has little or nothing to do with technology design. ABET criterion 3 c requires "an ability to design a system, component, or process to meet desired needs." As alluded to earlier, the air bag disaster in the American auto industry points out the error that occurs when gender is not considered in designing technology, given the "desired need" to avoid death from the lifesaving device itself.

The less dramatic example of the Joint Primary Aircraft Training System (JPATS) reveals the importance of unacknowledged or unrecognized gender bias in cockpit design (Weber 1997). The application of Military Standard 1472 of anthropometric data, which uses the ninety-fifth and fifth percentile of male dimensions, was applied in designing the cockpits of airplanes. This application meant that 90 percent of male military recruits, but only 30 percent of female recruits, had the dimensions to fit the cockpits. The policy decision by Secretary of Defense Les Aspin (1993, 1) to increase the percentage of women pilots uncovered this gender bias in cockpit design. Excluding by default only 10 percent of male recruits on the basis of their dimensions, the cockpit excluded 70 percent of women recruits. Exclusion of such large numbers of women, by dint of dimensions alone, made it extremely difficult to meet the military's policy goal of increasing women pilots. The officers initially reacted with an assumption that the technology reflected the best or only design possible and that the goal for the percentage of women pilots would have to be lowered or the number of tall women recruits would have to be increased. Instead, the policy decision to increase the numbers of women pilots led to a focus on gender, which changed the cockpit design to reduce the minimum sitting height needed (Weber 1997).

7. Undertake the investigation of problems of a more holistic, global scope rather than those traditionally considered, which are of a more reduced and limited scale.

The work of Gilligan (1982) suggests that adolescent girls often approach problem solving from the perspective of interdependence and relationship rather than from the hierarchical, reductionistic viewpoint favored by most adolescent boys. Further, on the Perry scale of student development (Perry 1970), the average eighteen-year-old female first-year college student scores higher than the average eighteen-year-old male student. This means that she is better able to deal with complex problems and ambiguity, while he is more comfortable dealing with dualisms and problems that have one correct or concrete answer. Thus, females are more likely to feel comfortable in approaching problems and laboratory experiments if they understand the relationship of the particular problem or experiment to the broader context of the bigger problem of which this solution may be a small part.

As suggested by ABET criteria 3 e and h, most engineering problems extend beyond a piece of equipment or technology. Within the engineering profession, sustainability of technology, human-computer interfaces, and systems design increasingly gain importance. These all require expansion of the definition of problem solving in engineering

(e) to include the short- and long-term impact of the technology and equipment on human beings and on the local and global environment (h). Studies on women in engineering document their attraction to the discipline when it is perceived as solving social problems and note their interest in technology in context as well as their desire to solve complex problems (Olsen 2000). Klawe recommends that to attract women, introductory college computer science courses should begin by discussing real-world problems and how computer science could help solve them, rather than focusing on abstract concepts (Olsen 2000). These interests and attractions conjoin nicely with the ABET criteria 3 e and h.

8. Use a combination of qualitative and quantitative methods in data gathering.

Some studies suggest that women engineers and scientists have demonstrated more interest in complex problems and more holistic approaches than have men. Systems, interdependence, and global approaches to problems may include both quantitative and qualitative methods to obtain the needed data. For example, the work in software systems development that starts from the understanding of a worker and her abilities and then focuses on how her professional competence can be augmented by the use of a system (Suchman and Jordan 1989) combines such quantitative and qualitative methods. Users are interviewed to ascertain their problems and satisfactions with particular software. The qualitative interview information is then combined with quantitative programming information to yield a better system. The qualitative/quantitative combination functions well for designing a system, component, or process to meet desired needs as required by criterion 3 c.

9. Use methods from a variety of fields or interdisciplinary approaches to problem solving.

Because the scope of problems in which women are interested tends to be broader, methods that cross disciplinary boundaries or include combinations of methods traditionally used in separate fields may provide more appropriate approaches. Women appear to be more attracted to engineering when they perceive its usefulness, relationship, and interdependence with other disciplines. For example, Mills College, a small liberal arts college for women, capitalized on this idea by developing a five-year dual-degree engineering program that permits students to receive bachelor's degrees in both liberal arts and engineering (Blum and Givant 1982). Klawe "recommends, first that colleges develop and publicize programs that combine computer science with biology, psychology, fine arts, and other fields that she says appeal to women" (Olsen 2000, A47).

The interdisciplinary approaches overlap exactly with ABET criterion 3 d, an ability to function on multidisciplinary teams. This criterion probably evolved because many of the current, most challenging engineering problems require interdisciplinary approaches, making these techniques, skills, and tools necessary for modern engineering practice (k).

10. Use females as subjects in experimental designs.

When women have not been subjects in the experimental designs of technologies created for use by people (both men and women), users may experience the technology as not useful, unsafe, or even lethal. The dramatic air bag example points out the error that occurs when a variety of women have not served as subjects during the technology design and underscores the significance of designing a system, component, or process to meet the desired need (c) of avoiding death. The JPATS example of cockpit design based upon male norms also reveals why a technology based upon norms that fit 95 percent of one sex may exclude the vast majority of the other.

When engineers become aware of the technological flaws that result from not using women, as well as men, as subjects in experimental designs, they should also increase their awareness of other groups— children, the disabled, the elderly—for whom technology designed around able-bodied, adult male norms may not work. Such recognition not only demonstrates knowledge of contemporary issues (j); it also leads to technology designs that may reduce legal liabilities for the designers and manufacturers.

11. Use more interactive methods, thereby shortening the distance between the observer and the object being studied.

Some studies (Gilligan 1982; Keller 1983) suggest that many women tend to prefer closer, more interactive approaches. In contrast, more men prefer distant, autonomous, and abstract approaches. Bodker and Greenbaum (1993) suggest that the "hard-systems" approach to computer systems may reflect the distant, autonomous, abstract approaches of the information technology (IT) designers, who are mostly men. The technical capabilities, constraints of the machines, and rational data flow become the focus and driver of the technology design. Since users do not contribute to the design of the system, their needs and suggestions are not included, and hard-systems design often does not function as well as desired in the real world of work.

Because women tend to place more emphasis upon relationships and interactions, some women scientists who work in computer design (Suchman 1994; Microsyster 1988) have attempted to link users more directly with systems design. They and others who use "soft-systems" human-factors approaches attempt to mediate the gap between users and the hardware. These interactive approaches correspond well with ABET criterion 3 in demonstrating an ability to design a system to meet desired needs (c) and to solve engineering problems (e).

12. Decrease laboratory exercises in introductory courses in which students must kill animals or render treatment that may be perceived as particularly harsh.

Geared toward biology and medical research, this suggestion does not have particular relevance for engineering and the ABET criteria. As engineering becomes increasingly interdisciplinary, however, and as increasing numbers of engineering students pursue courses in biology to undertake research in biomedical engineering and other related fields, this suggestion may become relevant.

13. Use precise, gender-neutral language in describing data and presenting theories.

Sensitivity to the use of gendered pronouns and the meanings of exclusion and inclusion implied by certain words extends beyond political correctness and making individuals feel included. Precise use of gendered or gender-neutral language conveys data and its conclusions accurately; imprecise use of such language may lead to inappropriate extrapolation of results to populations not included in the experiment or tests of the technology. For example, until a 1990 U.S. General Accounting Office (GAO) report uncovered that the National Institutes of Health failed to follow its protocols of requiring use of both male and female subjects in clinical trials of drugs, most drugs were tested on men only. A study published in September 1992 in the *Journal of the American Medical Association* surveyed the literature from 1960 to 1991 of more than one thousand studies of clinical trials of medications used to treat myocardial infarction. Women were included in only 20 percent of those studies (Gurwitz, Nananda, and Avorn 1992). Because the results of these trials were publicized as effects of a particular drug on "people" or "human subjects," the public remained largely unaware that most trials were run on men only. Physicians were placed in a precarious position, prescribing to both men and women drugs tested on the limited population of men only. When Congress, the GAO, and women's health activists (Rosser 1994) drew attention to the exclusion of women from clinical trials and its impact on women's morbidity and mortality in cardiovascular and other diseases where hormones and other factors appear to influence the effects of drugs and the etiology of the disease itself, women began to be included in the drug trials.

In a similar fashion, engineers may avoid bias and possible legal liability by precise use of gendered and gender-neutral language in describing the design and testing of technology. Recognizing and stating the sex of the test subjects in technical reports goes beyond demonstrating "a knowledge of contemporary issues" (ABET criterion 3 j). It extends to an understanding of professional and ethical responsibility (f). A statement that a particular technology was tested or designed using the body dimensions of only one sex as the norm raises the question of whether it is ethical to assume that the test results can be extrapolated to a broader population—both men and women.

14. Be open to critiques of conclusions and theories drawn from observations differing from those drawn by the traditional male scientists from the same observations.

Women researchers, consumers, and politicians raised the issues of gender and the use of language, which opened the door to changes in medical research, clinical trials, and conclusions drawn from data. Similarly, women have noted designs of technology and interpretation of technology test results that suffer from gender bias. Presumably, women's gender-based experiences, among them their ability to bear children, and their average size, all features in which they differ from men, provide the sources for their perspectives on the bias. ABET criterion 3 b implies that individuals putting together a multidisciplinary team will understand how diversity in race, class, nationality, disability, age, sexuality, and gender provide other experiences that may lead the team to function better in technology design and testing.

15. Encourage uncovering of other biases such as those of race, class, sexual orientation, ability status, and age that may permeate theories and conclusions drawn from experimental observation.

An engineering team or group composed of diverse individuals provides an environment where other biases besides those of gender in the design or testing of technology might be discovered. For example, in most technologies there is the assumption that the user will be an able-bodied adult. As the average age of the overall U.S. population becomes older, entrepreneurs are discovering the financial benefits of technologies designed for the elderly and for disabled populations. Designing and testing technologies for users from diverse backgrounds demonstrates more than an understanding of professional and ethical responsibilities (f) to nonmajority populations; this knowledge of contemporary issues (j) such as needs of users depending upon their age, ability status, race/ethnicity, and sexuality also correlates well with the demands of bottom-line profit margins.

16. Encourage development of theories and hypotheses that are relational, interdependent, and multicausal rather than hierarchical, reductionistic, and dualistic.

Just as women show particular interest in the investigation of problems that appear to be more holistic and global in scope, studies (AAUW 2000; Belenky et al. 1986; Gilligan 1982) also suggest that women demonstrate an interest in more complex, systemic solutions. Females are likely to be eager to learn how the specific bit of information provided by a particular experiment or data may influence and be influenced by other related factors; in contrast, males may be content to examine the bit of information out of context (J. Harding 1985). Hynes (1995) discusses the importance of providing complex contexts for studying problems in environmental engineering, not only to make the solutions more attractive to females, but also to provide a more realistic picture of how technology influences and is influenced by other parameters.

As twenty-first-century research moves engineering toward the interdisciplinary areas of human-computer interface, biomedical engineering, bioinformatics, and environmental engineering, the hypotheses and theories drawn from engineering research are changing and will not remain dualistic and reductionistic. More complex and systemic solutions result from an ability to use the techniques, skills, and modern engineering tools necessary for engineering practice (k).

17. Use less competitive models to practice science.

Although some women actively like and seek competition of the "I win, you lose" type, research over several decades (Horner 1969; Hoffman 1972; Belenky et al. 1986; Mouring et al. 1999) documents that more women prefer collaborative, cooperative approaches to problem solving. Some studies also document the deleterious effects of excessive competition, among them stress, fabrication of fraudulent data (Kohn 1986), and lost productivity from time spent jockeying for position rather than producing results. These harmful consequences of competition, although possibly with different manifestations for each gender, appear to be problematic for both men and women.

Modern engineering and science have become increasingly competitive. Struggles to obtain large grants to support postdoctoral researchers and students, to purchase major equipment to gather data, and to publish the results fuel the competitive research cycle that produces improved technology. Most laboratory activities are carried out by groups; going beyond this, however, working in functioning multidisciplinary teams, as required by industry and ABET criterion 3 d, cooperating in order to solve problems, calls upon collaborative skills, rather than competition. Most women excel at collaboration and teamwork, when roles within the group are monitored and rotated by the supervisor and when their contributions are recognized by others in the group (Rosser 1997). Some men may need to engage in lifelong learning (i) to understand possible gender differences in group dynamics, conversation, and cognitive styles that may either facilitate or inhibit team functioning.

18. Discuss the role of scientist as only one facet that must be smoothly integrated with other aspects of students' lives.

Despite the increasing numbers of women entering into engineering and science during the past thirty years, a major issue that continues to concern most women is the possibility and difficulty of combining a career in engineering or science with marriage, family, or both. In separate studies done on talented women in the 1980s, Arnold (1987), Matyas (1985), and Gardner (1986) found that women's decisions to switch majors to nonscience and nonengineering fields were related to issues surrounding marriage and family. Several studies (American Women in Science 1993; Humphries 1999; Rosser and Zieseniss 2000; Rosser and Montgomery 1999) underline that combining career and family is the predominant issue for women engineers and scientists at every step of the pipeline.

My own research on the National Science Foundation program Professional Opportunities for Women in Research and Education (POWRE), reveals that the challenge of balancing career and family is the overwhelming concern of the tenure-track academic engineers and scientists who receive most POWRE awards. For example, in response to an open-ended question solicited by email, "What are the most significant issues/challenges/opportunities facing women scientists/engineers today as they plan their careers?" 61.8 percent (42/68) of FY 1997 awardees and 72.0 percent (85/118) of FY 1998 awardees gave a response categorized as "balancing work with family responsibilities." Although the questionnaire permitted multiple responses, no other issue was cited by more than 23 percent of respondents. Women engineers and scientists want to pursue their research and careers, but they also want to have families (Rosser and Montgomery 1999).

Society as a whole has begun to understand that for most professionals balancing career and family may be the foremost issue of the twenty-first century. Clearly, it stands out as the predominant issue for women pursuing careers in engineering, science, and technology. ABET criterion 3 j, which requires a knowledge of contemporary issues, opens the door for engineering education to include strategies for dealing with this complex problem. The recognition of the need for, and an ability to engage in, lifelong learning (i) also provides a venue for individuals who have experienced career interruptions for family responsibilities to obtain reentry skills.

19. Put increased effort into strategies such as teaching and communicating with nonscientists to break down barriers between science and the layperson.
Engineering, scientific, mathematical, and technological terminology is intimidating and incomprehensible to many people in our society, particularly females (Bentley 1985). This terminology proliferates as research in an area becomes increasingly sophisticated and as its accompanying technology becomes more complex. Failure to communicate effectively about research, engineering, and technology not only leads to confusion for consumers and users of technology; ultimately it undermines the impact of the profession and its products.

When engineers and scientists do not communicate effectively to the public and politicians the potential of engineering and scientific research, politicians may withdraw support and funding from it, either not understanding or misunderstanding its implications. Genetically engineered food and the superconducting supercollider provide relatively recent examples of withdrawal of support from and public misunderstanding of scientific and engineering projects. President of the National Academy of Engineering William Wulf recommends that engineers now have a professional and ethical responsibility (f) to become involved in public policy in order to educate the public and politicians about the "larger effects" of engineering products and infrastructure (Wulf 2000).

Beyond Wulf's request to extend ABET criterion 3 f, an understanding of professional and ethical responsibility to encompass public policy, ABET criterion 3 g requires an ability to communicate effectively. Restructuring of the engineering curriculum to include more information on communication skills and ethics may have resulted from surveys of engineering seniors such as the one conducted at Purdue University (Daniels and LeBold 1982). Daniels and LeBold discovered that female students were more apt than males to place greater importance on educational goals stressing general education, communication skills, and the development of high ethical standards. "However, they were similar to the men in their perception that such goals were not achieved very well" (157). The new ABET criterion 3 emphasis upon ethics and communication is a response to deficits noted by women that should improve the image and understanding of engineering and technology held by the general public.

20. Discuss the practical uses to which scientific discoveries are put to help students see science in its social context.

A persuasive argument to attract women to engineering and technology is the tremendous usefulness they have for improving people's lives. The positive social benefits of technology, science, and engineering appear to be overwhelmingly important for women. Many studies on different ages of girls and women (AAUW 2000; J. Harding 1985; Rosser 1995; Miller et al. 2000), in different settings and career levels (Seymour and Hewitt 1994; Hynes 1995; Rosser and Zieseniss 2000) and of diverse cultures (Lie and Bryhni 1983; Frize et al. 1999; Sorenson 1992) support the assertion that women become particularly interested in and attracted to engineering and technology because of its social usefulness.

ABET criterion 3 h emphasizes the broad education necessary to understand the impact of engineering solutions in a global and societal context. This emphasis provides the impetus for courses such as the one developed at Case Western Reserve in which engineering students undertake socially useful projects to improve the community (Heller 2000). In helping students see engineering and technology in its social context, such projects also fulfill criterion 3 c of designing a system, component, or process to meet desired needs. In this case, the needs met are multiple: the needs of women to see the social usefulness of technology; the needs of the community, such as mounting a portable respirator on a juvenile wheelchair and developing a flood gauge for a stream in a nature center; and most important, to quote Bill Wulf, the needs of engineers to understand the larger effects "of the products and infrastructure we design."

Conclusion

A close comparison of the new ABET criterion 3 with twenty curricular ideas and pedagogical techniques that I suggested a decade ago (Rosser 1990) reveals considerable overlap and substantive correspondence between the subpoints of criterion 3 and the techniques. Although some criterion subpoints—d, f, g, h, i, and j—directly overlap and support a female-friendly agenda, all subpoints correspond at least partially. None runs directly counter to female-friendly suggestions, which bodes well for ABET Goal 5, to "expand the diversity of participation in ABET" (ABET 2000).

In sum, ABET criterion 3 lays the requirement groundwork for a curriculum with the potential to attract and retain more women in engineering. As always, the devil is in the details. Individual institutions may choose to implement the criteria by developing curricula that conform to criterion 3, but will remain unlikely to attract increased percentages of women. For example, they might interpret interdisciplinary teams in the limited sense of all white men who have a background in different disciplines within mechanical engineering, chemical engineering, and electrical engineering; they might limit ethical and professional responsibility to examining efficient ways to produce weapons of mass destruction. In contrast, however, another institution might broaden the definition of interdisciplinary to encompass gender, race, age, and ability status, along with social sciences and humanities, as the diversity needed on all interdisciplinary teams. This same institution might require that philosophers and public policy faculty be included in the design of projects, as well as their evaluation. These latter institutions would be applying criterion 3 in more female-friendly ways, likely to lead to increased diversity.

REFERENCES

Accreditation Board for Engineering and Technology, Inc. 1998. *Engineering Criteria 2000: Criteria for Accrediting Programs in Engineering in the United States.* 2d ed. Baltimore: Engineering Accreditation Commission.

American Association of University Women (AAUW). 2000. *Tech-Savvy: Educating Girls in the New Computer Age.* Washington, D.C.: AAUW Educational Foundation.

American Society of Engineering Education Task Force. 1987. *The National Action Agenda for Engineering Education.* Washington, D.C.: American Society of Engineering Education Task Force.

American Women in Science (AWIS). 1993. *A Hand Up: Women Mentoring Women in Science.* Washington, D.C.: AWIS.

Arnold, Karen. 1987. "Retaining High Achieving Women in Science and Engineering." Paper presented at the conference "Women in Science and Engineering: Changing Vision to Reality," University of Michigan, Ann Arbor, June. Sponsored by American Association for the Advancement of Science.

Aspin, Les. 1993. *Policy on the Assignment of Women in the Armed Forces.* 28 April. Washington, D.C.: Department of Defense.

Belenky, M. F., B. M. Clinchy, N. R. Goldberger, and J. M. Tarule. 1986. *Women's Ways of Knowing.* New York: Basic Books.

Bentley, Diane. 1985. "Men May Understand the Words, but Do They Know the Music? Some Cris de Coeur in Science Education." In *Supplementary Contributions to the Third GASAT Conference,* 160–68. London: University of London, Chelsea College.

Blum, Lenore, and Steven Givant. 1982. "Increasing the Participation of College Women in Mathematics-Related Fields." In *Women and Minorities in Science,* ed. S. Humphreys. AAAS Selected Symposia Series. Boulder, Colo.: Westview Press.

Bodker, S., and J. Greenbaum. 1993. "Design of Information Systems: Things Versus People." In *Gendered by Design: Information Technology and Office Systems,* ed. S. Green, J. Owen, and D. Pain. London: Taylor and Francis.

Commission on Professionals in Science and Technology. 1997. *Best and Brightest: Education and Career Paths of Top Science and Engineering Students.* Washington, D.C.: Commission on Professionals in Science and Technology.

Cockburn, Cynthia. 1981. "The Material of Male Power." *Feminist Review* 9: 41–58.

———. 1983. *Brothers: Male Dominance and Technological Change.* London: Pluto Press.

———. 1985. *Machinery of Dominance: Women, Men, and Technical Know-How.* London. Pluto Press.

Daniels, Jane, and William Lebold. 1982. "Women in Engineering: A Dynamic Approach." In *Women and Minorities in Science,* ed. S. Humphreys. AAAS Selected Symposia Series. Boulder, Colo.: Westview Press.

Fee, Elizabeth. 1983. "Women's Nature and Scientific Objectivity." In *Women's Nature: Rationalizations of Inequality,* ed. Marian Lowe and Ruth Hubbard, 9–27. New York: Pergamon Press.

Felder, R. M., G. N. Felder, M. Mauney, C. E. Hamrin, Jr., and E. J. Dietz. 1995. "A Longitudinal Study of Engineering Student Performance and Retention. III. Gender Differences in Student Performance and Attitudes." *Journal of Engineering Education* 84 (2): 151–63.

Fossey, Dian. 1983. *Gorillas in the Mist.* Boston: Houghton Mifflin.

Frasier, Jane M., and D. R. Ismail. 1997. "Analysis of Men and Women Engineering Students at Ohio State." *ASEE Annual Conference Proceedings, 1997.* Washington, D.C.: American Association of Engineering Societies.

Frize, Monique, Claire Deschenes, Elizabeth Cannon, Mary Williams, and Marie Klawe. 1999. "A Unique National Project to Increase the Participation of Women in Science and Engineering." In *Tackling the Engineering Resources Shortage: Creating New Paradigms for Developing and Retaining Women Engineers,* ed. Barbara Bogue, Priscilla Guthrie, Barbara Lazarus, and Steve Hadden, 83–90. Bellingham, Wash.: International Society for Optical Engineering.

Gardner, A. L. 1986. "Effectiveness of Strategies to Encourage Participation and Retention of Precollege and College Women in Science." Ph.D. diss., Purdue University.

Gilligan, Carol. 1982. *In a Different Voice: Psychological Theory and Women's Development.* Cambridge: Harvard University Press.

Goodall, Jane. 1971. *In the Shadow of Man.* Boston: Houghton Mifflin.

Gurwitz, J. H., F. C. Nananda, and J. Avorn. 1992. "The Exclusion of the Elderly and Women from Clinical Trials in Acute Myocardial Infarction." *Journal of the American Medical Association* 268 (2): 1417–22.

Hacker, Sally. 1981. "The Culture of Engineering: Woman, Workplace, and Machine," *Women's Studies International Quarterly* 4: 341–53.

———. 1989. *Pleasure, Power, and Technology.* Boston: Unwin Hyman.

Hamilton, Laura S. 1998. "Gender Differences on High School Science Achievement Tests: Do Format and Content Matter?" *Educational Evaluation and Policy Analysis* 20 (3): 179–95.

Harding, Jan. 1985. "Values, Cognitive Style, and the Curriculum." In *Contributions to the Third Girls and Science and Technology Conference.* London: University of London, Chelsea College.

Harding, Sandra. 1986. *The Science Question in Feminism.* Ithaca: Cornell University Press.

———. 1998. *Is Science Multicultural? Postcolonialisms, Feminisms, and Epistemologies.* Bloomington: Indiana University Press.

Heller, Scott. 2000. "Engineering 101: Case Western Reserve University Freshman Engineering Field Service Project." *Chronicle of Higher Education,* May 26, A18.

Hoffman, Lois W. 1972. "Early Childhood Experiences and Women's Achievement Motives." *Journal of Social Issues* 28 (2): 129–55.

Horner, Matina. 1969. "Fail: Bright Women." *Psychology Today* 3: 36–38.

Hrdy, Sarah. 1986. "Empathy, Polyandry, and the Myth of the Coy Female." In *Feminist Approaches to Science,* ed. R. Bleier, 9–34. Elmsford, N.Y.: Pergamon Press.

Humphries, Sheila. 1999. "Preparing for Long-Term Growth in the Profession." In *Tackling the Engineering Resources Shortage: Creating New Paradigms for Developing and Retaining Women Engineers,* ed. Barbara Bogue, Priscilla Guthrie, Barbara Lazarus, and Steve Hadden, 126–30. Bellingham, Wash.: International Society for Optical Engineering.

Hynes, H. Patricia. 1989. *The Recurring Silent Spring.* Elmsford, N.Y.: Pergamon Press.

———. 1995. "No Classroom Is an Island." In *Teaching the Majority,* ed. Sue V. Rosser, 211–19. New York: Teachers College Press.

Kahle, Jane B. 1985. *Women in Science.* Philadelphia: Falmer Press.

Keller, Evelyn F. 1983. *A Feeling for the Organism.* San Francisco: Freeman.

———. 1985. *Reflections on Gender and Science.* New Haven: Yale University Press.

Kohn, Alexander. 1986. *Fraud Prophets.* New York: Basil Blackwell.

Kunda, Gideon. 1992. *Engineering Culture.* Philadelphia: Temple University Press.

Lie, Svein, and Eva Bryhni. 1983. "Girls and Physics: Attitudes, Experiences, and Underachievement." *Contributions to the Second Girls and Science and Technology Conference.* Oslo: University of Oslo, Institute of Physics, 202–211.

Matyas, Marsha L. 1985. "Obstacles and Constraints on Women in Science." In *Women in Science,* ed. J. B. Kahle. Philadelphia: Falmer Press.

Microsyster. 1988. *Not Over Our Heads: Women and Computers in the Office.* London: Microsyster.

Miller, Patricia H., Sue V. Rosser, Joann P. Benigno, and Mireille Zieseniss. 2000. "A Desire to Help Others: Goals of High-Achieving Female Science Undergraduates." *Women's Studies Quarterly* 28 (1–2): 128–42.

Mitgang, Herbert. 1993. Review of *The Cold War and American Science*, by Leslie Stuart. *New York Times*, June 1, C11.

Mouring, Sarah, et al. 1999. "The ESTEAM Program: Changing the Paradigm on Engineering Students Teams from Forming for Diversity to Training for Diversity." In *Tackling the Engineering Resources Shortage: Creating New Paradigms for Developing and Retaining Women Engineers*, ed. Barbara Bogue, Priscilla Guthrie, Barbara Lazarus, and Steve Hadden, 119–25. Bellingham, Wash.: International Society for Optical Engineering.

Nair, Indira, and Sara Majetich. 1995. "Physics and Engineering in the Classroom." In *Teaching the Majority*, ed. Sue V. Rosser, 25–42. New York: Teachers College Press.

National Center for Educational Statistics (NCES). 1997. *NAEP 1996 Mathematics Report Card*. Washington, D.C.: NCES.

National Research Council, Board on Engineering Education. 1995. *Engineering Education: Designing an Adaptive System*. Washington, D.C.: National Academy Press.

National Science Foundation (NSF). 1995. *Restructuring Engineering Education: A Focus on Change. Report of an NSF Workshop on Engineering Education*. Arlington, Va. (National Science Foundation 9565).

———. 1999. *Women, Minorities, and Persons with Disabilities in Science and Engineering: 1998*. Arlington, Va. (NSF 99–338).

Olsen, Florence. 2000. "Institute for Women and Technology Works to Bridge the Other Digital Divide." *Chronicle of Higher Education*, April 7, A47.

Perry, William. 1970. *Forms of Intellectual and Ethical Development in the College Years*. New York: Holt, Rinehart, and Winston.

Rosser, Sue V. 1990. *Female Friendly Science*. New York: Pergamon Press.

———. 1993. "Female Friendly Science: Including Women in Curricular Content and Pedagogy in Science." *Journal of General Education* 42 (3): 191–220.

———. 1994. *Women's Health: Missing from U.S. Medicine*. Bloomington: Indiana University Press.

———. 1995. *Teaching the Majority*. New York: Teachers College Press.

———. 1997. *Re-engineering Female Friendly Science*. New York: Teachers College Press.

———. 1998. "The Next Millennium Is Here Now: Women's Studies Perspectives on Biotechnics and Reproductive Technologies." In *New Perspectives in Gender Studies: Research in the Fields of Economics, Culture, and Life Sciences*, ed. Boel Berner, 7–35. Stockholm: Almquist and Wilosell International.

———. 2000 *Women, Science, and Society*. Elmsford, N.Y.: Pergamon Press.

Rosser, Sue V. and Julie Montgomery. 1999. "Gender Equity Issues in Science Careers." *WEEA [Women's Educational Equity Act] Digest* (December): 3–8.

Rosser, Sue V., and Mireille Zieseniss. 2000. "Career Issues and Laboratory Climates: Different Challenges and Opportunities for Women Engineers and

Scientists (Survey of Fiscal Year 1997 POWRE Awardees)." *Journal of Women and Minorities in Science and Engineering* 6: 1–20.

Scott, Joan. 1988. *Gender and the Politics of History*. New York: Columbia University Press.

Seymour, Elaine, and Nancy Hewitt. 1994. *Talking about Leaving: Factors Contributing to High Attrition Rates Among Science, Mathematics, and Engineering Undergraduate Majors*. (Final report to the Alfred P. Sloan Foundation on an ethnographic inquiry at seven institutions.) Boulder, Colo.: Ethnography and Assessment Research, Bureau of Sociological Research.

Sorenson, K. 1992. "Towards a Feminized Technology? Gendered Values in the Construction of Technology." *Social Studies of Science* 22 (1): 5–31.

Suchman, L. 1994. "Supporting Articulation Work: Aspects of a Feminist Practice of Technology Production." In *Women, Work, and Computerization: Breaking Old Boundaries—Building New Forms*, ed. A. Adam, J. Emms, E. Green, and J. Owen. Amsterdam: North-Holland.

Suchman, L., and B. Jordan. 1989. "Computerization and Women's Knowledge." In *Women, Work, and Computerization: Forming New Alliances*, ed. K. Tijdens, M. Jennings, I. Wagner, and M. Weggelaar. Amsterdam: North-Holland.

Wajcman, Judy. 1991. *Feminism Confronts Technology*. University Park: Pennsylvania State University Press.

————. 1983. *Women in Control: Dilemmas of a Workers Co-operative*. Milton Keynes, U.K.: Open University Press.

Weber, Rachel. 1997. "Manufacturing Gender in Commercial and Military Cockpit Design." *Science, Technology, and Human Values* 22: 235–53.

Widnall, Sheila. 2000. "Digits of Pi: Why Do So Few Women Go into Engineering?" Lecture delivered for a National Academy of Engineering Regional Symposium, Georgia Institute of Technology, Atlanta, April 26.

Wulf, William. 2000. "The Societal Responsibility of Engineers (and Its Implications for Engineering Education)." The George W. Woodruff School of Mechanical Engineering Annual Distinguished Lecture, Georgia Institute of Technology, Atlanta, April 25.

Sue Rosser *is dean of Ivan Allen College, the liberal arts college at Georgia Institute of Technology, where she is also professor of History, Technology, and Society. She is the author of* Female Friendly Science *(1990) from Pergamon Press,* Feminism and Biology: A Dynamic Interaction *(1992) from Twayne Macmillan,* Women's Health: Missing from U.S. Medicine *(1994) from Indiana University Press, and* Teaching the Majority *(1995) and* Re-engineering Female Friendly Science *(1997), both from Teachers College Press. Her latest book is* Women, Science, and Society: The Crucial Union *(2000) from Teachers College Press.*

Women's Studies Online

Cyberfeminism or Cyberhype?

Ivy Schweitzer

It is the first day of class—Women's Studies 10: Sex, Gender, and Society—and although my co-teacher, Michelle Meyers, and I have taught this course before, this term is different: we have put a good deal of the course online. It took some wrangling with the registrar to get the particular classroom we needed to teach the course: one of a growing number of Dartmouth's "smart"—that is, technology-smart—classrooms. With some trepidation, we stand before the specially designed podium, and boot up the powerPC that is artfully fitted into it. The image of our computer desktop springs instantly onto the large screen at the front of the lecture hall.

As we navigate onto the Web, a hush falls over the one hundred or so students sitting expectantly in rows of bolted-down seats. There is a palpable edginess in the air, since none of us, students or teachers, knows exactly what this will be like. Instead of handing out syllabi and other paper notices, we begin by showing students step by step how to get, via the Dartmouth College homepage, to the Women's Studies 10 (WS 10) homepage, which gives access to the syllabus, course requirements, and writing assignments for the course. What we are doing on our Mac appears enlarged on the big screen at the front. Then the unexpected happens. As the image on the college's homepage takes shape, I gasp at what I see: a young woman in a tight white T-shirt sitting on a grassy spot in front of an immaculate eighteenth-century college building. She is bending over her books, evidently studying, but the layout cuts off part of her head and her lower body, so that the focus is—you can imagine where! I cannot resist pointing out the gendered politics of representation, in which even women who have proved their intellectual bona fides by matriculating at the college are objectified and fragmented in Dartmouth's choice of such an icon for its homepage. You can be sure we called College Computing directly after class.

We discovered that the headless, faceless coed was one of a rotating series of images of males, females, and college scenes that come up randomly on the Dartmouth homepage. We just happened to log on at the moment when a prime candidate for the wet T-shirt contest had her turn. This was small comfort, and in no way accounted for the *layout* of the image, which prevented the viewer from gazing anywhere else but at the faceless woman's midsection. Nor did this explanation stop us from using the image as an example for our largely privileged students in response to their (often repeated) protest that gender politics and oppression do not exist because *they* in particular do not experience them. On reflection, this moment also provided an immediate and concrete counterexample to the popular utopian myth of cyberspace, that it transcends differences such as gender, class, and race and that it allows users to operate as disembodied, and thus unmarked and equal, entities. On the contrary, Anne Balsamo concludes, citing the work of Sandy Stone, who studies electronic communities, "Cyberspace both disembodies and re-embodies in a gendered fashion," enabling "new forms of repression of the material body" (138–39). This was not a conclusion we were eager to reach as we initiated our students and ourselves into Web-assisted instruction, but it certainly buttressed the basic understanding of the operation of differences in mainstream U.S. culture that we were committed to interrogating in our introductory women's studies course.

Frankly, I had not known what to expect from this pedagogical experiment. Michelle Meyers, an art historian turned pop culture critic and feminist theorist, had put WS 10 online in summer 1997 to take advantage of the opportunities for research and interaction offered by the Internet and to make feminist-friendly students familiar with the latest Web technology. The following fall, when we co-taught the course, we intensified the Web interface, but aside from the novelty and excitement involved in using the smart classroom, and the reduction of some of the hard-copy clutter that comes with a big course, I did not expect momentous changes. However, after reflecting on our experiences, and doing more reading about cyberspace, I have come to believe that Web technology constitutes the greatest opportunity for feminism and progressive politics in the new century. With certain very important caveats, Web technology and Web-related teaching have the potential to actualize some of the basic goals of feminism and feminist pedagogy. As we discovered while teaching WS 10 that term, Web technology gave our abstract academic endeavor a virtual "space" that made it more "real" and more accessible than ever before, especially to a generation of students who grew up with computer technology. The Web interface empowered students by freeing them from the often inhibiting presence of authority figures. By providing these spaces, the Web has the capacity not merely to challenge, but also to change, the structures of power in the classroom and, perhaps, the world at large.

Feminist Pedagogy and Challenges

Dartmouth has been in the forefront in bringing computer technology to its campus and the college curriculum. As a result, we have an extensive infrastructure for Web-related teaching and learning, including a fast and reliable internal email system called "blitzmail," which students patronize for academic and, especially, social communications. We wanted them to use some of the enormous amounts of time they spend in cyberspace learning to think critically about sex and gender in contemporary U.S. culture, not just performing its rituals via their powerPCs. We also wanted to explore the opportunities offered by Web technology to modify the traditional classroom in ways that advanced our feminist goals. While there are probably as many definitions of *feminist pedagogy* as there are feminist teachers, practitioners in various fields agree on a few principles.

My co-teacher and I strive for the kind of feminist pedagogy articulated by bell hooks: an "engaged pedagogy" that fosters a "community of learning" and advances the "practice of freedom" not only in the classroom, but in the world.[1] A major feminist contribution to this kind of practice has been the emphasis on coming to voice: making ourselves visible, recognizing ourselves as the subject of knowledge production and not simply its object or receptacle, and granting others a similar validation. Such a pedagogy unfolds from the basic notion that, to use the well-worn expression, "the personal is political," that our private, individual, and subjective experiences are crucially important. Furthermore, these experiences comprise the many important bits of evidence that allow us to make that inductive leap and theorize about collective experiences and the larger structures of domination and subordination.

For this reason, a basic and crucial component of WS 10 is the application of critical paradigms to personal experience and what I call the "micropolitical climate" of the campus community. For example, in the past, students have read and critiqued such works as Deborah Tannen's on the linguistic theories of gendered conversation and applied them to their own experiences in the snack bar or the classroom. This is not a mere exercise. In almost a decade of my teaching WS 10, it never fails that after the Thanksgiving break, during my office hours I am swamped with students who complain, sometimes bitterly, that they could not sit at the holiday table with their family, or interact with their boyfriend or girlfriend, without seeing some of Tannen's principles at work. Similarly, in observing classroom dynamics, understanding the implications of who gets called on, who monopolizes the floor, who interrupts whom, and who is silenced, students see the limitation of Tannen's gendered approach, recognizing that race and class are also important determinants of classroom politics and the general politics of "space."

These kinds of critical investigations encourage students to question the dominant paradigms of power, to explore alternative forms of empowerment and interaction. As historian Robert J. Bezucha points out, feminism is threatening, precisely because it is not content with merely analyzing, but "seeks to undermine one of the most powerful and deeply held sets of distinctions drawn in Western thought and society: the separation of the public, the impersonal, and the objective, on the one hand, from the private, the personal, and the subjective on the other" (81). Students have to *unlearn* the false separation that dichotomizes their experiences and tells them—to take a sensational example—that marital rape is a "private" behavior inappropriately dealt with by courts, laws, or rules controlling international immigration. At the same time, students have to learn a critical approach toward the personal and private, how to analyze their own as well as others' experiences using different theoretical paradigms.

One of our constant challenges in teaching WS 10 is that we not replicate the destructive dynamics that all too often resurface in the women's studies classroom. These dynamics are exacerbated by large classes (made necessary in order for embattled programs such as women's studies to "prove" their relevance and popularity); impersonal lecture halls where all the rows face forward and the seats do not swivel; and course syllabi in which information is dispensed by the instructor/producer of knowledge, replicated by the student/consumer of knowledge, and rarely produced or shared among peers.

Another challenge is to foster critical thinking and self-awareness. One of the most effective strategies for this is to nudge students to become active participants in the creative dialectic of theory and practice, learning and doing. In an informal survey of his feminist colleagues, John Schib found that "a student-centered classroom, in some meaning of that term, lay at the heart of our pedagogical dreams" (257). Like bell hooks, Schib drew from the educational philosophy of Brazilian thinker Paulo Freire, whose thought appealed to him because it "connects true reciprocity in the educational process with a truly humanistic praxis in the larger world" and enables students to "attain a new power to distinguish the ineradicable laws of nature from the transient institutions of culture, along with a new optimism about the prospect of social change" (258). The slippery notion of "true reciprocity" is still, I think, a key term for our educational goals, and one made all the more possible by Web technology, which has untapped potential for creating connections.[2]

Frequently, when students "find their voices," they come to interrogate the very notion of authority, which leads them to question the authority figures in the classroom—the authors they read and the people who teach them. As hooks points out, in the early 1970s, feminist classrooms "were the one space where pedagogical practices were interrogated, where it was assumed that the knowledge offered students would empower them to be better scholars, to live more fully in the world beyond academe" (6). I do not want to give away entirely the authority of expertise, experience, or the evaluation of students. Rather, I think we should explore how feminists can model different ways of being authoritative, not authoritarian. One of the ways of subverting the structural effect of teacher authority that we established in WS 10 was to turn over to the students part of the process of coming to critical self-consciousnesss.

We found that what benefits this process of interrogation, and lets off steam that might otherwise cloud up the classroom atmosphere, is the existence of a space defined in students' own terms, and lots of nearly unstructured and unsupervised interaction with peers—a kind of free-form group exploration within the larger, governing themes and structure of the course. It has been my experience that students learn best what they need and want to know, and that this kind of learning often requires a long, and sometimes tedious, process of exploration, the endless conversational give-and-take that classroom structures cannot easily accommodate. In years past, I sent groups of students eager for this kind of extracurricular consciousness-raising to the women's resource center. I was concerned that women's studies classes not be branded as "touchy-feely" enclaves where students merely vented or talked about their menstrual cramps—our local stereotype of how feminists "bond." Such extracurricular exploration is absolutely necessary for the kind of learning and analysis that invites and requires students to think beyond the academic subject matter, the required reading, the parameters of the classroom.

Breaking large classes (usually between 100 and 150 students) up into smaller discussion groups has been the conventional means by which we provided this space. In years past, discussion groups have been led by the teachers and aided by a cadre of experienced women's studies students enrolled in the course whom we selected and trained and with whom we met on a weekly basis. Still teacher-initiated and structured around a discussion leader, these sections have only been marginally successful. No matter how freewheeling and spontaneous these discussions may be, they still feel constrained and scripted. This time, we hoped that the Web would make available new spaces that were somewhere between the teacher/lecture-centered classroom and the student-centered rap session, but that avoided the limitations of the discussion section.

We never imagined that our Web-assisted course would eliminate the instructor or the need for face-to-face (FTF) student-teacher or peer interaction, which some students feared when we explained to them the Web-interface format of the course. It is certainly true that these mainstays of traditional teaching are rendered superfluous by Internet innovations such as the Virtual On-line University (VOU), which was unveiled in September 1994; or the Women's International Electronic University (WIEU), which came online in December 1996. According to their announcement, VOU "operates within a Virtual Educational Environment using Multiuser-Object-Oriented environment database software (a MOO)" to produce various online virtual campuses from which students can choose (http://www.wvu.edu/~womensu/). This is called "distance learning"; students can "attend" any number of university environments, at any time they choose, and from any location they choose. There are enormous advantages from a feminist perspective to doing away with the traditional, physical classroom as the privileged site of academic instruction where a masculine ethos has, for a long time, held sway. Furthermore, "simulated inter-activity," as this kind of instruction is called, would significantly benefit individuals—mothers with small children, disabled people, people living far from academic institutions—who cannot physically attend traditional classes. However, these benefits depend upon people owning or having access to computers and network hookups—no small consideration, since the target groups of sites such as WIEU are precisely the undereducated, underskilled, and economically deprived. Still, if as Australian Net-tech booster, communication expert, and longtime feminist Dale Spender asserts, computer technology is here to stay, then what we need are "computer-competent women . . . to 'suss out' this new public space and pass on advice to the next generation" (xxiv). Our challenge was to explore the possibilities of this new public space precisely in order to "suss out" its potential from a feminist perspective.

We also believed that the vast resources of the Web would enhance the students' academic and intellectual experience. Feminist investigation is often interdisciplinary, operating in areas where knowledge evolves out of the interstices between disciplines and traditional methods. Such work tries to be self-conscious and self-critical about the way in which it produces knowledge and constitutes subjects of study. Both as a high-powered research tool and an efficient retrieval system for a vast and expanding "infosphere," the Web makes available an array of information that encourages students to design provocative connections to fields that might have otherwise been closed to them or hard to reach. It also opens up the possibility of creating multimedia and multidimensional research assignments—of encouraging new forms of knowledge and new ways of knowing that can embody feminist values.

The Web Site: A Location of Our Own

Because all the information about our course was posted on our Web site, the site served as a virtual information center and location for the course that did not depend on our literal presence. Students could visit the site at any time, including between office hours or late at night, this latter being the time when they often prefer to work. The advantage this arrangement had over the dissemination of hard-copy information is that it could accommodate the changes, updates, emendations, and additions we posted throughout the entire term. No longer was the course defined and ultimately limited by a syllabus that had been constructed before we even had had contact with the particular group of students who would be taking the course. The Web site allowed us to make changes to the skeletal structure of the course in response to student reactions to the material. Although it was a bit unnerving *not* to hand out a hard copy of the syllabus—our handing it out ensured that all students had it and thus absolved us of further responsibility—this became the first and most basic way we gave responsibility for learning to the students. We showed them (several times) how to get to the Web site and use its links. They could visit the site whenever they needed to check the syllabus for reading assignments, or for the contents of the course reading packet, or for the Additional Bibliography, a constantly expanding list of related readings that we updated as titles and subject matter came up in lectures or discussions. Dartmouth's Baker Library now has its online catalog in Web-based form, so that in the Web site's next incarnation, there will be direct links from the titles in these bibliographies to the library's electronic catalog. Essays listed in the bibliography that are in journals in Web-based form are immediately accessible to students on the computer.

The Web site also had a description of the written and Web assignments required for the course, as well as a short list of links to Web sites
important for the course content. But to merely detail the contents of
our homepage doesn't explain how its existence subtly affected how
we perceived and how the students reacted to the course. Instead of
existing on distributed photocopied sheets of paper that could be torn
or lost, WS 10 had a location—in cyberspace, it is true, but a location
nevertheless. It constituted a "space," a place to be visited and consulted; this Web site located us even when we were not in that Goddess-
forsaken classroom with its harsh lights and immovable seats, so that
the course existed, if only in potentia and until someone visited it, all
the time and extended beyond the three or four hours of in-class time
we were allotted by the college and registrar. At any time day or night,
there was a place where students could "go" called WS 10. And they
did, especially to post comments and reactions to the Open Discussion
forum we set up. By not giving students a hard copy of syllabi and
assignments, we asked them to acknowledge and validate this site as
the virtual space of our learning community. We also required students
to add links to the Web site, so that the site itself became theirs, the
sole and lasting evidence of this particular class's existence.

Links and the Gender Politics of the 'Electronic Frontier'

Our Web-linked assignment asked students to find a link relevant to
the course content, annotate it, and add it to the site. Through the
assignment, students created an account of our academic and intellectual interaction and what our temporary community collectively
produced. The Web site also held traces of other students and their
explorations via WS 10 in the form of a Student Links list—a long,
annotated list of links to Web sites that students from the previous WS
10 class had posted that formed a veritable, or more precisely "virtual,"
archaeology of links to issues of sex, gender, and society in the 1990s.
Such lists perform the function of "sifting and sorting" the overwhelming amount of information on the Web; but more important,
they reflect the interests of WS 10's students, who are at least a generation or two younger than its faculty. Many students reported that
their initial link led them to other sites, forming "links of association"
that Steven Johnson calls "trails." Although these trails were evanes-
cent, the process of linking that produced them is the key to the
Web's treasures.

Johnson, author of *Interface Culture: How New Technology Transforms
the Way We Create and Communicate,* explains that the link is "a tool that

brings multifarious elements together" to augment knowledge, rather than a fragmenting or dissociative element, as hypertext fiction has prompted many people to think of it (111). Trails, or groups of links, "imply a profound shift in the way we grapple with information." They move us away from a nineteenth-century "encyclopedic mentality" obsessed with ordering and cataloging small nuggets of information so that their value derives from the class or species in which they are placed. Trails of links, by contrast, allow us to "see the world the way a *poet* does: a world teeming with associations, minglings, continuities" (118–19). As Johnson and others contend, this aspect of Web technology brings us to the threshold of the new: "The link is the first significant new form of punctuation to emerge in centuries, but it is only a hint of things to come. Hypertext, in fact, suggests a whole new grammar of possibilities, a new way of writing and telling stories" (110–11). Hypertext creates texts or takes existing texts and builds in links that provide an almost endless set of narrative possibilities or informational connections, enabling what Michael Joyce calls the poetics of "hypertext pedagogy." While neither Johnson nor Joyce explicitly considers the gendered qualities of hypertext, Johnson finds links to be proletarian and potentially subversive: "More than any other interface element, the link belongs to the cultural peripheries and not to the high-tech conglomerates" (110). According to these critics, linking and hypertext have the potential to significantly change how we understand ourselves and our world, and how we produce knowledge.

Some students found the link assignment to be mechanical and uninteresting, while quite a few reported making far-flung associations, clicking themselves clear across the infosphere in what Johnson identifies as the "eureka moment" when Net users first experience the enormous possibilities of the technology and get "hooked" (110). This kind of exploration has been mislabled "surfing the Web," a term borrowed from the passive and random "channel surfing" associated with TV watching. But as Johnson argues, Web surfing, unlike channel surfing, explores the interstices between sites, uncovering the connections and thus "the relationships between them." Unlike bookmarks, which he compares to "snapshots or postcards mailed home from an overseas vacation," links that form trails preserve "the journey itself," the relationships between sites, associations that make that personal web intelligible to you" (122). Links allow a particular user to make her own unique connections—"to blaze your trail through information space" (123).

A collateral and unexpected effect of the links assignment was the examination and critique it precipitated of the very discourse we use to describe our activities in this new space, which led to a wider consideration of gender dynamics on the Web. Inexplicably, the term for Web surfing that has stuck is *surfing*, rather than *trailblazing*. Although Web surfing, as our students experienced it, is far removed from the couch potato clutching the remote, its connotations of passivity and randomness, according to Johnson, may prevent software designers from developing the means to preserve individual trails. His alternative, however, gave many of us pause. Although Johnson is carefully gender inclusive throughout his descriptions of Web activity, the imagery of "trailblazing" too easily and unproblematically invokes the analogy of the Web as frontier. Students were tickled by the idea of themselves as technophilic bushwhackers, but were stopped in their tracks, so to speak, by Laura Miller's canny analysis of the language of pioneering in her response to a controversial May 16, 1994, article in *Newsweek* in which the author declared cyberspace to be a "sexist" and hostile environment for women. Miller argues that the pervasive description of the Web as an "electronic frontier" evokes popular masculinist fantasies of rugged individualism, female vulnerability, and quintessential Americanness that not only stereotype and exclude women, but also justify the call on the part of conservative "civilizing" forces for Web regulation. Women, Miller believes, should resist an argument that plunges them back into the roles of helpless victim "especially when we are used as rhetorical pawns in a battle to regulate a rare (if elite) space of gender ambiguity" (57). We should also resist this imagery because it divides us in all too familiar ways: "As the schoolmarms arrive on the electronic frontier, their female predecessors find themselves cast in the role of saloon girls, their willingness to engage in 'masculine' activities like verbal aggression, debate, or sexual experimentation marking them as insufficiently feminine, or 'bad' women" (57). While recognizing the potential for gender stereotyping on the Web, which our students saw for themselves on the first day of class exemplified by our very own Dartmouth homepage, Miller also refuses *Newsweek*'s simplistic and reductive claim that "the gender gap is real" in cyberspace or has to be. As our students discovered, cyberspace allows for gender blurring and masking, for passing and experimentation, which rarely, if ever, occur in traditional classrooms.

Academic Exercises as Public Space

The most important advantage our Web site provided was the opportunity, on the one hand, to break down the traditional notion of the classroom as a limited physical space and, on the other, to intensify the sense of a shared location for the course. This dual effect was reinforced by our adaptation of "reading responses" to the Web. In years past, we asked students to choose a particular passage in the weekly reading, quote it, and make specific connections between the passage they cited and other course readings. They could discuss the relevance of the passage to their own experiences, but had to frame their ideas critically. I must admit I dreaded this aspect of the course, despite its considerable pedagogical value, because it inevitably became a logistical nightmare, trying to get more than one hundred responses, at first scrawled on note cards then later on word-processed sheets, collected, sorted by discussion groups, read by teams of student teaching assistants (TAs) who would be leading the small-discussion section for the week, and returned to the students. Having students post their reading responses to us via the Web site was an extremely convenient form of receiving, checking, and vetting a large number of responses.

More important, however, this Web posting of reading responses was public, so that students could read one another's responses. This created an instant, comprehensive public forum in which students wrestled with the material they had read. Although we did not insist that students read one another's responses, it was clear from postings in the Open Discussion (see below) that they did, and rather assiduously. The public nature of this pedagogical method may have inhibited some of the more extreme responses we had received in the past, when they had been private, but it also encouraged students to take more responsibility for their positions and their efforts. Students were on their toes when they knew they were being "checked out" by everyone else. Furthermore, the TAs and instructors could survey the entire class's responses, for a sense of the impact of certain readings or topics, and orient our discussion strategies accordingly.

For example, in the second week of the course, we launched into a consideration of the social construction of gender and race. The readings by Evelyn Brooks Higginbotham and Judith Lorber were complicated and demanding. We followed them up with a set of readings in our section "Doing Anti-racist, Anti-classist Work" that were more testimonial than the previous assignments, but concluded with Tessie Lui's complex meditation, "Teaching Differences among Women from a Historical Perspective." The reading responses for that week clearly indicated that most students grasped a constructed notion of gender but had trouble with what Higginbotham labeled "the metalanguage of race." Because we could easily survey the responses, we could pinpoint concepts students struggled with, ideas that riled them up, or notions they couldn't grasp, and adjust the topics for the group discussions. We could also identify which discussion group needed work in which area, and coach the TAs accordingly. One certainly does not need Web technology to accomplish the same kind of pedagogical oversight; the following year, the women's studies program decided to offer this course every term with a limited enrollment of thirty. The use of Web technology, however, transformed the reading responses from individual analytical exercises into public exercises with a wide range of pedagogical applications. More important, the transformation created another level of public space—localized and controlled—in which a diversity of student opinions could be aired.

An Example of the 'Real': Riot Grrls

For many of the class meetings, we worked from the course Web site. By this I mean that we had the Web site up on the large screen, and as we lectured, we linked to other sites, exploring their contents to enhance the materials presented in the lectures. Our most successful class in this regard was an exploration of "riot grrls" and their relationship to feminisms past and present, presented by guest lecturer Susan Marine, the coordinator of Dartmouth's Sexual Abuse Awareness Program. Susan used examples from music and a personal collection of rare riot grrl "zines" to bring to life for us not only the sounds but also the powerful, gut-level feminism of these women. In addition, she steered the class through the history and politics of riot grrls and other related girl groups, illustrated by their out there and in-your-face homepages. Throughout this presentation, Susan emphasized how subversive, countercultural, and politically empowering self-created homepages could be as sites for the expression of radically charged feminine and feminist subjectivity and sexuality—as well as feminist activism. During this class, I was struck by the continuity between theory and practice, traditionally seen as distinct from each other. These women used their sites to declare positions, especially on sexual violence against women, and urge action of a personal as well as a public and communal nature. Neither an abandonment of the real world for cyberspace, nor the moral detachment feared by critics as a consequence of cyberspace, was anywhere in evidence.

In an email conversation with Michelle Meyers after the class, Susan elaborated on the differences between the feminisms and feminist activism of riot grrls and other forms of feminism, such as ecofeminism, sex radical feminism, the feminism of Third World women, and that of women of color in the United States, which dominated our syllabus:

> I think those are essentially "academically developed" forms of fem-
> inism. riot grrl isn't about thought or deconstruction or close reflec-
> tion . . . most riot grrl musicians are high school dropouts . . . i think
> it's the rawest, purest form of feminism even tho it isn't very well
> thought out. it's getting in touch with that carnal sense of injustice
> as a gendered being and saying "fuck this, im not gonna take this."
> Is it lacking in multilayered understanding? yep! but it's raw and
> pure, i think, and still meaningful because of it.

Showing these sites allowed Susan to bring extremely powerful and,
in terms of our syllabus, unique feminist incarnations into the classroom, as well as explore links to other related sites of "indie" music for
a contextualized discussion of the politics of music production and
marketing. We saw how these sites give the particular grassroots politics of the riot grrl fanzines—their self-generated mode of communication—a high-tech immediacy and national range made possible only
by Web technology.

A challenge for our next version of the course would be to structure
a series of Web-based research questions or group projects that would
facilitate students' use of the Web as an information resource. These
assignments could specify a broad topic such as riot grrls, or women's
reproductive health, or a historical event, such as the 1851 Women's
Rights Convention in Akron, Ohio, at which Sojourner Truth gave—
or, according to Nell Irvin Painter, didn't give—her famous speech.
Using the Web would permit students to gather a wide array of information about the social, cultural, and political contexts of these events
from sources that might not be readily available in traditional forms.
We could also design Web exercises that are text centered, focusing
on specific historical documents or literary texts, and ask students to
produce hypertextual readings and analyses of texts, creating links to
an array of explanatory and corroborating materials, and producing
a "virtual-library effect." These innovations do not merely augment
interdisciplinary research; they produce new, nonlinear ways of knowing. Web technology would allow us to encourage students to do more
research on contemporary and international issues. For example, electronic bulletin boards have been crucial to the peace movement in
Croatia, in which women have played a central role (Wilding and
Critical Art Ensemble 58). The Web helps students gain access to and
participate in grassroots movements, such as riot grrls or the peace
movement in Croatia, which are largely ignored by the mainstream
press and in academic criticism. Despite their relative invisibility, these
movements exist at the cutting edge of feminist activism, unsettling a

strictly academic perspective, and reshaping the way we conceive of feminist politics.

The Open Discussion: Prototype for a 'Public Sphere'

The aspect of our Web-assisted course that most advanced feminist pedagogies was the Open Discussion. In cyberspeak, this was a disintermediated site for synchronous and asynchronous interaction—that is, an unrestricted public space for discussion of topics related to sex and gender in society. Although the site was open to contributors willing to identify themselves and easily accessible from the Dartmouth College homepage, mostly students in the course and some visitors posted comments. As the course instructors, we monitored and occasionally contributed to the discussion, but we did not guide or grade it. There were no rules for this site except the community standards that prevail at Dartmouth that we also enforce in our small-discussion sections: toleration and respect for diverse viewpoints. Students were not required to post a response in the Open Discussion. Some never did, while others contributed frequently. Nevertheless, as a localized version of a public sphere, this site played a crucial role in reinforcing the student-centeredness of the course experience.

Students who logged on to the Open Discussion contributed detailed and often passionate postings in response to several different stimuli: class reading assignments, class or section discussions, the postings of other students on the Open Discussion, or events on campus and in the nation that touched on issues of sex and gender. Some specifically indicated that they were responding "emotionally" to issues raised during class, differentiating their posting from a reading response, which had to be "critical." Thus, the Open Discussion had the effect of continuing, but also expanding, the conversation initiated by classroom lectures, the reading responses, and discussion sections on a less formal, more individualized basis. Several postings took off from the reading responses for that week. One especially controversial comment from a male student about gender equality began, "Im gonna toss this onto the table and see what happens." He had obviously read many reading responses that supported the notion of the social construction of gender; he argued against gender "sameness" and for a reconsideration of "nature" and "biology" in the shaping of gender differences. Although students argued vehemently against his ideas, they did not attack or dismiss him. Their responses were not flip or flaming, as comments sometimes are in online chat rooms or less formal email interactions. One student agreed with him, but argued

for a "celebration of 'natural' differences" of sex, gender, and race—
not exactly what he had in mind. These students were working out separate understandings of the material and defining positions for
themselves in response to other students' opinions.

In several postings, students expressed their sense that the Open
Discussion encouraged new, self-conscious kinds of intellectual/criti-
cal thought that went beyond the academic. For example, one student
began: "I was struck by a phrase in the Milton reading, "Paradise Lost"
[for a Gender and Religion class] but didn't think the RR [reading
response] was the right format for my comment." She went on to
quote the passage in book 4 in which Satan resolves to "excite" the
minds of Adam and Eve "with more desire to know, and to reject /
Envious commands, invented with designe / To keep them low whom
knowledge might exalt" (lines 522–25). She related God's command
forbidding Adam and Eve to eat of the Tree of Knowledge, which
Satan deliberately subverts, to a notion discussed in our readings about
education as a "commodity which has been intentionally withheld
from women and minorities," and concluded: "Perhaps ignorance
would have been bliss, but from my standpoint as a Chinese American
woman enrolled in a liberal arts college, I am grateful to Satan, that
first dark professor who introduced a commodity, education, far
greater than any soft mossy knoll or scented bower."

Another example illustrates the advantages of the disembodied virtuality of the public space created by a site such as the Open
Discussion. A woman visiting the class posted this comment after seeing "Dreamworlds II," a video critique by Sut Jhally that juxtaposes
MTV's representation of women with the gang rape scene in *The
Accused* (we always have a counselor on hand for this screening): "I pass
Ivy consoling a group of very upset women and she says to no one in
particular, 'What, no one wishes to stay and discuss.' And since I am
no one in particular I say, 'We wanted to leave and collect our
thoughts.' To discuss something like this we need, what is it called? A
safe place. And that place is not safe enough to discuss such things. Or
is it perhaps unsafe by virtue of the things we saw there? I am looking
for a safe place to collect my thoughts." This woman makes painfully
clear that the violence and hard revelations of Jhally's video rendered
the physical coed classroom an unsafe and uncomfortable place for
her, and other women, to discuss and debrief. She could not "revert"
to an analytical or critical mode, nor could she be fully emotional
there. But quite soon after the screening (judging from the rawness
of her reactions), she logged on to the Open Discussion to express that
powerful realization. Although it was the most public space of the

course, it felt "safer" to her then the classroom of her peers precisely because she could be quasi-anonymous and disembodied.

In reviewing the postings at the conclusion of the course, I found a similar trend: students were voluble in cyberspace on issues that elicited little or no commentary in class. For example, sexual orientation was a major issue in many of the readings and lectures. Although a selection on lesbian motherhood produced some shocked, resistant, but also sympathetic reading responses, students in class consistently avoided sexual orientation as a category of analysis and experience. When we asked students, in response to the final reading by Dorothy Allison, what were "the two or three things you know for sure" as a result of this course, many confidently cited issues of gender, race, ethnic identity, even class status, a category practically off limits at a place like Dartmouth. Not one person mentioned sexual orientation, as if that were the issue that these liberal, privileged young people wanted most to forget or deny. This attitude persisted, despite our unremitting efforts to frame issues from a queer perspective, and despite the presence in class of several out lesbians, gay men, and bisexuals, one of whom was an outspoken, shaven-headed (and thus, unmistakable) TA who, as a discussion leader, would have been familiar to all the students. However, a long thread of postings raised the question of the pervasive discrimination faced by gay, lesbian, bisexual, and transgendered people at Dartmouth and in society at large. In this conversation, students called one another out for essentialism, homophobia, insensitivity, tokenism, PC-ism, and apathy. They debated the effectiveness of action, and the differences between "anger" and "rage." They challenged and critiqued one another in ways that were inappropriate for discourse between professors and students. They took risky positions and defended them passionately. They had their say in ways inappropriate for class discussions, but essential for personal growth.

Although students were not anonymous in the Open Discussion, as one can often be in Web chat groups, the virtuality of their interaction provided enough disintermediation to produce a comparatively safer space in which to speak frankly and confront one another constructively—a hint of the "true reciprocity" with which we would like to characterize our feminist endeavors in the classroom and outside of it. Students who never spoke up in class and rarely made comments in discussion sections were brash and articulate. Colleagues who use or have studied the effects of online pedagogies and discussion sites confirm that these noticeably increase the participation of women and other silenced groups. This increase may result from the fact that

online interaction uniquely combines aspects of the aural and the textual. The speed with which one can communicate online lends it some
of the immediacy, informality, and frisson of face-to-face interactions
while suppressing some of FTF's potentially threatening or inhibiting
qualities, such as tone, depth or strength of voice, physical size or body
language, and facial expression. Aggression in cyberspace has to be
mainly textual, and in that realm, physicality is not necessarily a determining factor. However, the textual nature of these interactions—reading others' responses and formulating one's ideas in words—provides
a time lag that can promote a thoughtfulness we associate with written
interaction and want to preserve as we enter the media-drenched
twenty-first century.

Not only did the space of the Open Discussion allow students to
interact with one another; it also gave them a site for a collective experience—an important aspect of any women's studies course. In many
ways, this space was antithetical to the classroom: the usual "authority"
figures were not immediately visible, and students dominated. They
wrestled intellectually and emotionally with one another, in their own
time, not limited to the artificial and abbreviated class sessions three
times a week. We could monitor and join in, but it was definitely not
our space. Rather, it was a space where students had relatively equal
access (in the sense that they all had the software and hardware to log
on and a common set of questions and resources) and opportunity to
explore, debate, and learn from one another. In this sense, the Open
Discussion was a prototype of the democratic forums many of us hoped
and still hope the Web would provide—free from e-commercialism
and the unequal access to resources that presently contaminate it.

A Conclusion

Without much hard evidence, both Michelle and I *sensed* that our use
of Web technology, especially the creation of a virtual location for the
course, the posting of reading responses, and the Open Discussion,
created a new, potentially transformative public dimension for the
course. A majority of students reported in their final evaluations that
the Web interface was a "challenging" and "extremely valuable" aspect
of the course. A few were wildly enthusiastic, and a few were indiffer-
ent; no one dismissed it outright. But, of course, we were just sampling
some of the possibilities that Web technology makes available to educators, possibilities I am eager to pursue and expand. Before we sign
on wholeheartedly to this "revolution," however, we need to consider
more fully whether Web technology can advance feminist pedagogies.

Ultimately, this depends on one's attitude toward the Web's potential as a liberatory space.

It is indicative, I think, of our resistance to cyberspace that the Virtual On-line University includes on its menu of distance learning environments "a traditionally designed university campus" that can simulate FTF instructor-and-peer contact (Spender 137). The question arises—and it is one that feminists and media critics alike are asking about the entire so-called information revolution—why substitute a simulation when you can have the real thing? One very important reason, as WIEU points out in its Web-site rationale, is that many people, especially nontraditional female students worldwide, cannot physically come to a university. The organizers of WIEU argue that "electronic education holds the greatest hope and possibility for the Two-thirds World where poverty, isolation and gender bias disempower so many women. It is the first technology since the industrial age which has the potential to transcend class barriers." No longer a physical place, this electronic university is intended as "an experience" in employing the feminist values of "connection and collaboration between learners and mentors" that will empower women and democratize education. This is a large, and attractive, claim that founders on the problem of access to technology education and hardware—what has been called "the digital divide."

By emphasizing "connection and collaboration," WIEU's discourse about distance learning ties Web technology to a basic feminist perspective. Although the "new grammars" of links and hypertext are frequently associated with postmodernist modes of interstitiality and nomadism, with poststructuralist intertextuality and the rhizomatic imagery of theorists Gilles Deleuze and Félix Guattari (Joyce 5), it is difficult *not* to hear how descriptions of hypertext and simulated interactivity resemble the particularly feminine ways of thinking described by Carol Gilligan in her well-known study of women's moral development, *In a Different Voice.* Gilligan gives copious evidence that in approaching moral dilemmas, women have been conditioned to construct "a network of connection, a web of relationships that is sustained by a process of communication" (32). WIEU alludes to the pedagogic counterpart of Gilligan's work, "women's ways of knowing," to explain the student-mentor connection they feature: "These 'ways' are believed to be more collaborative and more friendly to the protection of earth and of life itself."

In several recent books and on the Web site Women Weaving Webs, inspired by Sally Helgesen's *The Female Advantage,* there is agreement that "communicating in cyberspace is particularly suited to women's

ways of acting—using cooperation, collaboration, sharing and constant communication" (http://www.women.weavingwebs.com/wom-
enweavingwebs.html). The assumption, which seems simplistic to me,
is that the current male domination of the Web is a result of social con-
ditioning that can be reversed. Spender makes a similar argument for
the feminist and democratic benefits of virtuality in her book *Nattering
on the Net: Women, Power, and Cyberspace.* She speculates that the "virtual
classroom has many distinct advantages" and may provide "the best
opportunity yet for solving the problem of boys getting more than
their fair share of teacher attention" (143). In her optimism, however,
she sidesteps her own conclusion that "when it comes to cyberspace,
men have the power" (xxiv)—that information technology as it has
developed and in the ways it is represented is a stereotypically masculine realm that reinscribes and may even intensify current offline ideologies of difference and power.

Spender's boosterism also ignores deeper concerns raised by such
self-proclaimed Luddites as James Brook and Iain A. Boal. In their collection, *Resisting the Virtual Life: The Culture and Politics of Information,*
they call for an intelligent resistance to "machine fetishism" and the
ritual worship of the "free market" and its analogous "free flow of information." From their materialist perspective, the flight to cyberspace
looks like "white flight" to the suburbs, where "hanging-out" in virtual
reality allows users to avoid the unpleasantness that may be going down
on their street corners or in their downtowns. They also question
whether it is not multinational corporations and global capitalism—
the very and already privileged few—that benefit most when we all get
on the "information superhighway." This loudly touted avenue offers
only some of us helpful prosthetic extensions at the same time that it
advances globalization at the expense of local communities and promotes alienated experiences that steamroll over cultural diversity.
Socialist feminist Zilla Eisenstein mounts a similar critique in her
recent book, *Global Obscenities: Patriarchy, Capitalism, and the Lure of
Cyberfantasy.* Not only is there a digital divide between those who have
access to the Web and those who do not, but the control of access to
information, she argues, is becoming more significant than the "fac-
tual" content of information. Furthermore, the way the "cyber-media-
corporate complex" controls and packages information on the Web
diverts us from the demise of democracy and advances new forms of
domination under the seductive banner of "freedom" rather than
equality (70). Paradoxically, she concludes, cyberspace also has the
potential to create new decentralized and unmediated public spaces
that can further the democratic process and facilitate progressive

activism. It is not yet clear whether the democratic potential of the Web is worth the risk posed by the proliferation and popularity of sites containing pornography, violence, hate speech, and the unchecked consumerism that e-commerce encourages.

It is important to remember that the use of Web technology as an adjunct to the classroom does not inevitably lead to virtual education. By extending the opportunities for student-centered interaction, we muted some of what we feel to be the hierarchical effects of the traditional, physical classroom. We can take this even further, still leaving open the question of whether and how Web technology can help to realize feminist and radical democratic goals by benefiting marginalized groups and changing dominant structures of power. Can this technology, despite the problems I have outlined, help to create, as Spender envisions, a "virtual sisterhood"? In determining the answer to this, we need to carefully distinguish the goals of social change from the loudly touted "liberation" offered by the Web, since we must always ask, Whose liberation and from what? If we accept Spender's argument that this technology is here to stay, then we can work on shaping the technology or demanding that it be shaped to serve specific ends. Introducing students, and especially large numbers of women and pro-feminist students, to the Web has the potential of making them informed users who can also become active resisters, critics, and even shapers of future cyberspace technology.

Technology, as feminists who work on reproductive technologies have found, while not politically neutral, is not inherently good or bad for women, the poor, or people of color. Its effects depend on who owns and controls it, who determines the trajectory of its development and its research agenda. At present, according to Faith Wilding, a member of Critical Art Ensemble and a feminist artist/activist since the early second wave, "real world social stratifications are, in general, reflected and replicated in cyberspace" (Wilding and Critical Art Ensemble 50). Attending the proceedings of the first Cyberfeminist International held in Kassel, Germany, in September 1997, Wilding reported that these self-declared cyberfeminists reject the two popular "utopic myths of the internet: that the Internet transcends hierarchies because there is a free interchange of information across boundaries and that the Net is ungendered so that you can create any way you want without regard to body and sex." On the contrary, they argue, "the Net is a contested zone" and is "not automatically liberating" (55). In order to see through the "cyberhype" of marketing, male-oriented software, and dumbed-down commercial sites for women, "women need to experiment in developing their own working and learning spaces in this postfeminist decolonization of cyberspace" (51).

Wilding, who enthusiastically embraces the new technology for art as well as for political organizing, nevertheless calls for a therapeutic and politically strategic and pedagogic "separatism" that would help women escape from "a false universal" and foster "a cyberspace of difference" as a means of undermining structures of domination (51). This sounds like second-wave arguments for separatism and consciousness-raising, but Wilding's use of the term *decolonization* suggests a cagey politics borrowed from and allied with postcolonial discourse. Homi Bhabha's theory of interstitiality makes claims for the contested spaces of colonialism that can be applied to the Web as a "terrain for elaborating strategies of selfhood—singular and communal—that initiate new signs of identity, and innovative sites of collaboration, and contestations, in the act of defining the idea of society itself" (1–2). Susan Damarin puts it more simply:

> There is a very real question as to whether the computer is so heavily valenced against feminist values . . . that it precludes the development of useful feminist approaches. . . . In some circles the question is regularly asked: "Are computers ultimately liberatory or are they essentially disempowering?" An answer is that computers will be whatever we make them. (367)

In other words, we and our students need to be savvy enough about Web technology to tell the cyberhype, which is inevitable, from the cyberfeminism, and demand or create it ourselves.[3]

Without being aware of its relevance to WS 10 online, we assigned as the final reading for the course Dorothy Allison's poignant memoir, *Two or Three Things I Know for Sure.* There are many ways in which Allison's text was a fitting conclusion for a course that investigated sex and gender in U.S. society. What I hadn't understood, until I began to formulate my ideas about our use of the Web in WS 10, was that Allison ends her meditation on storytelling as "an act of love" with a hypertext dream. She tells of being at a reading in Providence, Rhode Island, when two very intense young people approach her with the proposition of putting "everything you've every published . . . in hypertext" (90). "It's the latest thing," the thin young man says, but the young woman is beyond trends, transformed by hypertext's multidimensional nature: "'It's so beautiful,' she said. 'After a while it's like a skin of oil on water. If you look at it from above it's just one thing, water and oil in a spreading shape. But if you looked at it from the side, it would go down and down, layers and layers. All the stories you've ever told. All the pictures you've ever seen'" (91). Overwhelmed by the prospect, Allison demurs, but that night dreams of herself, aged and debilitated, walking through corridors, and coming finally to a brick wall that is composed of all the stories of her life. Touch one brick and it opens a window into that story. . . . I don't want to ruin with paraphrase the pleasure of reading this sequence. Suffice it to say that Allison's dream, while it acts out the very tensions in the idea and reality of women and the Web, also suggests new ways of looking at old truths that feminist educators and students will want to ponder, pursue, and shape to our collective needs and desires.

NOTES

An earlier version of this essay, inspired by my participation in the year-long Crossroads Project on Learning and Technology in the American Culture and History Classroom, appeared first online as "Putting Sex and Gender On-Line," <http://www.georgetown.edu/crossroads/conversations/>, and then in expanded and revised form in *Works and Days 31/32 Intentional Media: The Crossroads Conversations on Learning and Technology in the American Culture and History Classroom* 16, nos. 1 and 2 (1998): 347–72. I would like to thank Michelle Meyers; Sarah Horton, our tech expert; Susan Marine, our riot grrl; and all the students in WS 10, fall 1997, especially the TAs, and Tom Luxon, my personal computer troubleshooter.

1. hooks combines her early experience of black teachers with the feminist pedagogy of the early second wave and the ideas of Brazilian thinker Paulo Freire, whose work *Pedagogy of the Oppressed* has been influential in shaping radical notions of education. I cite hooks's work for its foregrounding of issues of race and class consciousness. For more accounts of feminist pedagogy, see Culley and Portuges; Gabriel and Smithson; Luke and Gore.

2. According to several recent commentators, "connectivity" in the form of communications technology, rather than information technology, is what distinguishes women's attraction to the Web. See the introduction to Hawthorne and Klein 5–6; Pollock and Sutton 35.

3. Guymer, who has pioneered online teaching in Australia, comes to similar conclusions, arguing that "we must acknowledge that not only can we influence cyberspace but we can develop a whole new way of using it so that women are included, interested and benefit from cyberspace" (75).

REFERENCES

Allison, Dorothy. *Two or Three Things I Know for Sure*. New York: Penguin Books, 1995.

Balsamo, Anne. "Feminism for the Incurably Informed." In *Flame Wars: The Discourse of Cyberculture*, ed. Mark Dery, 125–56. Durham: Duke University Press, 1994:

Bezucha, Robert J. "Feminist Pedagogy as a Subversive Activity." In *Gendered Subjects: The Dynamics of Feminist Teaching*, ed. Margo Culley and Catherine Portuges, 81–95. Boston: Routledge & Kegan Paul, 1985.

Bhabha, Homi. *Location of Culture*. New York: Routledge, 1994.

Brook, James, and Iain A. Boal, eds. *Resisting the Virtual Life: The Culture and Politics of Information*. San Francisco: City Lights Books, 1995.

Culley, Margo, and Catherine Portuges, eds. *Gendered Subjects: The Dynamics of Feminist Teaching*. Boston: Routledge & Kegan Paul, 1985.

Damarin, Suzanne. "Where Is Women's Knowledge in the Age of Information?" In *The Knowledge Explosion: Generations of Feminist Scholarship*, ed. Chris Kramarae and Dale Spender, 362–70. New York: Teachers College Press, 1992.

Eisenstein, Zilla. *Global Obscenities: Patriarchy, Capitalism, and the Lure of Cyberfantasy*. New York: New York University Press, 1998.

Freire, Paolo. *Pedagogy of the Oppressed*. Translated by Myra Bergman Ramos. New York: Continuum, 1970.

Gabriel, Susan L., and Isaiah Smithson, eds. *Gender in the Classroom: Power and Pedagogy*. Urbana: University of Illinois Press, 1990.

Gilligan, Carol. *In a Different Voice: Psychological Theory and Women's Development*. Cambridge: Harvard University Press, 1982.

Guymer, Laurel. "Online Teaching: No Fear of Flying in Cyberspace." In *CyberFeminism: Connectivity, Critique, and Creativity*, ed. Susan Hawthorne and Renate Klein, 362–70. Melbourne: Spinifex Press, 1999: 51–78.

Hawthorne, Susan, and Renate Klein, eds. Introduction to *CyberFeminism: Connectivity, Critique and Creativity*. Melbourne: Spinifex Press, 1999.

Higginbotham, Evelyn Brooks. "African-American Women's History and the Metalanguage of Race." *Signs* 17, no. 2 (1992): 251–74.

hooks, bell. *Teaching to Transgress: Education as the Practice of Freedom*. New York: Routledge, 1994.

Jhally, Sut. "Dreamworlds II: Desire, Sex, Power in Music Video." Amherst, Mass.: Media Education Foundation, 1991.

Johnson. Steven. *Interface Culture: How New Technology Transforms the Way We Create and Communicate*. New York: HarperCollins, 1997.

Joyce, Michael. *Of Two Minds: Hypertext Pedagogy and Poetics*. Ann Arbor: University of Michigan Press, 1995.

Liu, Tessie. "Teaching Differences among Women from a Historical Perspective: Rethinking Race and Gender as Social Categories. *Women's Studies International Forum*, 14, no. 4 (1991): 265–76.

Lorber, Judith. *Paradoxes of Gender*. New Haven: Yale University Press, 1994.

Luke, Carmen, and Jennifer Gore, eds. *Feminisms and Critical Pedagogy*. New York: Routledge, 1992.

Miller, Laura. "Women and Children First: Gender and the Settling of the Electronic Frontier." In *Resisting the Virtual Life: The Culture and Politics of Information*, ed. James Brook and Iain A. Boal, 49–57. San Francisco: City Lights Books, 1995.

Pollock, Scarlet, and Jo Sutton. "WomenClick: Feminism and the Internet."
  In *CyberFeminism: Connectivity, Critique, and Creativity*, ed. Susan Hawthorne
  and Renate Klein, 33–50. Melbourne: Spinifex Press, 1999.
Schib, John. "Pedagogy of the Oppressors?" In *Gendered Subjects: The Dynamics
  of Feminist Teaching*, ed. Margo Culley and Catherine Portuges. Boston:
  Routledge & Kegan Paul, 1985.
Spender, Dale. *Nattering on the Net: Women, Power, and Cyberspace*. Melbourne:
  Spinifex Press, 1995.
Stone, Allucquere Rosanne. "Will the Real Body Please Stand Up? Boundary
  Stories about Virtual Cultures." In *Cyberspace: First Steps*, ed. Michael
  Benedikt, 81–118. Cambridge: MIT Press, 1992.
Tannen, Deborah. *You Just Don't Understand: Women and Men in Conversation*.
  New York: Ballantine Books, 1990.
Virtual On-line University. Available: <http://www.wvu.edu/~womensu/>.
Wilding, Faith, and Critical Art Ensemble. "Notes on the Political Conditions
  of Cyberfeminism." *Art Journal* 57, no. 2 (summer 1998): 47–59.
Women's Electronic International University. Online. Available: <http//
  www.wvu.edu/~womensu>.
Women Weaving Webs. Online. Available: <http://women.weavingwebs.com/
  womenweavingwebs.html>.

SYLLABUS: INTRODUCTION TO WOMEN'S STUDIES— SEX, GENDER, AND SOCIETY

Michelle Meyers and Ivy Schweitzer

Unit 1: Genealogies

Week 1: Introduction

In-class video: *A Place of Rage*. By Pratibha Parmar. England, 1991.
  Women Make Movies, <http://www.wmm.com/catalog/pages/
  c287.htm>.

Week 2

A History of Women's Movements

Nancy Cott. Conclusion to *The Grounding of Modern Feminism*. New
  Haven: Yale University Press, 1989, pp. 271–83.
Betty Friedan. Epilogue to *The Feminine Mystique*. 20th anniversary ed.
  New York: Bantam Doubleday Dell, 1983, pp. 379–95.

Paula Giddings. "Preface: A History of Our Own"; "The Women's Movement and Black Discontent." In *When and Where I Enter: The Impact of Black Women on Race and Sex in America.* New York: Bantam Books, 1988, pp. 5–8, 299–324.

Toni Cade Bambara, foreword; Cherríe Moraga, preface; Kate Rushin, "The Bridge Poem"; Cherríe Moraga and Gloria Anzaldúa, introduction; Cherríe Moraga, "Refugees of a World on Fire: Foreword to the Second Edition"; Gloria Anzaldúa, "Foreword to the Second Edition." In *This Bridge Called My Back: Writings by Radical Women of Color,* ed. Cherríe Moraga and Gloria Anzaldúa. New York: Kitchen Table/Women of Color Press, 1981; 2d ed., 1983, pp. vi–viii, xiii–xix, xxiii–xxvi.

Intersectionalities I

Gloria Yamato. "Something about the Subject Makes It Hard to Name." In *Changing Our Power: An Introduction to Women's Studies,* ed. Jo Whitehorse Cochran, Donna Langston, and Carolyn Woodward. Dubuque, Iowa: Kendall-Hunt, 1988, pp. 3–6.

Peggy McIntosh. "White Privilege and Male Privilege: A Personal Account of Coming to See Correspondences Through Work in Women's Studies." In *Race, Class, and Gender: An Anthology,* ed. Margaret Anderson and Patricia Hill Collins. 2d ed. Belmont, Calif.: Wadsworth, 1995, pp. 76–87.

Audre Lorde. "The Master's Tools Will Never Dismantle the Master's House" (1979). *Sister/Outsider: Essays and Speeches.* Freedom, Calif.: Crossing Press, 1984, pp. 110–13.

Cherríe Moraga. "La Güera." In *This Bridge Called My Back: Writings by Radical Women of Color,* ed. Cherríe Moraga and Gloria Anzaldúa. New York: Kitchen Table: Women of Color Press, 1981; 2d ed., 1983, pp. 27–34.

Intersectionalities II

Lisa Kahaleole Chang Hall. "Eating Salt." In *Names We Call Home: Autobiography on Racial Identity,* ed. Becky Thompson and Sangeeta Tyagi. New York: Routledge, 1996, pp. 241–63.

June Jordan. "Report from the Bahamas." In *On Call: Political Essays.* Boston: South End Press, 1985, pp. 39–49.

Dorothy Allison. "A Question of Class" (1993–94). In *Skin: Talking about Sex, Class, and Literature.* Ithaca: Firebrand Books, 1994, pp. 13–36.

Unit 2: The Social Construction of Gender and Race

Week 3

The Social Construction of Gender

Judith Lorber. "'Night to His Day': The Social Construction of Gender"; "Seeing Is Believing: Biology and Ideology." In *Paradoxes of Gender.* New Haven: Yale University Press, 1994, pp. 13–54, 304–7.

Gloria Steinem. "If Men Could Menstruate." *Ms.,* October 1978.

Evening video: *Pumping Iron II: The Women.* Dir. George Butler, U.S.A., 1985.

The Social Construction of Race

Evelyn Brooks Higginbotham. "African-American Women's History and the Metalanguage of Race." *Signs* 17, no. 2 (1992): 251–74.

Tessie Liu. "Teaching Differences among Women from a Historical Perspective: Rethinking Race and Gender as Social Categories." In *Unequal Sisters: A Multicultural Reader in U.S. Women's History,* ed. Vicki Ruiz and Ellen Carol DuBois. 2d ed. New York: Routledge, 1994, pp. 571–83. (Originally published in *Women's Studies International Forum* 14, no. 4 [1991]: 265–76.)

Discussion 1

Unit 3: Gendered Systems of Knowledge

Week 4

Language

Deborah Tannen. *You Just Don't Understand: Women and Men in Conversation.* New York: Ballantine Books, 1990, chaps. 2, 3, 7; pp. 49–95, 188–215, 301–3, 306–7.

Gloria Anzaldúa. "How to Tame a Wild Tongue." In *Borderlands La Frontera: The New Mestiza.* San Francisco: spinsters/aunt lute, 1987, pp. 53–64, 96–97.

Evening video: *Battle for the Minds: A Film about Fundamentalism and Women.* Dir. Steven Lipscomb. PBS Point of View series, U.S.A., 1996.

Religion and Gender

King James Bible. Genesis 1–3, Corinthians.

John Milton. *Paradise Lost.* Books 4, 8.

Discussion 2

Unit 4: Sex and Sexualities

Week 5

Compulsory Heterosexuality

Adrienne Rich. "Compulsory Heterosexuality and Lesbian Existence" (1980). In *Blood, Bread, and Poetry: Selected Prose, 1979–1985.* New York: W. W. Norton, 1986, pp. 23–75.

Monique Wittig. "One Is Not Born a Woman" (1981). In *The Straight Mind and Other Essays.* Boston: Beacon Press, 1992, pp. 9–20, 101–2.

Sexualities

Amanda Udis-Kessler. "Notes on the Kinsey Scale and Other Measures of Sexuality." In *Closer to Home: Bisexuality and Feminism,* ed. Elizabeth Reba Weise. Seattle: Seal Press, 1992, pp. 311–18.

Evening video: *Forbidden Love: The Unashamed Stories of Lesbian Love.* Dir. Lynne Fernie and Aerlyn Weissman. Canada 1992, http://www.nfb.ca/FMT/E/MSN/30/30473.html.

Body Politics/Sexual Politics

Jason Shultz. "Getting Off on Feminism." In *To Be Real: Telling the Truth and Changing the Face of Feminism,* ed. Rebecca Walker. New York: Anchor Books, 1995, pp. 107–26.

Amber Hollibaugh and Cherríe Moraga. "What We're Rolling Around in Bed With: Sexual Silences in Feminism—a Conversation Toward Ending Them." In *The Persistent Desire: A Femme Butch Reader,* ed. Joan Nestle. Boston: Alyson, 1992, pp. 242–53. (Originally published in *Heresies* 12 [1981]).

Jeannine Delombard. "Femmenism." In *To Be Real: Telling the Truth and Changing the Face of Feminism,* ed. Rebecca Walker. New York: Anchor Books, 1995, pp. 21–33.

Pat Califia. "Public Sex" (1982). In *Public Sex: The Culture of Radical Sex.* Pittsburgh: Cleis Press, 1994, pp. 71–82.

Amber Hollibaugh. "Desire For the Future." In *Pleasure and Danger: Exploring Female Sexuality,* ed. Carole Vance. London: Pandora (1989) 1992, pp. 401–10.

Week 6

Discussion 3

Unit 5: The Reproduction of Gender and Sexuality in Popular Culture

The Beauty Myth

Naomi Wolf. "Culture." In *The Beauty Myth.* New York: Random House, 1990, pp. 42–64.

Wendy Chapkis. *Beauty Secrets: Women and the Politics of Appearance.* Boston: South End Press, 1986, pp. 37–58, 164–68.

Nellie Wong. "When I Was Growing Up." In *This Bridge Called My Back: Writings By Radical Women of Color,* ed. Cherríe Moraga and Gloria Anzaldúa. 2d ed. New York: Kitchen Table/Women of Color Press (1981) 1983, pp. 7–8.

Ekua Omosupe. "In Magazines (I Found Specimens of the Beautiful)." In *Making Face/Making Soul Haciendo Caras: Creative and Critical Perspectives by Feminists of Color,* ed. Gloria Anzaldúa. San Francisco: aunt lute books, 1990, p. 169.

Week 7

Advertising and Fashion

Sander Gilman. "Black Bodies, White Bodies: Toward an Iconography of Female Sexuality in Late Nineteenth-Century Art, Medicine, and Literature." In *"Race," Writing, and Difference,* ed. Henry Louis Gates, Jr. Chicago: University of Chicago Press, 1986, pp. 223–61.

bell hooks. Introduction; "Eating the Other." In *Black Looks: Race and Representation.* Boston: South End Press, 1992, pp. 1–7, 21–39.

Angela Davis. "Afro Image: Politics, Fashion, and Nostalgia." In *Names We Call Home: Autobiography on Racial Identity,* ed. Becky Thompson and Sangeeta Tyagi. New York: Routledge, 1996, pp. 87–91.

Evening video: *Dreamworlds II: Desire/Sex/Power in Music Video.* Dir. Sut Jhally. Amherst, Mass.: Media Education Foundation, 1991.

MTV

Tricia Rose. "Bad Sistas: Black Women Rappers and Sexual Politics in Rap Music." In *Black Noise: Rap Music and Black Culture in Contemporary America.* Middletown: Wesleyan University Press, University Press of New England, 1994, pp. 146–82, 210–12.

Discussion 4

Unit 6: Family Politics

Week 8

The Family in History

Friedrich Engels. *The Origin of the Family, Private Property, and the State* (1883). In *The Feminist Papers: From Adams to Beauvoir,* ed. Alice S. Rossi. New York: Bantam Books (1973) 1981, pp. 478–95.

Angela Davis. "The Legacy of Slavery: Standards for a New Womanhood." In *Women, Race, and Class.* New York: Vintage Books, 1983, pp. 3–29, 247–52.

Connie Young Yu. "The World of Our Grandmothers." In *Making Waves: An Anthology of Writing by and about Asian American Women.* Ed. Asian Women United of California. Boston: Beacon Press, 1989, p. 33–42.

Family Politics, 1950s/1990s

Betty Friedan. "The Happy Housewife Heroine"; "The Sexual Sell" (1963). In *The Feminine Mystique.* 20th anniversary ed. New York: Bantam Doubleday Dell, 1983, pp. 33–68, 206–32.

Barbara Ehrenreich. "Breadwinners and Losers: Sanctions Against Male Deviance." In *The Hearts of Men: American Dreams and the Flight from Commitment.* New York: Anchor Books, Doubleday, 1984, pp. 14–28, 184–85.

Ellen Herman. "Still Married after All These Years?" (1990). In *Front Line Feminism, 1975–1995: Essays from* Sojourner's *First Twenty Years,* ed. Karen Kahn. San Francisco: aunt lute books, 1995, pp. 175–82.

Discussion 5

Week 9

Gender and Poverty

Angela Davis. "Slaying the Dream: The Black Family and the Crisis of Capitalism." In *Women, Culture, and Politics.* New York: Random House, 1989, pp. 73–90.

———. "Racism, Birth Control, and Reproductive Rights." In *Women, Race, and Class.* New York: Vintage Books, 1983, pp. 202–21, 268–70.

Annelise Orleck. "'If It Wasn't for You, I'd Have Shoes for My Children': The Political Education of Las Vegas Welfare Mothers." In *The Politics of Motherhood: Activist Voices from Left to Right,* ed. Alexis

Jetter, Annelise Orleck, and Diana Taylor. Hanover, N.H.: University Press of New England, 1997, pp. 102–18.

Albelda, Randy. "The Misogyny of Welfare Reform: Corporate America's Cycle of Dependency" (1994). In *Front Line Feminism, 1975–1995: Essays from* Sojourner's *First Twenty Years,* ed. Karen Kahn. San Francisco: aunt lute books, 1995, pp. 121–25.

Evening film: *To Protect Mother Earth: Broken Treaty II.* Dir. Joel L. Freedman. New York: Cinnamon Productions, 1989.

Fighting to Protect Mother Earth: The Dann Sisters' Case

Shanley, Kate. "Thoughts on Indian Feminism." In *A Gathering of Spirit: A Collection by North American Indian Women,* ed. Beth Brant. Ithaca: Firebrand Books, 1988, pp. 213–15.

Discussion 6

Week 10

Queering the Family

Moraga, Cherríe. "Waiting in the Wings: Reflections on a Radical Motherhood." In *The Politics of Motherhood: Activist Voices from Left to Right,* ed. Alexis Jetter, Annelise Orleck, and Diana Taylor. Hanover, N.H.: University Press of New England, 1997, pp. 288–310.

Mulley, Linda. "Lesbian Motherhood and Other Small Acts of Resistance." In *The Politics of Motherhood: Activist Voices from Left to Right,* ed. Alexis Jetter, Annelise Orleck, and Diana Taylor. Hanover, N.H.: University Press of New England, 1997, pp. 311–21.

Brant, Beth. "A Long Story." In *A Gathering of Spirit: A Collection by North American Indian Women,* ed. Beth Brant. Ithaca: Firebrand Books, 1988, pp. 100–106.

Unit 7: Writing Lives

Local Lives (handouts from a collegewide study of students' lives conducted by the education department)

Week 11

Allison, Dorothy. *Two or Three Things I Know for Sure.* New York: Penguin Books, 1995.

Conclusion

Ivy Schweitzer *is an associate professor of English at Dartmouth College and past cochair of the women's studies program and also teaches in the comparative literature and Jewish studies programs.* Most recently, she has coedited The Literatures of Colonial America: An Anthology *with Susan Castillo and has joined the editorial board for the* Heath Anthology of American Literature. *She is currently working on a study of narratives of women's interracial friendships, titled* Milk Sisters.

Michelle Meyers *is an adjunct instructor of women's studies and the associate director of equal opportunity and affirmative action at Dartmouth College. Her teaching interests include women's studies, queer studies, and cultural studies.*

Teaching for Peace in a Digital Age

Asking 'What' and 'Why' of Technology

Lori E. Amy and Laura A. Milner

Across the country, educators are redefining ourselves in the wake of the 1996 Telecommunications Act, the presidential mandate to connect public schools to the national information infrastructure (NII), and in reaction to the subsequent Technology Literacy Challenge, a "national literacy challenge aimed to make all young Americans technologically literate by 2000" (Selfe 1999, 59). The mandate to ground education initiatives and reforms in the NII and global information infrastructure (GII) inevitably—and problematically—links education, technology, private sector business, and national and international politics and economics in unprecedented ways. At micro and macro levels, the changes in our professional and personal practices are enormous and frequently oppressive.

At the micro level, we are increasingly being told that we must use technology in our courses. If we do not, we are marked as "unqualified" to educate students for the technological challenges of the twenty-first century and hence as "unemployable." As a consequence, we are contorting our classes, our bodies, our energies, and our intellects to fit the shape of the technology designed not by and for us, but by and for corporate and political structures that are often at odds with the goals and purposes of education. We are prematurely being forced to fragment our time between computer labs and traditional classrooms; to rush to include technology components in our courses; and to frenziedly research and learn the rapidly developing education software packages churned out by private sector businesses eager to cash in on the technological literacy challenge. We are all caught in this race to attain technological literacy, a race in which Boards of Regents (BOR) need to secure funding for their institutions, administrators need to please the BOR, teachers need to keep our jobs, parents want their children to be marketable when they finish college, and students want good grades and good jobs.

It seems as though we are all rats about to topple off this wheel that is spinning faster than we can run. We must stop this frenetic motion, even if for just a few reflecting moments, and ask *what* we are doing in rooms dominated physically and spiritually by machines and *how* we are using the technologies culturally inscribing us. We must, as Cynthia Selfe argues, pay attention to the fact that "technology supports social divisions along race, class, and gender," that our uses of technology in the classroom are implicated in national and international politics and economics, and that, unless we critically analyze and actively shape our uses of technology, we are doomed to reinscribe the exploitative social and economic conditions in which we presently exist. This essay, then, is a gesture toward reflection. As two university professors of English confronting the micro-level changes brought by the technological literacy challenge at our institution, we pause to ask: What are we doing and why? And, more important, how can we work for positive productive social change (Selfe 1999, xxiii) through the technologies writing us?

Teaching for Peace

When Mary Rose O'Reilley taught the course War and the Modern Imagination in the early 1980s at St. Thomas University in St. Paul, Minnesota, she wanted to explore twentieth-century war literature with her students to see how we have all been marked by war, how the history or imminent possibility of violent confrontation defines us as humans. The course was inspired, in part, by a question she was asked by a professor in graduate school: "'Is it possible to teach English so that people stop killing each other?'" (O'Reilley 1993, 20). By studying poetry and fiction depicting war in the twentieth century, her students discovered "a progressive abandonment of the world of nature for the world of technology, radical dislocation of relationships between men and women, and the emergence of new attitudes toward religion and spirituality" (25). This study of the literature of twentieth-century war revealed that embracing technology almost always means rejecting the natural world.

O'Reilley's findings are especially important to American educators working under the technological literacy mandate at the beginning of the twenty-first century. Given the scope and magnitude of this mandate, it is imperative that we confront the larger social and cultural ramifications of the technologies we have been charged with integrating into our personal and professional lives. As Cynthia Selfe argues, "The real work facing teachers involves transforming our current limited discussions about technological literacy into more fully informed debates acknowledging the complex relationships between technology, literacy, education, power, economic conditions, and political goals. It is only after we have undertaken this work that we can make productive change" (xxi–xxii). Indeed, *without* this work we are *guilty* of enacting forms of violence through "unthought participation in political agendas" (Gastells 1997, 160).

Unfortunately, a critical consideration of our uses of technology is impeded by academia's bifurcated rhetoric pitting "technophiles" against "Luddites." Within this language, there are either technology enthusiasts or technology resisters, those who want to use it or those who do not. A critical confrontation with the impact of educational technologies on our lives requires that we first deconstruct this false binary: the question is not, Should we use computers? Rather, our multiple questions are, How will we use them, under what circumstances, and to what ends, and what does it mean when we choose to use them? Resisting technology is like building a wall of pebbles to block the ocean at high tide. We and our students *are* using computers for writing, research, and electronic communications, and we will continue to explore methods for using them to enhance communication and critical thinking. But asking what we are doing and why forces us to ask what good this technology is doing us and what it is costing us. This critical interrogation of the benefits and costs of technology that should be the hallmark of academic inquiry has been appallingly absent from the educational technology movement.

In the interests of critical inquiry, we ask in this essay: What is the computer—more specifically, our round-the-clock absorption in the (online) world—doing to us and our students? What is our addiction to and dependence on keyboard, screen, and modem doing to our bodies, minds, and souls, individually and collectively? How can we use educational technologies in ways that resist the cultural and economic violences out of which they evolve and in which they are complicit? What are the ways that these technologies might work as more than just instruments for skills learning and proficiency demands requisite to the education of privileged students in an advanced technological culture? Is it possible to use educational technologies not just to increase the advantage of the privileged few, but also for the humanistic education necessary for individuals to live peacefully and hence to act for the mutual good of people across the globe and for the world we all share?

Technology's Costs: What We Need to Be Afraid Of

In the tradition of bell hooks and Paulo Freire, *teaching* means creating a space where every voice is heard and valued; where students read and respond to a variety of texts, including one another's, on paper and online; where the room is arranged in a way that decentralizes authority and supports a collaborative, dynamic center where "something can rush in, something we did not plan and cannot control" (O'Reilley 1998, 6); where students and teachers, male and female, gay and straight, urban and rural, black, white, and "other" can see and hear and begin to know and, hopefully, respect and value one another. In the best of cases, our classrooms, like the educational journey itself, can constitute sacred space; in them, we can create what O'Reilley calls "islands of quiet" where each of us is able to sit or write in silence. Indeed, for many of our students, the classroom "may be the only site of reflection" (7) in their day. Our classrooms may be one of the few safe, quiet places where students can tell the stories that are "caught in [their] throats" and blocking their spirits' "longing to participate in the world" (25). In the peaceable classroom O'Reilly advocates, students have time for silence, for examining texts, for reflecting on what they know and what others know, and ultimately, for asking the questions that will move them closer to what they need to discover. Often, what students need to discover does not necessarily conform to the agenda the university curriculum dictates. As O'Reilley notes,

> Struggling for identity in a materialistic culture, young people run the risk of becoming robots. . . . In leisure hours students deliver their brains to the Walkman and their hands to the controls of video games. At school they present themselves as passive vessels to be filled by the lecturer; they "interface" with computers, and in a variety of "learning labs" they are willingly plugged in and turned on. At what point do they stumble on an inner life? When do they discover the questions of the heart and the leadings of the intuition? (1993, 32)

Our classrooms, then, can be a site of the silence and reflection necessary for all those gestations of self through which we grow as individuals and from which we act in the world. Without inner retreat, how can we progress? Without silent spaces, how can we begin to hear our own voices, much less anyone else's? And without doing this, how can we move into the world and act for the good of it? In more than twenty years of teaching, O'Reilley has discovered that "if we allow enough quiet, a diversity of voices begins to be heard" (7). If we don't allow for the silence of reflection, we risk chaos and ultimately death: of the individual spirit, of the community, and of the earth. Teaching for *human being*, then, requires that we take notice of the here and now; *be in this* time, in *this* place, with *these* students and texts. Our uncritical and unthought participation in the technology infusion can obstruct our ability to pay full attention to where we *are*. When computer technology, not individuals and voices, directs the classroom, what are we teaching?

And computerized technology, no matter how we resist or subvert it, *is* implicit in the corporatization of the university. Everything from the Internet browsers installed on our PCs to the software that students use for word processing entails global economic and political implications. For instance, as a condition of receiving Microsoft grant money to develop their technology infrastructure, academic departments and sometimes entire campuses are prohibited from using Netscape browsers and other competitors' software. This is just one of the many examples of corporations "investing hundreds of millions of dollars in the infrastructure for new media they hope will make them billions of dollars" in the long run (Rheingold, qtd. in Selfe 1999, 31). This is the insidious loop in which the national technology mandate, educational technology infusion, and the booming technology business combine to inscribe even the best-intentioned of us in cycles of exploitation, oppression, and global imperialism. We are, as Chellis Glendinning (1999) describes us, a "newly colonized" people enslaved by technology:

> How deeply and yet subconsciously [we] inhale and exhale the breath of empire: technoglobalization is in the air! Just as the lord of yesterday's dominion controls the servant's every move, so the machines tell the newly colonized when to get up, what to wear, how to lift their thighs to achieve a sculptured look. Machines do everything for them from chopping vegetables to reporting their financial options. They are accessorized in wearable chips interlocking them to every electronic device in the house—cell phone, digital assistant, beeper, personal stereo, vacuum cleaner. . . . [C]omputers dictate their schedules, and they need computers to keep up the pace. . . . The whole thing is maddening, disorienting, beyond the capabilities of human nerve cells to withstand. And so the newly colonized take drugs. Uppers. Downers. In-betweeners. Tea from India. Coffee from the former colonies. Prozac. Sugar. Codeine. Heroin. Valium. Cocaine. (117–18)

In a Dark Room, with No Windows and No Walls, but Working for a Way Out Anyway

There are, clearly, real dangers to our uncritical infusion of technology across the curriculum and throughout our lives. But we are already inscribed in them, and there is no way to unwrite the history that has led us to this point. Our question, then, is, *How* do we use technology? To acknowledge the problems inherent in the technologies we are using and then to move beyond them is not to dismiss these problems; rather, it is to ask: How can we, operating from within our American university sites of (relative) privilege, act? How can we teach, live, and function through and with the technologies that write our lives and culture so that we resist inasmuch as we can the multiple violences inherent in the evolution and deployment of these technologies and on behalf of global justice and women's rights? (Amy 2000a).

Using the Internet and digital technologies for global justice and women's rights requires a two-tiered approach. We must begin in the here and now, at the local level. But we must also connect the local to the global, link the lived experience of our daily lives to the larger worlds in which we live. In our classrooms, we can give students the opportunity to sit down and reflect, to find a coherent language developed with logic and compassion, heart and mind, with which to express themselves, and then to come together with their classmates to dialogue about what they are discovering through their writing. That's something we can give them in fifty-minute segments: opportunities to connect with themselves and others who are breathing the same air, reading the same text, angling for the same grade. A crucial part of our teaching is to facilitate students' access to their inner lives, to a deeper sense of personal meaning.

But we must also show students how to use available technologies to turn the meanings they develop and the futures they imagine into *action* in the world. In part, this means opening them to differences, to a more nuanced understanding of global social, political, and economic contexts. Often, our classrooms are too monolithic, and in them we and our students do not always have the possibility of meeting or hearing the points of view of the myriad wo/men marked as "other" in the dominant white patriarchal culture in which we live. And if, in our predominantly white and all too patriarchal universities, we do find ourselves in classes with the "other," we cannot assume that the "other" will be willing and or able to voice "difference" within the multiple and conflicting power zones of the classroom. Developing empathetic connections that allow us all to know and value one another, in all our differences, is thus a hit-and-miss and always difficult task. Even with the best-case scenario of a multiethnic classroom that forms empathetic bonds, though, how do we enable students to generalize the empathy they develop in the classroom to the larger world, and, even more crucially, *to action in the world?*

Especially in the context of Western technoimperialism, mobilizing students to conscientious action *in the world* is imperative if we hope to educate a citizenry interested in something more than maintaining their own individual levels of comfort (comfort enabled by the technologies structuring our lives), security (financially linked to the growth of transnational corporations), and individual well-being (inevitably purchased through the exploitation of the disenfranchised workers picking our coffee beans, making our clothes, working in NAFTA and GATT factories[1]). Our classrooms must open students to their full potential as human beings, and part of this opening is an opening to the responsibilities of citizenship in a world structured by the multiple violences of "a post-colonial world characterized by the growth of transnational corporations, a Western information economy exporting material production to third world sites, an inexhaustible number of goods produced with exploited third-world, immigrant, and child labor, and a dramatic increase in the numbers of people in this country living below the poverty line" (Amy 2000b, 54–55).

We must ask, then, how we can use information and educational technologies to make our classrooms the site of the healthy conversation and dialogue that English-composition theorist Kenneth Bruffee (1997) says is essential to the process of writing and maturing, of naming and knowing ourselves and others. In order to "think well as individuals we must learn to think well collectively—that is, we must learn to converse well. The first steps to learning to think better, therefore, are learning to converse better" (399). These conversations may occur in person or online, perhaps both: "We establish knowledge or justify belief collaboratively by challenging each other's biases and presuppositions; by negotiating collectively . . . new paradigms of perception, thought, feeling, and expression; and by joining larger, more experienced communities of knowledgeable peers through assenting to [their values]" (405). This process of challenging paradigms is crucial, for, as Gillian Young (1999) points out, we are bounded by the knowledges that construct us. "Boundaries of many kinds shape the processes by which knowledges are developed and established, understood and communicated. These boundaries are physical, organizational and symbolic" as well as ideological and potentially threatening in their ability to limit our lines of inquiry (56–58).

Henry Giroux (1992) calls for just such a practice of challenging paradigms, one in which public intellectuals "engage pedagogical practice as a form of cultural politics" (2). He insists on a "theoretical practice by which to engage in forms of transgression that challenge knowledge and social relations structured in dominance" (22). This means, ultimately, a collective remaking of knowledges, a reorganization of the boundaries of knowledge and hence of the identities corollary to knowledge structures. Strategic instructional uses of the Internet and electronic communication can provide one avenue for these boundary crossings that are essential to our collective growth. These technologies allow countless individuals and groups to produce, publish, and disseminate information about their experiences, values, beliefs, and knowledges and social, political, and economic conditions. Thus, they can greatly expand our ability to question our own knowledge bases and to critically interrogate the ways in which we are constructed by them and complicitous in larger global violence through them.

We must acknowledge that there is no "innocent" use of these technologies—they evolved through and in the interests of an elite and oppressive power structure. Acknowledging this, we can conscientiously develop strategic (and subversive) uses of new technologies, such as the Internet, that can help us to challenge the limits of the knowledges constructing our identities. Using the World Wide Web, our students can access the Web sites of social activist and human rights organizations. And, creating their own Web sites as writing projects, students can connect the insights gained in the classroom to the larger world they inhabit. Through Web-based reading and writing projects, our classes can begin the "collective knowledge-building and strategizing in circumstances which can connect local and global sites and issues" (Young 1999, 60). Web projects bring students' writing out of the classroom and into the world: they can enable students to organize social action through email discussion groups, letter writing campaigns, and participation in and initiation of support groups. Students can also publish their own narratives and research. Because students own and use their Web sites in ways that exceed the temporal limits of the classroom and overturn the teacher as primary audience/consumer/judge of student writing, they can use their writing to refigure the traditional institutional relationship between knowledge and power.

Several students in a recent freshman composition course at Georgia Southern University developed a wide range of Web sites demonstrating the possibilities that Web projects hold for our teaching. Students were asked to develop final projects that situated issues vital to their own lives within larger social, cultural, and historical contexts. In one particular instance, an African American woman struggling with racism created a Web site, Sister to Sister, for herself and other "young black women in the world . . . [who] . . . need to be motivated and told that they can achieve success just as well as the next man" (Burks 2000). As Burks says, many "young black women degrade themselves and they live by the standards that other people set for them." Because of this, she wanted to create a site that would "allow these women to see how other successful black women" had "paved the way for them" and to "inspire young black women like [herself] to regain possession of their lives and continue to pave the dirt road that [their] ancestors started. In other words, take authority!" (Burks 2000 online).[2]

We can also help students to connect their individual lives and local sites to the larger world in which we all live through projects such as the United Nations CyberSchoolBus and the Network of Educators on the Americas (NECA). These educational Web sites allow us to engage our students with writing in the interests of social justice. For instance, the aims of the United Nations CyberSchoolBus project are to

1. Create an on-line global education community;
2. Create educational action projects to show students that they have a role in finding solutions to global problems;
3. Give students a voice in global issues;
4. Provide high-quality teaching resources to a wide range of educators in a cost-effective manner (United Nations CyberSchoolBus 2000b).

Specifically targeting youth across the world, the United Nations Human Rights Project is collecting "inspiring stories of classes or schools defending and promoting human rights in their own communities, neighborhoods and cities." Many of these stories then "become part of a global atlas of student actions compiled and published on the World Wide Web by the UN CyberSchoolBus." The hope underlying this project is that "by bringing together the stories of student action," the site will become "a resource that will provide concrete examples to emulate and will inspire new and original actions" (United Nations CyberSchoolBus 2000a). Similarly, the NECA is a nonprofit "organization that promotes peace, justice, and human rights nationwide through critical, anti-racist, multicultural education" (NECA 2000).

Still in the Dark Room, Still Looking for the (Impossible) Way Out

Using the technologies available to us to engage students with projects such as these opens up possibilities for resisting the violences out of which these technologies emerge and that they can all too easily reinscribe. Computer literacy is a much needed skill, "but it cannot solve our many social and cultural problems, let alone all the world's problems as some 'technophiliacs' want us to believe" (Inayatullah and Milojevic 1999, 82). Indeed, the material conditions of the technologies forcing our pedagogies at times exacerbate these problems. When we are uncritically forced into badly designed rooms infused with the heat and hum of machines, the tyranny of technology that says "click here to connect," "click there to join the global community," then students can become nameless, faceless bodies emitting strings of typed characters with little room for white space, little room for tone and gesture. These dangers are especially apparent in email communications that, as Sohail Inayatullah and Ivana Milojevic argue, can give "the mirage of connection and community" (82). One of the real dangers of email and other forms of electronic communication is that, unless there is occasional face-to-face communication, they "can transform friendships into antagonistic relationships" (77).

Indeed, the entire terrain of "relationship"—to one another, to information, to meaning—is especially crucial to a consideration of gender and technology. At one level, as Inayatullah and Milojevic argue, "just as words lose the informational depth of silence, E-mail loses information embedded in silence and face to face gestures" (77). And "as the urgent need to respond to others quickens," we lose the ability to assimilate and reflect on what we have read; what we are saying; what we, together, might *mean*. We lose "the intuition and insight needed to make sense of intellectual and emotional data" (77). In this high-speed data-driven environment, "women's time, slow time, lunar time, spiritual timeless time, cyclical rise and fall time and circular seasonal time, are among the victims, leading to temporal impoverishment, a loss of temporal diversity where 'twenty-first century' as a temporal demarcation is for all, instead of peculiar to Western civilization" (Inayatullah and Milojevic 1999, 77).

Thus, while the Internet can connect the local with the global, it also "repeats a specific form of cultural violence. While it intends to create a global community of equals, making identification based on age, looks, race, (dis)ability, class or gender become less relevant, it also, by promoting, enhancing and cementing current ways of communicating, silences billions of people" (82). The language of the Internet "prevents all other forms of knowing and experiencing this world. There is little space for communicative poetry, and for feeling what is unsaid, for reading other signs, for weaving with another presence" (82).

In order to use these technologies in the interests of our students and for the good of our society, then, *we*, not school administrations and private enterprises, need to choose when to focus on the local, when to connect to the global. As feminist poet Marge Piercy (1979, 497) reminds us in "Right to Life," "Without choice, no politics, no ethics lives." In all our classes, and especially liberal arts classes, aren't we teaching ethics and politics? English teachers know especially well, as Ann Berthoff argues in *The Making of Meaning*, that the act of composing is all about choosing what to include and what to omit. Indeed, Berthoff goes so far as to argue that the extent to which we are free is determined by the extent to which we are able to choose. As teachers, *we* need to choose when to come together to sit at this desk, in this circle, writing our lives, practicing being here. And we need to choose which technologies we will use, when, how, and why.

English and language arts educators at all levels cannot afford to abandon poetry and silence, and we cannot afford to ignore the real life around us. Nor can we forget that the real lives around us are often suffering the injustices of the political and economic systems we inhabit and, by virtue of our nonrecognition, help to maintain. If our pedagogies are committed to *recognizing* others and *acknowledging* inequalities and differences, we might just be able to mine the potential of the Internet and electronic communications for positive productive social change. The reports through email and Internet channels of the Zapatistas' challenge to the official government of Mexico and South Africa's Truth and Reconciliation Commission's Web site provide two telling examples of the transformative potential of textual production and dissemination in the digital age. The Zapatistas, members of an indigenous population of Mexico, used the Internet and global communications technologies to gain international support in their successful uprising against the Mexican government's oppressive policies toward the Indians. Similarly, South Africa's Truth and Reconciliation Commission's Web site both disseminates information and invites readers to contribute to the Web site: it hosts an email register for readers around the world to publicly mourn the emotional, spiritual, and intellectual effects of apartheid. This proliferation of Web-based information constitutes an immediate and up-to-the-minute "text."

Clearly, those of us who are committed to critical pedagogies that call for education as liberation must remain aware of the limits to which we can engage students with themselves, one another, or the larger world. We must demand the right to critically interrogate the structures, purposes, and motives of technology in our classrooms, and we must play an active role in shaping our technology infrastructure and policy. Those of us who see learning as a road to self-actualization for students and teachers—and self-actualization as a process that can build hope and lead to meaningful lives—must critique the presence and uses of computers in our classrooms and confront the impact of educational technologies on our lives. It is only through this critical interrogation that we can freely choose teaching strategies that can create classrooms for peace- and knowledge-making, not war- and data-mongering.

NOTES

1. NAFTA is the acronym for the North American Free Trade Agreement; GATT, the General Agreement on Tariffs and Trade.
2. See <http://www2.gasou.edu/facstaff/lamy/studproj.html> for the language/world project description and a sample of student projects.

REFERENCES

Amy, Lori. 2000a. "The Internet and Feminist Activism: Changing Cultural Narratives of Memory and Identity." Paper presented at the "Computers and Composition" conference, Fort Worth, Texas.

———. 2000b. "Violent Matters, Classroom Practices: Teaching Etel Adnan's *Sitt Marie Rose*." *Concerns* 23, no. 4: 54–72.

Berthoff, Ann E. 1981. *The Making of Meaning: Metaphors, Models, and Maxims for Writing Teachers*. Montclair, N.J.: Boynton Cook.

Brufee, Kenneth. 1997. "Collaborative Learning and the 'Conversation of Mankind.'" In Victor Villanueva, Jr., ed., *Cross-Talk in Composition Theory*. Urbana, Ill.: National Council of Teachers of English (NCTE).

Burks, Latoya. 2000. "Sister to Sister." Online. Available: <http://www2.gasou.edu/student/gsi22631/prop.html>. May 29.

Gastells, Manuel. 1997. *The Power of Identity*. Vol. 2 of *The Information Age: Economy, Society, and Culture*. Oxford: Blackwell Publishers.

Glendinning, Chellis. 1999. *Off the Map: An Expedition Deep into Imperialism, the Global Economy, and Other Earthly Whereabouts*. Boston and London: Shambhala.

Giroux, Henry. 1992. *Border Crossings: Cultural Workers and the Politics of Education*. New York: Routledge.

Inayatullah, Sohail, and Ivana Milojevic. 1999. "Exclusion and Communication in the Information Era: From Silences to Global Conversations." In Wendy Harcourt, ed., *Women@Internet: Creating New Cultures in Cyberspace*, pp. 76–90. London: Zed Books.

Network of Educators on the Americas (NECA). 2000. Homepage. Online. Available: <http://www.teachingforchange.org/>. May 29.

O'Reilley, Mary Rose. 1993. *The Peaceable Classroom*. Portsmouth, N.H.: Boynton/Cook Publishers, Heinemann.

———. 1998. *Radical Presence: Teaching as Contemplative Practice*. Portsmouth, N.H.: Boynton/Cook Publishers, Heinemann.

Piercy, Marge. 1979. "Right to Life." In Pamela J. Annas and Robert C. Rosen, eds., *Literature and Society: An Introduction to Fiction Poetry, Drama, Nonfiction*, 2d. ed. Englewood Cliffs, N.J.: Prentice Hall.

Selfe, Cynthia. 1999. *Technology and Literacy in the Twenty-First Century: The Importance of Paying Attention.* Carbondale: Southern Illinois University Press.

United Nations CyberSchoolBus. 2000a. "Human Rights in Action." Online. Available: <http://www.un.org/Pubs/CyberSchoolBus/humanrights/about/about.htm>. May 29.

———. 2000b. "Mission Statement." Online. Available: <http://www.un.org/Pubs/CyberSchoolBus/homepage/miss.html>. 29 May 2000.

Young, Gillian. 1999. "Virtual Voices: Real Lives." In Wendy Harcourt, ed., *Women@Internet: Creating New Cultures in Cyberspace,* pp. 55–68. London: Zed Books.

Lori E. Amy, *assistant professor of writing and linguistics at Georgia Southern University, specializes in narrative and discourse theory, particularly theories of narrative, memory, and trauma. Her teaching and research interests include writing for social justice and critical pedagogy, feminist and psychoanalytic theory, and cultural studies. She has published several articles analyzing the discourses of social violence and is currently working on a book,* Letters to My Father, *that examines the ways in which families of military men inherit the violences of war.*

Laura A. Milner *is an assistant professor in the Department of Writing and Linguistics at Georgia Southern University. Her teaching, poetry, and writing are informed by her Zen practice and her passion for truth-telling; as a doctoral student in composition at Indiana University of Pennsylvania, she is exploring the role that writing plays in personal and cultural healing and peacemaking.*

Cyberfeminism and Technoculture Studies

An Annotated Bibliography

Sidney Eve Matrix

The number of courses in women's studies that focus on gender and computer technologies is steadily increasing. In response, what follows is an annotated bibliography of resources contributing to this curriculum. The bibliography is divided into five sections, with the largest collection of texts falling into the categories of cyborg theory and cyberspace. Also included are sections on technoculture and the genetic revolution, and a final category of work on new medical imaging technology and visual electronic culture. The selections included do not constitute an exhaustive bibliography on these subjects, but rather are representative of recently published texts in the emerging fields of cyberfeminism and technoculture studies. The majority of writings described below are anthologies, although works by single authors are also included, as are student-authored online texts.

Keywords

The following list of keywords is useful for cross-referencing texts in the bibliography that follows, and for searching library and online indexes for related resources: biotechnology, cyberculture, cyberfeminism, cyberpunk, cybersex (or "tinysex"), cyberspace, cyborg, digital, embodiment, feminism, genetics, gender, Haraway, imaging,informatics, Internet, postfeminism, posthuman, reproductive technology, science fiction, technoculture, technofeminism, technoliteracy, technology, virtual reality.

Technoculture

Bell, David, and Barbara M. Kennedy, eds. *The Cybercultures Reader*. New York: Routledge, 2000. Highly recommended for classroom use, this anthology contains forty-eight (reprinted) essays organized into nine sections, including cyberfeminisms, cybersubcultures,

cyberbodies, cybersexuality, and cybercolonization. Lengthy intro-
ductions to the volume and to each section synthesize the wealth of
material. As with other Routledge readers, this volume collects the
canonical and emerging scholarship that is defining the field.
Authors include Donna Haraway, Arthur and Marilouise Kroker,
Vivian Sobchack, Scott Bukatman, Andrew Ross, Sadie Plant,
Claudia Springer, Chela Sandoval, Anne Balsamo, Jennifer
González, Lisa Cartwright, Ananda Mitra, and Lisa Nakamura
among others. Indexed and illustrated.

Conley, Verena Andermatt, ed. *ReThinking Technologies*. Minneapolis:
University of Minnesota Press, 1993. Collection of twelve pieces with
speculation on the relationships between science and culture,
technology and the environment, science and the arts. Presents a
"complex rapport" between postmodern and poststructural
humanities-based theory (including psychoanalysis), technoscientific discourses and practices, and artistic expression. Includes work
by Paul Virilio, Felix Guattari, Katherine Hayles, Teresa Brennan,
and others. Advocates increased cross-disciplinary dialogue and the
development of technoliteracy to avoid the extremes of technode-
terminism or technofetishism. Philosophical tone of the pieces
derives from their engagement with Martin Heidegger's "The
Question Concerning Technology."[1] Includes sections on cyberspace, virtual reality, cybernetics, and virtual embodiment. For
another philosophical view of technoculture and cyberspace, see
Michael Benedikt, ed. *Cyberspace: First Steps*. Cambridge: MIT Press,
1994.

Hopkins, Patrick D., ed. *Sex/Machine: Readings in Culture, Gender, and
Technology*. Bloomington: Indiana University Press, 1998. Thesis of
volume is that technology, gender, and culture are interlinked, such
that (for instance) computers and the Internet can be used as tools
to reify or transgress/rewrite gender norms. Twenty-seven (mostly
reprinted) articles, including work by Sherry Turkle, Donna Haraway,
Allucquére Rosanne (Sandy) Stone, Judith Halberstam, Autumn
Stanley, Suzanne Kessler, Kathryn Morgan, Janice Raymond, and
Claudia Springer. Topics covered include surgical construction of
gender, artificial reproduction technologies, cyborgicity, bioethics,
cybersex, computer-mediated communication technologies, and
others. Highly recommended as course reader.

Penley, Constance, and Andrew Ross, eds. *Technoculture*. Minneapolis:
University of Minnesota Press, 1991. Collection of thirteen essays
argues for the importance of developing cultural "technoliteracy"
by examining various discourse communities including hackers,

cyberpunks, and computer programmers. See especially "Cyborgs at Large: Interview with Donna Haraway"; Haraway's companion piece, "The Actors Are Cyborg, Nature Is Coyote, and the Geography Is Elsewhere"; and Valerie Hartouni, "Containing Women: Reproductive Discourse in the 1980s."

Terry, Jennifer, and Melodie Calvert, eds. *Processed Lives: Gender and Technology in Everyday Life.* New York: Routledge, 1997. Twenty-three contributions ask: How can technology be used to transform cultural conceptions of gender and embodiment? Considers contradictions inherent in women's ambivalent relationship to science and machines, understood as a "complex territory" between pleasure/desire and fear/suspicion of technology. Notable essays by Margaret Morse and Sara Diamond on virtual embodiment and gender politics in cyberspace; by Lisa Cartwright and Evelynn Hammonds on imaging technologies and the production of gendered and racial identities, bodies, and cultural norms. Includes work by female technoartists interpreting intersections between sexuality, gender, bodies, and technoscience. Seventy illustrations and images.

The Women's Research Group, eds. *Desire by Design: Body, Territories, and New Technologies.* London: I. B. Taurus, 1999. Sixteen essays bring together cyberfeminists (see especially Technowhores' Manifesto) with digital media artists; software and graphic designers; and feminist theorists and historians of space, architecture, and science to consider how gender factors into design decisions and principles. Contributors critically and creatively celebrate and interrogate how new design technologies are being utilized and consider how these (material, conceptual, and virtual) processes and practices can upgrade our current thinking about gender, the body, nature, identity, space, diaspora, and difference.

Wood, John, ed. *The Virtual Embodied: Presence, Practice, Technology.* New York: Routledge, 1998. Seventeen chapters in this volume ask, "What is 'human nature' in a technocentric era of globalized capital and consumerism?" Employs the concept of embodiment to consider (in theoretical essays, often heavily illustrated) how "nature" gets constructed and sold, to examine the claims of freedom and autonomy inherent in virtual reality, to analyze how "information," knowledge, and data are constructed and circulated. Considers technoethics, techno-utopianism, and other philosophical issues. Volume is intentionally "provocative" and editors (un)apologetically admit that "some of our perceptions . . . must remain implicit." Similar to Women's Research Group, *Desire by Design,* and Terry and Calvert, *Processed Bodies* (annotated above), this volume includes work by (mostly female) technoartists and creative writers. For additional philosophical writing on techno-utopianism, see Richard Coyne, *Technoromanticism: Digital Narrative, Holism, and the Romance of the Real.* Cambridge: MIT Press, 1999.

Cyborg Theory

Balsamo, Anne. *Technologies of the Gendered Body: Reading Cyborg Women.* Durham, N.C.: Duke University Press, 1996. Poststructural feminist analysis of cultural-technical processes/practices and discourses that construct the body as a gendered entity. Includes chapters on bodybuilding, cosmetic surgery, artificial reproduction technologies, and virtual reality. Views these activities as cyborg technologies, insofar as Haraway suggests that they denaturalize modes of gender embodiment. Also analyzes science fiction, cyberpunk, and biomedical discourses to unearth the assumptions and equations about gendered embodiment present there.

Braidotti, Rosi, and Nina Lykke, eds. *Between Monsters, Goddesses, and Cyborgs: Feminist Confrontations with Science, Medicine, and Cyberspace.* London: Zed, 1996. Thirteen essays consider the relationship between gender, science, and nature; how the discourse of monstrosity fits into cyborg genealogy; and the contested boundaries demarcating the natural from the artificial. Chapters examine the "postmodernification" of menopause and reproductive technologies, highlight the use of gendered metaphors in physics, theorize virtual embodiment and sexual violence online, and underscore the relationship between ecofeminism and cyberfeminism. Lykke's introduction situates current feminist science studies work in relation to feminism's second-wave (1970s) positions on gender and technology. Braidotti's postface restates the central theoretical concern of the volume, namely, questioning what counts as nature, continuing the inquiry developed in Donna Haraway's "Manifesto."[2]

Crary, Jonathan, and Sanford Kwinter, eds. *Zone 6: Incorporations.* New York: Zone, 1992. Half postmodern and feminist theoretical analysis, half full-color photographs and artwork, this glossy volume of six hundred–plus pages serves double duty as a coffee-table book and a cutting-edge collection of creative and philosophical pieces. Includes work by Haraway (early version of chapter in *Modest_ Witness*), Elaine Scarry, Eve Sedgwick, Lisa Cartwright, Allucquére Rosanne (Sandy) Stone, and thirty-seven other authors and artists (mostly male and not explicitly feminist). Examines the history of technology, computerization, and the rise of "biotechnics" (cybernetic corporeal states), through analysis of moments in "the mechanization of life and the vitalization of the machine." Considers modernity and postmodernity, embodiment, the construction and control of human life by info- and biotechnologies. Chapters on artificial life research, medical imaging, the automaton, postmodern architecture, the metropolis, cyberspace, and other issues.

Critical Art Ensemble. *Flesh Machine: Cyborgs, Designer Babies, and New Eugenic Consciousness.* New York: Autonomedia, 1998. Theoretical manifesto-type political tract considers innovations in biotechnological research and development in relation to the history of eugenics, speculating that digital embodiment and the posthuman condition will give rise to new and improved forms of technobiological determinism. Considers medical imaging technology as an exercise in "mapping" the human body, designed to extend sociomedical control over the body and subjectivity. Complements work on the Visible Human Project (see Imaging section below).[3] Influenced by Jean Baudrillard, Paul Virilio, Michel Foucault, Gilles Deleuze, and other postmodern and poststructural philosophers. Not explicitly feminist in focus, the volume contributes to a feminist analysis of the production of the "data-body" by technoscience and cyberspace. Provocative text, very short (approximately 150 pages), fully illustrated, and accessibly written; suitable for classroom use.

Davis-Floyd, Robbie, and Joseph Dumit, eds. *Cyborg Babies: From Techno-Sex to Techno-Tots.* New York: Routledge, 1998. Sixteen essays contribute to "cyborg anthropology." Volume considers human reproduction through the lens of the cyborg concept, acknowledging its power, pleasure, promise, and threat. Essays discuss medicotechnological interventions in conception and contraception, including production of "technosemen." Includes work by Emily Martin, Rayna Rapp, and others, examining gestation and the use of medical imaging (ultrasound) and screening (amniocentesis) technologies to produce "normal" and "healthy" fetuses. Other pieces examine the phenomenon of technobirth, focusing on the medical monitoring and management of the mother's body. Concludes with discussion of child rearing in the digital age, including essay by Sherry Turkle on cyborg offspring in a culture of simulation and simulacra.

Dixon, Joan Broadhurst, and Eric J. Cassidy, eds. *Virtual Futures: Cyberotics, Technology, and Post-Human Pragmatism.* New York: Routledge, 1998. Thirteen essays explore intersections between postmodern theory (Virilio, Deleuze, Haraway) and the information age, with special attention to concepts of becoming cyborg, virtual embodiment, and the posthuman. Philosophical and creative/poetic essays contemplate cultural ramifications of "the increasingly synthetic and virtual world" and resulting technophobia, or technophilia, or both. Notable cyberfeminist contributions from VNS Matrix (the utopic and in-your-face manifesto "All New Gen") and Sadie Plant focus on gender, sexuality, embodiment, cyberspace, and possibilities for political resistance and social transformation through electronic interfaces.

Downey, Gary Lee, and Joseph Dumit, eds. *Cyborgs and Citadels: Anthropological Interventions in Emerging Sciences and Technologies.* Santa Fe, N.M.: School of American Research Press, 1998. Authors of eleven essays contribute to cyborg anthropology delivering ethnographies about how computer technology is used in everyday life in the United States. Fieldwork sites include a prenatal sonogram clinic, an inner-city AIDS clinic, a center for brain imaging technology, a particle physics lab, and the academic field of science, technology, and society studies. Contributors include Donna Haraway, Rayna Rapp, Emily Martin, Sharon Traweek, David Hess, and Paul Rabinow. In a detailed methodological introduction editors argue the need to develop interventionist strategies for studying technoculture. Concluding chapter offers practical advice on publishing, grant writing, and professionalizing in cyberculture studies. Extensive bibliography. For another ethnographic study of cyberspace, see David Hakken, *Cyborgs@Cyberspace: An Ethnographer Looks to the Future,* New York: Routledge, 1999.

Goodeve, Thyrza Nichols, *How Like a Leaf: An Interview with Donna Haraway.* New York: Routledge, 2000. Composed of a series of interviews Goodeve conducted with Donna Haraway, serving to introduce and contextualize her oeuvre. Includes explanation of Haraway's methodology and key concepts (for example, cyborg, OncoMouse[tm]). Distills and synthesizes theses of her works and narrates the progression of Haraway's ideas. Accessible, conversational style. Essential background reading. Excellent companion text to *Modest_Witness* and *Simians.*

Gray, Chris Hables, ed. *The Cyborg Handbook.* New York: Routledge, 1995. Highly recommended as course reader. Forty-two articles provide historical, cultural, and scientific context for cyborg science and studies. Includes work by Donna Haraway, Joseph Dumit, Cynthia Fuchs, Philip K. Dick, Katherine Hayles, David Hess, Allucquére Rosanne (Sandy) Stone, and Jennifer González among others. See especially Chela Sandoval's "New Sciences: Cyborg Feminism and the Methodology of the Oppressed" for a rereading of Haraway's "Manifesto" through the lens of third-world feminism. Extensive bibliography. Fully illustrated.

Haraway, Donna. *Modest_Witness@Second_Millennium.FemaleMan(c) Meets_ OncoMouse*[tm]: *Feminism and Technoscience.* New York: Routledge, 1997. This text expands and develops ideas from Haraway's earlier work in *Simians.*[4] Considers genetics, artificial reproduction technologies, the scientific construction of race and gender, the global impact of biotechnology on what counts as "nature" and "human," patenting of organic life, cyborgs, cyberpunk (e.g. Marge Piercy's *He, She, and It*),[5] cyberspace, and infotechnology. Introduction decodes the unconventional title of the text. Includes reproductions of artwork by Lynn Randolf, which interpret the central topics of the book.

Hayles, N. Katherine. *How We Became Posthuman: Virtual Bodies in Cybernetics, Literature, and Informatics.* Chicago: University of Chicago Press, 1999. Considers the problem of embodiment in the information age. Central concepts include cybernetics, virtual culture, cyborgs, artificial life research, and cybersubjectivity. Detailed historical overview of early moments in communication science explains terms such as *digital, entropy, informatics.* Chapter on Philip K. Dick's novels, including *Do Androids Dream of Electric Sheep?*[6] (the inspiration for science fiction cyborg film *Blade Runner*).[7] Framed by theoretical speculations on the concept of the posthuman, which Hayles uses as a metaphor for rethinking gender, embodiment, identity, and the self.

Kirkup, Gill, and Linda Janes, Kath Woodward, and Fiona Hovenden, eds. *The Gendered Cyborg: A Reader.* New York: Routledge, 2000. Highly recommended as a course reader, nineteen (abridged and reprinted) essays on women/technology/science, SF film, the monstrous feminine, artificial reproduction technologies, artificial intelligence research, and cyberspace. Includes work by Mary Ann Doane, Barbara Creed, Sadie Plant, Alison Adam, Londa Shiebinger, Nancy Stepan, Nina Lykke, and others. See especially Evelynn Hammonds's analysis of representations of racial identity as configured through computer imaging technology and the concepts of "shapeshifting" and "morphing" (also appears in Terry and Calvert, *Processed Lives*; see above) and Jennifer González on the female automaton as predecessor to feminized replicants/cyborgs (also appears in Gray, *Cyborg Handbook*; see above). Reprints Haraway's "Manifesto." Editors include detailed introductory remarks to each section of the volume, situating and contextualizing the essays. Content overlaps (two essays) and complements Wolmark, *Cybersexualities* (see below).

McNally, Amy. "Gendered Creatures: The Sexual Function and Reproductive Ability of Computers in Science Fiction Film." Senior thesis. Online. Available: <http://www.tc.umn.edu/~mcna0094/thesis.html>. Examination of cyborg images in science fiction and cyberpunk film. Tracks evolution of cyborgs in popular imaginary, noting how they are increasingly sexualized and given reproductive capabilities and recognizably gendered features. Contributes to feminist visual culture studies. (See also Andrea Slane, "Romancing the System: Women, Narrative Film, and the Sexuality of Computers," in Terry and Calvert, *Processed Lives*; see above.)

Wolmark, Jenny, ed. *Cybersexualities: A Reader on Feminist Theory, Cyborgs, and Cyberspace.* London: Edinburgh University Press, 1999. Excellent choice for a course reader. Contains seventeen essays on science fiction and cyberpunk, cyborgs, monstrosity, the female automaton, gender performativity and virtual reality, postmodernism and the posthuman, and others. Contributors include Mary Ann Doane, Claudia Springer, Alluquére Rosanne (Sandy) Stone, Sadie Plant, Elizabeth Grosz, Anne Balsamo, Katherine Hayles, Veronica Hollinger, Donna Haraway, and others. See especially Chela Sandoval's rereading of Haraway's "Manifesto" in terms of its use for "third world feminism." Content significantly overlaps both *The Gendered Cyborg* and *The Cyborg Handbook.* All essays are abridged reprints.

Cyberspace

Blair, Kristine, and Pamela Takayoshi, eds. *Feminist Cyberscapes: Mapping Gendered Academic Spaces.* Greenwich, Conn.: Ablex, 1999. Thirteen essays provide introduction to key issues in cyberfeminism through the lens of composition theory and practice. Focus on the construction of virtual embodiment, online identities, and discourse communities through computer-mediated writing technologies. Several essays discuss how women use the Internet to forge connections/relationships, and to counter or reinvent/reinterpret popular representations of gender and sexuality.

Braidotti, Rosi. "Cyberfeminism with a Difference" Online. Available: <http://www.let.ruu.nl/womens_studies/rosi/cyberfem.htm>. Manifesto-like essay on cyberbodies, postmodernism, and the utopic potential of cyberfeminism. Braidotti's passionate call for women to occupy and reinvent the "all-male terrain" of cyberspace echoes Donna Haraway's advocation of irony as political strategy. Includes analysis of science fiction, cyberpunk, female artists, riot- and guerrilla grrls, and the discourse of the monstrous feminine cyborg.

Cherny, Lynn, and Elizabeth Reba Weise, eds. *Wired Women: Gender and New Realities in Cyberspace.* Toronto: Seal Press, 1996. Fifteen essays consider gender relations in cyberspace, including sexual harassment online, cybercensorship, the culture of *Wired* magazine, the erotic potential of the Internet, virtual reality, community, and virtual embodiment.

Ferrari, Michele Ierardi. "The Polychromatic Girl Confronts the Virtual Boy: Questioning the Construction of Gender in Virtual Reality." Master's thesis. Online. Available: <http://www.people.virginia.edu/~mli5e/thesis.html>. Discusses the cultural fascination with virtual reality as part of a historical climate of fear and desire for disembodiment and transcendence of the flesh and real life. Asks: "What is the relationship between the physical body and the 'virtual' body? Does the virtual reality experience fundamentally destabilize the nature of gender and embodiment or does it merely reinscribe traditional or conservative perspectives onto the new 'non-space' it creates?" Includes reading of William Gibson's cyberpunk classic novel *Neuromancer,*[8] science fiction film *The Lawnmower Man,*[9] and various video games.

Harcourt, Wendy, ed. *Women@Internet: Creating New Cultures.* New York: Zed, 1999. Seventeen essays provide analysis of global Internet culture, emphasizing women's use of computer-mediated communication to form communities for political action and personal change. Preface by Haraway. For more about how women are using computer-mediated communication technologies, see Dale Spender, *Nattering on the Net: Women, Power, and Cyberspace.* Toronto: Garamond Press, 1995.

Hawthorne, Susan, and Renate Klein, eds. *Cyberfeminism: Connectivity, Critique and Creativity.* Melbourne: Spinifex, 1999. Nineteen essays serve as introduction to feminist studies of cyberspace and Internet culture. Considers online feminist community and women's use of the Internet for personal and educational (including classroom) purposes. Engages with Haraway's cyborg metaphor, hypertext theory, and global studies, covering topics such as virtual reality, "the virtual traffic in women," and computer gaming.

Jones, Steven G., ed. *Virtual Culture: Identity and Communication in Cybersociety.* London: Sage, 1997. Eleven essays study use of the Internet by "socially disadvantaged" groups, including the homeless. Although essays are not explicitly feminist in tone, they are accessibly written, and together provide a solid analysis of the construction of social relationships through computer-mediated communication. Includes chapters on the discourse of cyberhate, the "techno-erotic" (cyborg) woman, and cybersex.

Kolko, Beth E., Lisa Nakamura, and Gilbert B. Rodman, eds. *Race in Cyberspace.* New York: Routledge, 2000. Twelve essays form a ground-breaking collection of work on the dynamics of race and ethnicity as they are manifested in Internet culture. Acts as a corrective to the Net-utopianism that would suggest that the cultural markings of embodiment and identity can be erased in the flow of information online. Considers access issues, language, transnational virtual culture and capital, cyborgs and avatars, advertising and media, virtual community and science fiction, among other issues.

Morse, Margaret. *Virtualities: Television, Media, Art, and Cyberculture.* Bloomington: Indiana University Press, 1998. Analyzes the utopic and dystopic effects of the virtual relationships forged between computerized machines and humans in the information age. Considers impact of cyberspace on our ideas of embodiment, identity, and interpersonal relations. See especially "What Do Cyborgs Eat? Oral Logic in an Information Society" (complements Hayles's *How We Became Posthuman*; see above).

O'Farrell, Mary Ann, and Lynn Vallone, eds. *Virtual Gender: Fantasies of Subjectivity and Embodiment.* Ann Arbor: University of Michigan Press, 1999. Authors in interdisciplinary collection of ten essays consider cyberfeminism (see Kay Schaffer on VNS Matrix), transgenderism, and virtual reality (see essay by Bernice Hausman), sexuality, cyberspace, computer-mediated communication, online "gender fantasies" and the creation of virtual discourse communities (see Robyn Warhol on electronic bulletin boards for soap opera fans). Also includes several historical pieces on subjectivity, gendered embodiment, self-representation, and women's relationships to technology and machines.

Plant, Sadie. *Zeros + Ones: Digital Women + The New Technoculture.* New York: Doubleday, 1997. Historical perspective on women and the development of computer technologies; considers gender relations on the Internet and previews the emergence of cyberfeminism.

Reid, Elizabeth. "Text-Based Virtual Realities: Identity and the Cyborg Body." Online. Available: <http://www.rochester.edu/College/ FS/Publications/ReidIdentity.html>. Reid suggests that gender, sexuality, and corporeality are problematized and made uncertain, even "unresolvable," in a virtual reality environment where users are anonymous and have the ability to reinvent themselves through identity "play." Argues that multiuser domain (MUD) participants do not simply "enter" the virtual environment, but are configured by it. Essay characterized by a Net-utopia suggesting unlimited possibilities to escape the flesh and the particularities of the body in cyberspace. Argues that MUD players have the ability to experiment with gendered, sexual, and racial identities in spite of the cultural fixity of these markers in real life (see also Christine Tamblyn, "Remote Control: The Electronic Transference," in *Processed Lives* above; for an opposing view see Kolko, Nakamura, and Rodman, *Race in Cyberspace*, above).

Scott, Krista. "Girls Need Modems! Cyberculture and Women's Ezines" Senior thesis. Online. Available: <http://krista.tico.com/mrp.html>. Study of gender, cyberfeminism, and cyberspace through in-depth analysis of two electronic zines (*Brillo* and *Girlrights*), both of which present feminist and "Riot Grrrl-style politics." Includes rhetorical/textual analysis, interview material, and theoretical engagement with Haraway and Turkle's work (see also Nina Wakeford, "Networking Women and Grrrls With Information/Communication Technology: Surfing Tales of the World Wide Web" in Terry and Calvert, *Processed Lives*, above).

Springer, Claudia. *Electronic Eros: Bodies and Desire in the Postindustrial Age*. Austin: Texas University Press, 1996. Feminist popular-culture analysis of imagery of "techno-erotics," or human pleasure in and desire for machines, and cyborg envy. Includes discussion of science fiction and cyberpunk films and literature, comic books, television. Accessible writing style. Discusses tinysex, cyborgs, virtual reality, postmodernism, fantasies of bodily transcendence, history of computing technologies.

Stone, Allucquére Rosanne (Sandy). *The War of Desire and Technology at the End of the Mechanical Age*. London: MIT, 1995. Fuses transgender politics, feminist theory, and analysis of computer-mediated communication. Poetic, personal, experimental essays discuss the performances, subversions, and negotiations of gender and embodiment in a series of virtual spaces in Internet culture. Includes analysis of "virtual rape" and online sexual harassment.

Turkle, Sherry. *Life on the Screen: Identity in the Age of the Internet*. New York: Simon & Shuster, 1995. Accessibly written sociological, ethnographic, and philosophical study of how people use computer technologies, and how machine-man (*sic*) interfaces affect the construction of identity online. Explains gender dynamics in virtual communities (MUDs, MOOs), artificial intelligence research, cybersex, and related topics. Argues that Internet culture is making psychoanalytic, postmodern, and poststructural theory accessible, through the real life experience of users living multiple, fragmented, and invented virtual selves/lives.

Wilding, Faith, and Critical Art Ensemble. "Notes on the Political Condition of Cyberfeminism" Online. Available: <http://www.obn.org/cfundef/condition.html>. Thorough examination of the issues and politics of third-wave, postfeminist cyberfeminism. Makes connections to second and first waves of feminist movement (see also Faith Wilding, "Where Is Feminism in Cyberfeminism?" Online. Available: <http://www.obn.org/cfundef/faith_def.html>).

Genetics

Condit, Celeste Michelle. *The Meanings of the Gene: Public Debates about Human Heredity.* Madison: University of Wisconsin Press, 1999. Rhetorical analysis of popular-press representations of genetics in the twentieth century; describes what has elsewhere been called "gene angst" or public fear and skepticism about genetics, eugenics, selective breeding and genetic engineering, sociobiology and genetic determinism. Complements and overlaps Nelkin and Lindee, *The DNA Mystique*; and Van Dijck, *Imagenation*; see below.

Keller, Evelyn Fox. *Refiguring Life: Metaphors of Twentieth-Century Biology.* New York: Columbia University Press, 1995. Three essays consider the power of discourse in shaping scientific knowledge. Analyzes the language of DNA as "the master molecule" and the chromosome as "code-script"; examines "the discourse of gene action" and other cybernetic metaphors adopted by biologists and geneticists, which popularized an understanding of the human organism as a cyborg entity. Complements Hayles's and Haraway's work (see above).

Lindee, Susan, and Dorothy Nelkin. *The DNA Mystique: The Gene as a Cultural Icon.* New York: Freeman, 1995. Argues that the gene is not only a biological entity but also a controversial cultural "icon" in popular culture, signifying our historical fascination with DNA and the ongoing currency of biologically determinist (or reductionist) explanations for human behavior and social conditions (for example, inequity). Analyzes comic books, media, films, television, and advertising for genetic discourses, metaphors, images. For related analysis, see Jon Turney, *Frankenstein's Footsteps: Science, Genetics, and Popular Culture.* New Haven: Yale University Press, 1998.

Rothman, Barbara Katz. *Genetic Maps and Human Imaginations: The Limits of Science in Understanding Who We Are.* New York: W. W. Norton, 1998. Blends philosophical analysis with autobiographical insight to discuss the relationship of genetic research to the dangers of genetic determinism. Discusses the Human Genome Project, sociobiology and racial science, the politics of screening for inherited breast cancer, prenatal genetic testing, and the controversy over "the gay gene."[10] Critically analyzes the power of genetic explanations for social behaviors, and the predominance of a "prism of heritability."

Van Dijck, José. *Imagenation: Popular Images of Genetics.* New York: New York University Press, 1998. Historic-cultural study of public and popular representations of genetic science from its eugenic beginnings to contemporary discourses surrounding the Human Genome Project. Analyzes the struggle to determine/define the meaning of genetic research in public relations material, popular press, science journalism, and science fiction.

Wingerson, Lois. *Unnatural Selection: The Promise and the Power of Human Gene Research.* New York: Bantam, 1998. Accessible background reading on genetic science, genetic engineering and screening, cloning, gene therapy, and genethics. Considers the social ramifications of the genetic revolution, the digitalization of the body, and the commodification of genetic information.

Imaging

Cartwright, Lisa. *Screening the Body: Tracing Medicine's Visual Culture.* Minneapolis: University of Minnesota Press, 1995. Historical feminist study of medical cinema's role in constructing gendered (and normative) models of human embodment. Considers the power of imaging technology in defining "healthy" and "normal" body-states. Argues that the authority of information produced by X-ray technologies (including those used in the Visible Human Project) is used to determine the cultural hierarchy of subjects and create a "visual ordering of bodies," in which specific (racialized, sexualized, gendered) bodies are differently targeted as objects of the medical gaze.

Druckrey, Timothy, ed. *Electronic Culture: Technology and Visual Representation.* New York: Aperture, 1996. Twenty-nine (reprinted) essays consider how new media is transforming visual culture and subjectivity. Preface by Allucquére Rosanne (Sandy) Stone. Includes work by Katherine Hayles on the posthuman body (see above), Critical Art Ensemble on "the flesh machine" (see above), and a host of essays on representation, technology, the visual, cyberspace, digitality, and the cultural ramifications of technoscientific advances in genomics and cybernetics. Complements Mary Anne Moser's edited collection *Immersed in Technology: Art and Virtual Enviroments,* Cambridge: MIT Press, 1996.

Kelves, Bettyann Holtzmann. *Naked to the Bone: Medical Imaging in the Twentieth Century.* Reading, Mass: Addison-Wesley/Helix Books, 1997. Cultural-historical analysis documenting the invention of X-ray technology in 1890s and the use of related medical imaging technologies in the 1990s and beyond. Describes the impact of the invention of the "transparent" body and the corresponding cultural upheavals in notions of corporeal boundaries and privacy that resulted. Chapters on ultrasound imaging (also see Davis-Floyd and Dumit, *Cyborg Babies,* above) and the use of X-ray images in popular culture and art. Stops short of considering the Visible Human Project, but explains the science and technologies involved in it.

Treichler, Paula, Lisa Cartwright, and Constance Penley, eds. *The Visible Woman: Imaging Technologies, Gender, and Science.* New York: New York University Press, 1998. Excellent choice for course reader. Thirteen essays politicize and interrogate the "spectacle" of the human body as it is produced by medical imaging research, discourses, and technologies. Thesis of volume is "visibility is not transparency." Authors illustrate how medico-scientific representations of corporeality are contested in a struggle over the authority of interpreting images. Strength of volume lies in several essays on AIDS/immune system discourses, and reproductive imaging technology/fetal photography, which discuss the struggles for agency and control around defining the concepts of health, normalcy, and disease. Introduction by editors provides concise theoretical overview of volume's concerns and situates content politically, culturally, and historically.

Waldby, Catherine. *The Visible Human Project: Informatic Bodies and Posthuman Medicine.* New York: Routledge, 2000. Book-length study of the Visible Human Project, contextualizes the project historically and explains scientific background. Places the project within larger context of digital culture, comparing it to the Human Genome Project and other biomedical technologies and ventures, including cloning. Argues, like Haraway, that the Visible Human Project effectively destabilizes distinctions such as virtual and actual, organic and mechanistic. Contains extended consideration of the gendered implications of the creation of these virtual bodies.

NOTES

1. Martin Heidegger, *The Question Concerning Technology and Other Essays,* trans. William Lovitt (New York: Harper & Row, 1977).
2. Donna Haraway, "A Manifesto for Cyborgs," in *Simians*; see note 4.
3. For more information about the National Library of Medicine's Visible Human Project, visit their Web site <http://www.nlm.nih.gov/research/visible/visible_human.html>.

4. Donna Haraway, *Simians, Cyborgs, and Women: The Reinvention of Nature* (New York: Routledge, 1991).
5. Marge Piercy, *He, She, and It* (New York: Fawcett Columbine, 1991).
6. Philip K. Dick, *Do Androids Dream of Electric Sheep?* (New York: Del Ray, 1968).
7. *Blade Runner,* dir. Ridley Scott, screenplay Philip K. Dick (1982).
8. William Gibson, *Neuromancer* (New York: Ace Books, 1984).
9. *The Lawnmower Man,* dir. Brett Leonard, screenplay Stephen King (1992).
10. For more information about the U.S. Department of Energy's Human Genome Project, visit their Web site <http://www.ornl.gov/Tech Resources/Human_Genome/home.html>.

SYLLABUS: CYBERFEMINISM AND TECHNOCULTURE

Cyberfeminism and Technoculture was taught at the University of Minnesota in the women's studies department in May 2000. The course was an accelerated one, completed over a three-week period, with third-year students meeting Monday through Friday for three hours each day. The course materials included theory, cultural studies, and feminist essays; films; popular novels; advertisements; and Internet sites. The course was organized into three modules, each lasting five meetings, or one week. Each day's discussion was facilitated by a student volunteer. Students' writings, full course syllabus, and links to online resources are available on the course Web site, http://www.sites.netscape.net/sidneyevematrix/syllabi.

Required Texts

Cartwright, Lisa. "The Visible Male: The Male Criminal Subject as Biomedical Norm." In *Processed Lives: Gender and Technology in Everyday Life,* ed. Jennifer Terry. New York: Routledge, 1997.
Cook, Robin. *Chromosome 6.* New York: Berkley Books, 1997.
Dibble, Julian. "My Tiny Life: A Rape in Cyberspace" Online. Available: <www.levity.com>.
Dick, Philip K. *Do Androids Dream of Electric Sheep?* New York: Del Ray, 1968.
Gibson, William. *Neuromancer.* New York: Ace Books, 1984.
Goodeve, Thyrza Nichols. *How Like a Leaf: An Interview with Donna Haraway.* New York: Routledge, 2000.
Gray, Chris Hables, ed. *The Cyborg Handbook.* New York: Routledge, 1995.
Halberstam, Judith. "Introduction: Posthuman Bodies." In *Posthuman Bodies,* ed. Judith Halberstam, and Ira Livingston. Bloomington: Indiana University Press, 1995.

Hammonds, Evelynn M. "New Technologies of Race." In *The Gendered Cyborg.* ed. Gill Kirkup, Linda Janes, Kath Woodward, and Fiona Hovenden. New York: Routledge, 2000.

Haraway, Donna. "The Actors Are Cyborg, Nature Is Coyote, and the Geography Is Elsewhere: Postscript to 'Cyborgs at Large'" In *Technoculture,* ed. Constance Penley and Andrew Ross. Minneapolis: University of Minnesota Press, 1991.

———. *Modest_Witness@Second_Millennium.FemaleMan(c) Meets_Onco Mouse*(tm). New York: Routledge, 1997.

———. "A Manifesto for Cyborgs: Science, Technology, and Socialist Feminism in the 1980s." In *The Gendered Cyborg: A Reader,* ed. Gill Kirkup. New York: Routledge, 2000.

Haraway, Donna, Constance Penley, and Andrew Ross, "Cyborgs at Large: Interview with Donna Haraway." In *Technoculture,* ed. Constance Penley and Andrew Ross. Minneapolis: University of Minnesota Press, 1991.

Hayles, Katherine. "Toward Embodied Virtuality." *How We Became Posthuman.* Chicago: University of Chicago Press, 1999.

Ierardi, Michele. "The Beautiful (Broken) Woman's Body: *Neuromancer* as a Neo-Romantic Celebration of the Female Body in Pain." Online. Available: <http://prometheus.cc.emory.edu/panels/4E/M.Ierardi.html>.

Lewontin, Richard. "The Dream of the Human Genome." *Biology as Ideology: The Doctrine of DNA.* New York: HarperPerennial. 1991.

Nelkin, Dorothy, and M. Susan Lindee. "Creating Natural Distinctions." *The DNA Mystique: The Gene as a Cultural Icon.* New York: W. H. Freeman, 1995.

Piercy, Marge. *He, She and It.* New York: Fawcett Columbine, 1991.

Sandoval, Chela. "New Sciences: Cyborg Feminism and the Methodology of the Oppressed" In *The Cyborg Handbook,* ed. Chris Hables Gray. New York: Routledge, 1995.

Spitzer, Lisa, and David G. Whitlock. "Introduction: The Visible Human Male." In *National Library of Medicine Atlas of the Visible Human Male: Reverse Engineering of the Human Body,* ed. Victor Spitzer and Davia Whitlock. Sudbury, Mass: Jones and Bartlet, 1998.

Stelarc. "From Psycho-Body to Cyber-Systems," In *Virtual Futures,* ed. Joan Broadhurst. New York: Routledge, 1998.

Technowhores. "Technowhores Manifesto." In *Desire by Design: Body, Territories, and New Technologies,* ed. Cutting Edge: The Women's Research Group. New York: I. B. Tauris, 1999.

Turkle, Sherry. "The Cyberanalyst" In *Digerati: Encounters with the Cyber Elite,* ed. John Brockman. San Francisco: Hardwired, 1996.

————. "Tinysex and Gender Trouble." In *Sex/Machine: Readings in Culture, Gender, and Technology,* ed. Patrick Hopkins. Bloomington: Indiana University Press, 1998.

VNS Matrix, "All New Gen." In *Virtual Futures: Cyberotics, Technology, and Post-human Pragmatism,* ed. Joan Broadhurst-Dixon and Eric J. Cassidy. New York: Routledge, 1998.

Filmography

Blade Runner. Directed by Ridley Scott. Screenplay by Philip K. Dick. Warner Brothers, 1982. Director's cut.

Gattaca. Directed and screenplay by Andrew Niccol. Columbia Pictures, Jersey Films, 1997.

The Matrix. Directed and screenplay Andy Wachowski and Larry Wachowski. Warner Brothers, 1999.

Terminator 2: Judgment Day. Directed and screenplay by James Cameron. Columbia TriStar Productions, 1991.

Course Schedule

Module 01: Cyborgicity: Feminism and Technoscientific Fiction

Day 1: "Introduction." Film screening and discussion: *Terminator 2: Judgment Day*

Day 2: Theme: "Cyborgian Beginnings." Readings: Selections from "Part 1: The Genesis of the Cyborg," in *The Cyborg Handbook.*

Day 3: Theme: "Replicants." Film screening: *Blade Runner.* Reading: Philip K. Dick, *Do Androids Dream of Electric Sheep?*

Day 4: Theme: "Cyborgian Theory." Discussion of Donna Haraway's cyborg metaphor. Readings: Donna Haraway, "A Manifesto for Cyborgs"; Donna Haraway, Constance Penley, and Andrew Ross, "Cyborgs at Large"; Donna Haraway, "The Actors Are Cyborg, Nature Is Coyote, and the Geography Is Elsewhere"; Chela Sandoval, "New Sciences."

Day 5: Theme: "Monstrocity: Cyborgs and Golems." Reading: Marge Piercy, *He, She and It.*

Module 02: Cybersubjectivity

(Note: Due to a university holiday, this week's material was covered in four days instead of five.)

Day 1: Theme: "Consensual Hallucination: Cyberspace and Cyberpunk." Readings: William Gibson, *Neuromancer;* and Michele Ierardi, "The Beautiful (Broken) Woman's Body."

Day 2: Theme: "There Is No Spoon: Virtual Reality." Film screening and discussion: *The Matrix.*

Day 3: Theme: "Online Community, Cybersex, and Virtual Gender." Readings: Julian Dibble, "My Tiny Life: A Rape in Cyberspace"; Sherry Turkle, "The Cyberanalyst"; Sherry Turkle, "Tinysex and Gender Trouble."

Day 4: Theme: "Cyberfeminism." Visit virtual newscasters' Web sites: Ananova.com and Mya at Motorola.com. Readings: VNS Matrix, "All New Gen"; Technowhores, "Technowhores Manifesto"; Stelarc, "From Psycho-Body to Cyber-Systems."

Module 03: The Posthuman

Day 1: Theme: "Biotechnology, Informatics, and the Digital Body." Visit the Human Genome Project Web site. Readings: Dorothy Nelkin and M. Susan Lindee, "Creating Natural Distinctions"; Richard Lewontin, "The Dream of the Human Genome."

Day 2: Film screening and discussion: *Gattaca.*

Day 3: Theme: "Genomics and Genethics: Xenotransplantation and Cloning." Reading: Robin Cook, *Chromosome 6.*

Day 4: Theme: "Medical Imaging Technologies and the Construction of the Body as Digital Image-Map." Visit the Visible Human Project Web site. Readings: Judith Halberstam, "Introduction: Posthuman Bodies"; Katherine Hayles, "Toward Embodied Virtuality"; Lisa

Cartwright, "The Visible Male"; Lisa Spitzer and David G. Whitlock, "Introduction: The Visible Human Male"; Evelynn Hammonds, "New Technologies."

Day 5: Theme: "Cyberfeminism and Technoscience." Readings: Selections from Donna Haraway, *Modest_Witness* and *How Like a Leaf.*

Sidney Eve Matrix *(sidneyevematrix@yahoo.com) is completing her Ph.D. in feminist studies at the University of Minnesota.*

Copyright © 2001 by Sidney Eve Matrix

Strategies for Teaching/Strategies for Change

WOMEN'S STUDIES QUARTERLY

An Educational Project of The Feminist Press at The City University of New York
in Cooperation with Rochester Institute of Technology

"Valuable . . . authentic."
—Council of Editors of Learned Journals

Since 1972 *Women's Studies Quarterly* (*WSQ*) has been an internationally recognized and celebrated forum for the exchange of new ideas on women's issues and a vehicle for creative and engaging classroom discussion.

Accessible

In jargon-free language, each thematically based volume explores current issues such as violence against women and women's environmental concerns. *WSQ* is a vital resource for anyone engaged in education, research, or feminist action.

International

Committed to publishing international perspectives and exploring the intersections of race, class, and gender, *WSQ* brings its readers reports from around the globe, blending multiple feminist cultures and actions across boundaries.

Interdisciplinary

Combining the most recent developments in feminist theory and pedagogy with vibrant selections of women's poetry, fiction, and memoir, *WSQ* aims to bring the material fabric of women's lives before its readers.

Series Editor: Diane S. Hope, William A. Kern
Professor of Communication, Rochester Institute of Technology

Subscription Rates: U.S.: Individuals, 1 year—$30; 3 years—$70; Institutions: 1 year—$40; 3 years—$100. **Outside the U.S.**: Individuals, 1 year—$40; 3 years—$100; Institutions, 1 year—$50; 3 years—$120. Visa, MasterCard, and AmEx payments are accepted. To order, send check or credit card information (acct. no., exp. date, phone no., and signature) to the address below, or call us at 212-817-7920.

The Feminist Press at the City University of New York
The Graduate Center, 365 Fifth Avenue, New York, NY 10016
www.feministpress.org

ᴛʜᴇNATIONAL
COUNCILꜰᴏʀ
RESEARCH
ᴏɴWOMEN

BALANCING THE EQUATION:
WHERE ARE WOMEN AND GIRLS IN SCIENCE,
ENGINEERING, AND TECHNOLOGY?

"This report is a must for every educator, policy maker, and business leader in America. *Balancing the Equation* makes a major contribution by looking for better ways to incorporate girls and women at every stage of the education and employment process."

> Janet L. Holmgren   President, Mills College; Chair, Women's
> College Coalition; Board Chair, American Council on Education

This new report explores the lessons, challenges, and fresh directions that have emerged after a decade of activism by and for women and girls in science, engineering and technology. *Balancing the Equation* identifies areas where we have succeeded and points to moments when intervention can make a significant difference. Woven throughout the report are the voices of leaders responsible for changing the terrain of the sciences – as well as recommendations for action and an extensive Resource Guide.

> "There is room for cautious optimism at the beginning of this new century. It is up to all of us to put in place practices and ways of thinking that will enable women and girls to thrive in the sciences, and the sciences to thrive because of women's and girls' heightened participation."
> Linda G. Basch, NCRW Executive Director, from *Balancing the Equation*

For more information
Please visit www.ncrw.org or call 212 785-7335, ext. 22

"Inspirational."—*Multicultural Review*

For ages ten and up

WOMEN CHANGING THE WORLD

This one-of-a-kind biography series for younger readers introduces women leaders from around the globe and their struggles for social and environmental justice. These accessible and engrossing volumes are supplemented with vivid photographs and inset boxes that offer historical context and explain key political and social concepts.

"Combining detailed biography with thorough descriptions and well-designed layout...these titles provide more information for this age group than other single sources."
—*School Library Journal*

AUNG SAN SUU KYI:
Standing Up for Democracy in Burma

RIGOBERTA MENCHÚ:
Defending Human Rights in Guatemala

MAIREAD CORRIGAN AND BETTY WILLIAMS
Making Peace in Northern Ireland

MAMPHELA RAMPHELE:
Challenging Apartheid in South Africa

ELA BHATT
Uniting Women in India

New to the Series! Biographies of Two Indigenous Environmental Activists!

MARINA SILVA:
Defending Rainforest Communities in Brazil

WINONA LADUKE
Restoring Land and Culture in Native America

Order individual volumes or enjoy a *special discount* on a complete set of seven. Receive a free classroom teaching guide with any purchase:

Per Book	$10.95 paper	Per Set	$49.00 paper
	$19.95 library hardcover	(7 vols.)	$99.00 library hardcover

For additional information, visit our web site: www.feministpress.org

To place orders, call or write to: The Feminist Press at The City University of New York, 365 Fifth Avenue, New York, NY 10016; phone (212) 817-7920; fax (212) 817-1593.

Journal of Gender Studies

EDITORS
Ros Billington, Diane Dubois and **Jenny Wolmark**
All at University of Lincolnshire & Humberside, UK

Supported by an International Editorial Advisory Board

The *Journal of Gender Studies* is a refereed interdisciplinary journal which publishes articles relating to gender from a feminist perspective within a wide range of subject areas including the Social and Natural Sciences, Arts and Popular Culture. Reviews of books and details of forthcoming conferences are also included.

The journal seeks articles from international sources and aims to take account of a diversity of cultural backgrounds and differences in sexual orientation. It encourages contributions which focus on the experiences of both men and women and welcomes articles, written from a feminist perspective, relating to femininity and masculinity and to the social construction of relationships between men and women.

The *Journal of Gender Studies* is the journal of the Hull Centre for Gender Studies, which organises seminar programmes and day schools and is jointly sponsored by the Universities of Hull and Humberside.

This journal is also available online.
Please connect to http://www.tandf.co.uk/online.html for further information.

SUBSCRIPTION RATES
2001 – Volume 10 (3 issues)
Print ISSN 0958-9236
Online ISSN 1465-3869
Institutional Rate: US$298; £179 (includes free online access)
Personal Rate: US$41; £24 (print only)

- -

ORDER FORM
cjgs

PLEASE COMPLETE IN BLOCK CAPITALS AND RETURN TO THE ADDRESS BELOW

Please invoice me at the ☐ **institutional rate** ☐ **personal rate**

☐ Please send me a sample copy

Name _____

Address _____

_____

_____

E-mail _____

Please contact Customer Services at either:
Taylor & Francis Ltd, Rankine Road, Basingstoke, Hants RG24 8PR, UK
Tel: +44 (0)1256 813002   **Fax:** +44 (0)1256 330245   **E-mail:** enquiry@tandf.co.uk   **www:** http://www.tandf.co.uk

Taylor & Francis Inc, 325 Chestnut Street, 8th Floor, Philadelphia, PA 19106, USA
Fax: +1 215 625 2940   **E-mail:** info@taylorandfrancis.com   **www:** http://www.taylorandfrancis.com

MICHIGAN FEMINIST STUDIES

ISSUE NO. 14

{Masculinities}

AVAILABLE NOW

THE CURRENT ISSUE presents scholarship on narratives of female masculinity in Charles Dickens' *David Copperfield*, masculinity and Englishness in Olaudah Equiano's *An Interesting Narrative*, and reimagined masculinity in the fiction of Stephen King. Articles also explore anxious manhood on *Seinfeld* and high-altitude mountaineers' narratives of masculinity, and Michael Kimmel offers his reflections on the current debates surrounding the future of American boys.

{Masculinities}

AN INTERDISCIPLINARY JOURNAL *of gender studies,* MFS *has been edited and published by graduate students at the University of Michigan since 1975.*

TO ORDER THIS or a previous issue ($5 per issue for individuals, $12 for institutions), please contact *Michigan Feminist Studies,* 1122 Lane Hall, 204 South State Street, University of Michigan, Ann Arbor, Michigan, 48109-1290.

Email us at mfseditors@umich.edu,
or visit our website at http://www.umich.edu/~mfsed.

*Write for a **free** 2 - issue trial subscription*

Name

Address

City, State, Zip

Only $25 subscription

■ *Cutting edge*

Irreverent ■

■ *Activist*

Controversial ■

■ *Visionary*

Woman-centered ■

■ *Radical*

Subversive ■

off our backs

The feminist newsjournal for over 30 years

off our backs
2337B 18th Street, NW
Washington, D.C. 20009

web: www.igc.org/oob
email: offourbacks@cs.com